Harmonic Elliott Wave

The Case for Modification of R. N. Elliott's Impulsive Wave Structure

Harmonic Elliott Wave

The Case for Modification of R. N. Elliott's Impulsive Wave Structure

IAN COPSEY

WILEY

John Wiley & Sons (Asia) Pte. Ltd.

Copyright © 2011 John Wiley & Sons (Asia) Pte. Ltd.
Published in 2011 by John Wiley & Sons (Asia) Pte. Ltd.
2 Clementi Loop, #02–01, Singapore 129809

All rights reserved.

No part of this publication may be reproduced, stored in a retrieval system, or transmitted in any form or by any means, electronic, mechanical, photocopying, recording, scanning, or otherwise, except as expressly permitted by law, without either the prior written permission of the Publisher, or authorization through payment of the appropriate photocopy fee to the Copyright Clearance Center. Requests for permission should be addressed to the Publisher, John Wiley & Sons (Asia) Pte. Ltd., 2 Clementi Loop, #02–01, Singapore 129809, tel: 65–6463–2400, fax: 65–6463–4605, e-mail: enquiry@wiley.com.

This publication is designed to provide accurate and authoritative information in regard to the subject matter covered. It is sold with the understanding that the publisher is not engaged in rendering professional services. If professional advice or other expert assistance is required, the services of a competent professional person should be sought.

Neither the authors nor the publisher are liable for any actions prompted or caused by the information presented in this book. Any views expressed herein are those of the authors and do not represent the views of the organizations they work for.

Other Wiley Editorial Offices

John Wiley & Sons, 111 River Street, Hoboken, NJ 07030, USA
John Wiley & Sons, The Atrium, Southern Gate, Chichester, West Sussex, P019 8SQ, United Kingdom
John Wiley & Sons (Canada) Ltd., 5353 Dundas Street West, Suite 400, Toronto, Ontario, M9B 6HB, Canada
John Wiley & Sons Australia Ltd., 42 McDougall Street, Milton, Queensland 4064, Australia
Wiley-VCH, Boschstrasse 12, D-69469 Weinheim, Germany

Library of Congress Cataloging-in-Publication Data
ISBN 978-0-470-82870-0 (Hardcover)
ISBN 978-0-470-82872-4 (ePDF)
ISBN 978-0-470-82871-7 (Mobi)
ISBN 978-0-470-82873-1 (ePub)

Typeset in 11/14pt, Century-Book by Thomson Digital, India
Printed in Singapore by Toppan Security Printing Pte. Ltd.
10 9 8 7 6 5 4 3 2 1

Contents

Introduction   vii

CHAPTER 1   **R. N. Elliott's Findings: Impulsive Waves**   1

CHAPTER 2   **R. N. Elliott's Findings: Corrective Waves**   15

CHAPTER 3   **Impulsive Wave Modification**   37

CHAPTER 4   **Projection and Retracement Ratios**   71

CHAPTER 5   **Working with the Modified Wave Structure in Forecasting**   119

CHAPTER 6   **A Case Study in EURUSD**   159

CHAPTER 7   **The Modified Structure in Other Markets**   181

Index   225

Introduction

It has been 20 years since I began to learn and apply the Elliott Wave Principle to the markets. I bought two books on the topic, read them thoroughly, and thought I could begin to predict price movements more effectively. Of course, as anyone will tell you, it's not as simple as that.

I studiously attempted to apply the principle to daily forex movements, but finding no success I gave it up . . . several times. What drove me forward was that of all analysts, it was those who utilized this principle that produced the most accurate forecasts. Other analysts simply had no clue, and this prompted me to continue the quest to conquer the challenge.

It took me a full 18 months before I felt that I had mastered the technique to an extent where I could generally provide more accuracy to my forecasts, but I was not yet at the stage where there was a high level of consistency. This led me to believe that it was a technique that demanded a great deal of dedication and practical experience to achieve success. Strangely enough, even then others still seemed to appreciate my attempts.

Around 16 years ago, I left trading to join the second largest real-time data vendor, Dow Jones Telerate, to provide specialist analytical support for their clients. I began to hold seminars for traders in Tokyo, which of course included Elliott Wave. It was a marvelous experience that deepened my knowledge of technical analysis in general, but it also took me away from the front line of having to analyze and forecast every day.

It wasn't until around 2004 that I returned to full-time analysis, writing a daily report which has now developed into *The Daily Forecaster*, subscribers coming from retail traders, corporate treasurers handling forex exposures, bank traders, and hedge funds. Being independent, the need for accuracy was pressing. Subscribers paid up their bucks and wanted profits. The days of having the backing of a large bank's name, a good salary, and less risk had passed.

Utilizing R. N. Elliott's wave structure, I became aware that things were not quite right. The same anomalies in the wave structure repeated themselves over and over again. The normal Fibonacci projections that are widely quoted didn't work all that often. Impulsive waves all too often stalled early and missed out a wave. So I began to adapt the way in which impulsive wave structures develop and to research the common ratios in projections. After a few months, it was clear that my adaptations produced far more accurate results in both the projection ratios and the manner in which impulsive wave structures develop.

It was at this point that the number of subscribers who kindly wrote to compliment the accuracy of both my forecasts and the daily support and resistance rose considerably. Another quite common comment was how other market analysts seemed to have no idea of what will happen next. As one subscriber wrote:

> *I am also extremely happy that I stuck with you. At the time, you twisted my rubber arm to continue with the original subscription I had been suffering from a string of advisors, many of whom were well-intentioned but could not unfortunately, for me, chew gum and walk straight at the same time—I mean from an analysis point of view. It was a bit like dining "al fresco" in the middle of a hurricane . . .*

By no means am I perfect and I still have varying degrees of success in forecasting, but the consistency is higher with my approach, and one factor I have noted is that the "derivatives" of both Fibonacci and harmonic ratios I employ do often provide

Introduction

powerful reversal signals if my forecasts prove incorrect. The mere fact that support and resistance levels are more accurate provides more focused points in price action that identify both trade entry and stop loss/reversal levels that can assist in reducing the size of losses and thus provide more effective maintenance of capital.

In writing this book to describe my findings I do not wish to imply that R. N. Elliott failed. In my opinion he was brilliant to make such observations in the first place. I do not for one moment believe I could have identified and quantified the Wave Principle if I had no prior foundation on which to work. The ability for me to identify this different structure of impulsive waves could really only have been managed with the benefit of modern calculators and charting software. With a few touches of the keyboard I am able to generate a full range of retracement levels and projections in my spreadsheet. While Elliott did have access to hourly charts, his ability to scrutinize wave relationships was limited due to the fact that he would have had to calculate a range of ratios long hand. Spreadsheets allow these to be available almost instantaneously. All that is needed is to tap in a few highs and lows. Therefore I prefer to label my findings as a modification only. R. N. Elliott's work still remains a remarkable feat of observation and diligence.

Having mentioned to other market professionals that I feel Elliott's structure is incorrect I have encountered a significant degree of resistance. It's like I have touched a raw nerve, almost challenging a religious dogma! Therefore, in suggesting this re-appraisal of the impulsive wave structure I realize that I need to offer suitable substantiated evidence to support my claim, and this I do through the use of wave relationships. The key to this evidence comes from the fact that the Fibonacci or harmonic ratios must be present not only within each wave but also within the entire fractal sequence of waves, so that the waves of lower degrees must generate projection targets that fit harmoniously into the larger degrees. Each in turn contributes to the next larger degree.

I have provided a great number of actual examples of analysis and of the different methods of wave development, and substantiated them all through wave relationships so there can be no doubt that the modification to the harmonic structure is valid.

Clearly with a new modified harmonic structure some of the rules that have been used with Elliott's structure have changed and the methodology of recognizing a correct structure needs a shift in perception and application to forecasting. I have therefore included a chapter dedicated to providing practical guidance in using the harmonic structure, how to recognize certain common wave developments, and hints and tips on how to approach the task of deciphering wave recognition.

I have also included a section on confirming the retracement and projection levels when reached. While Elliott's observations on alternation and degree are still mainly valid, very clearly there are multiple potential retracement ratios or projection targets. Often they can be identified by matching projections from the wave structure of lower degree, but there can often be situations where two areas can be potential targets, both garnered from different wave degrees. Use of momentum can clarify these in the majority of instances.

It is still not the "Holy Grail." I even doubt that there is such a thing. There are still enough occasions where it is very difficult to identify the individual waves either due to exceptionally erratic price development or a rapid move in one direction that makes the identification of waves nigh on impossible. Extended trending moves are still a big challenge so there is still more work to do.

In Chapter 5, I have attempted to provide a practical approach to working with Harmonic Elliott Wave, highlighting some of the problems that arise and how to cope with or understand methods of recognizing when the analysis is going astray. This is extended in Chapter 6, which covers what I feel were a sequence of unfortunate calls in EURUSD. It may sound unusual to point out one's own pitfalls but analysis and forecasting is not a straightforward or simple matter. During much of the development in price I held the correct direction, but I made reversal calls at the wrong moments. One can try to ignore such events, but the manner in which these occurrences are handled is important in order to quickly get back onto the right track. Chapter 6 is an attempt to provide some guidelines on how this may be done.

In this book I therefore offer my own observations; others more capable than I can add to the evidence I will present. I am convinced that changes need to be made and that they provide a much more reliable structural framework in which to forecast future price movements. Having worked with this approach for several years and slowly realized what adjustments need to be made in both price structure and wave relationships, I have found the changes invaluable in providing forecasts.

One final point I should make is that since I am a foreign exchange analyst, necessarily the working examples are from the foreign exchange market. However, I have been asked by subscribers to comment on other markets on occasion. On the first occasion I was uncertain whether my changes would actually apply in other markets. However, I have been pleasantly surprised with the results, and have dedicated a chapter to providing evidence from a range of markets that substantiates my methodology. The first non—foreign exchange markets to which I applied Harmonic Elliott Wave were the Dow Jones Industrial Index and gold. The initial wave counts were generated at the commencement of writing the book. By the time I came to completion these markets had progressed a long way and followed the anticipated structural progress implied by the original analysis. I have therefore extended the original analysis to demonstrate the accuracy of the adaptations made to Elliott's original principle.

Ian Copsey
www.harmonic-ewave.com

CHAPTER 1

R. N. Elliott's Findings: Impulsive Waves

RALPH NELSON ELLIOTT

Ralph Nelson Elliott was a distinguished businessman, an accountant whose career began at the age of 25 in 1896. He was a renowned organizer, fastidious in his approach, and over the following 25 years he rescued a number of distressed companies and brought them back into profitability. In 1924 he was appointed by the U.S. State Department as chief accountant for Nicaragua—then under the control of the United States—to reorganize the finances of the entire country.

However, in 1929 he became seriously ill with pernicious anemia, which kept him confined to his bed. It was at this time, while recuperating, that he studied stock market charts, examining price behavior across all time frames. It took over five years for him to draw his conclusions. In March 1935, as the Dow Jones Average closed almost at its lows, he published his findings by declaring that the index was making its final bottom. The accuracy of his findings was impressive, and they were published in his first book *The Wave Principle*. He followed up in the early 1940s with an addendum on the application of the Fibonacci sequence of ratios to his findings on the structure of wave development.

This became known as the Elliott Wave Principle, and it is applied by what may be millions of traders around the world in today's markets. Before offering my modifications to this principle, I will present Elliott's findings and observations, which still remain the basis of what I consider the most accurate tool in forecasting markets.

The Wave Principle can be loosely separated into two basic market characteristic types: trends and consolidation (or correction). Elliott named the trending phase *impulsive* while the rest were classed as *corrective*. I shall reproduce these in full in order that the original theory is provided, as it still forms the basis of what is a brilliant example of observation and collation into a methodical tool that can be applied even to modern markets.

Those readers who are familiar with the principle may wish to move on to Chapter 3.

THE IMPULSIVE WAVE STRUCTURE

Elliott proposed that when price movements demonstrate an underlying trend, they will always develop in five distinct waves: three in the direction of the trend and two as corrections to the underlying trend (as shown in Figure 1.1). The three directional waves are labeled Waves 1, 3, and 5, and the corrective waves as Waves 2 and 4.

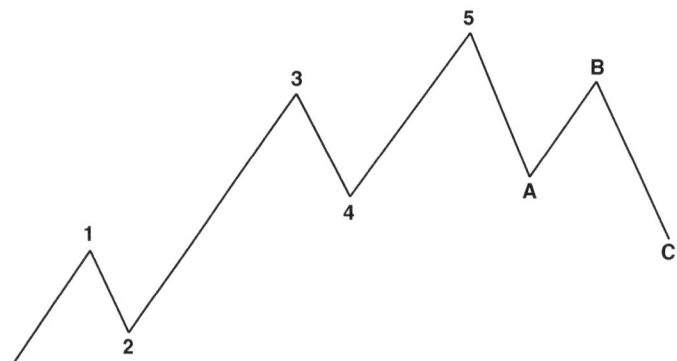

FIGURE 1.1 The Simple Wave Structure

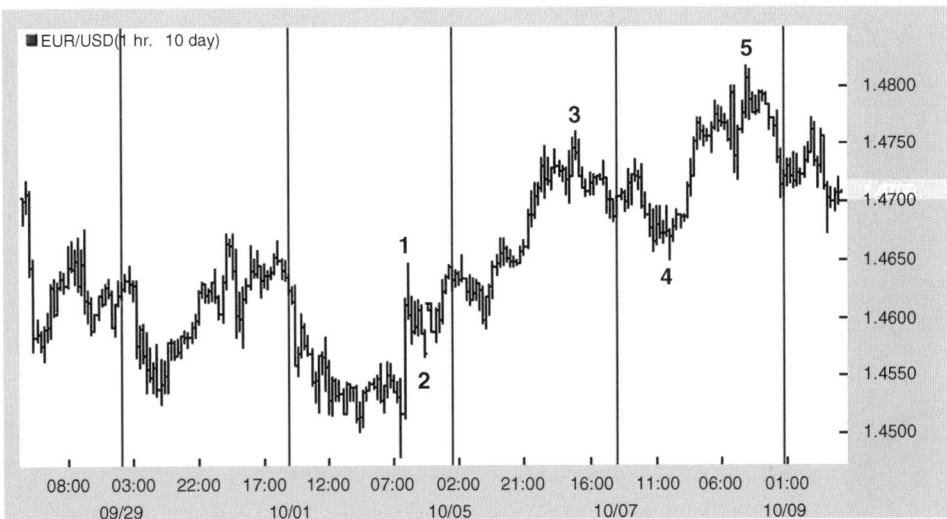

FIGURE 1.2 An Impulsive Wave in EURUSD
Source: FXtrek IntelliChart™ in collaboration with FX-Strategy.com Pro Charts™

The directional waves in a trend are normally referred to as *impulsive waves*. Once this five-wave sequence has been completed, a correction will be formed. While a fuller description of corrective waves will follow, for now I shall simply say that they develop in three waves and refer to these as Waves A, B, and C.

Figure 1.2 shows how a five-wave move would appear on a chart, the example being the hourly EURUSD chart.

Elliott's findings, which were observed over multiple time frames (daily, weekly, and monthly), were that waves are fractal. This meant that the basis of all movements, whether in five-minute charts or monthly, are intrinsically related as the shorter time frames form the building blocks for the larger time frames. This can be observed in the complex wave structure shown in Figure 1.3.

Thus, a simple five-wave move at the beginning of a new sequence will form a Wave (1) and the three-wave correction will then become Wave (2), followed by Wave (3), Wave (4), and Wave (5). Indeed, this larger five-wave move will form Wave [1] of the next higher degree, followed by a Wave [2].

Note: In a simple corrective move, Wave A and Wave C will consist of five waves due to the fact they are *counter-trending*

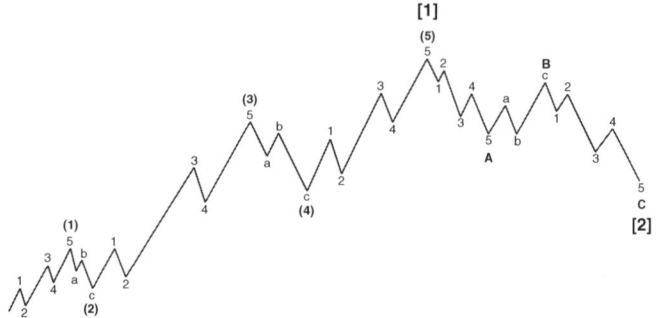

FIGURE 1.3 The Complex Wave Structure

moves. Wave B will always consist of three waves, or—as we will find later—a combination of three-wave moves.

Already it becomes apparent that where you see a five-wave directional move—with the exception of Wave 5—it will always be followed by another five waves.

Figure 1.4 shows how a complex five-wave decline would appear on a chart, the example being the daily GBPUSD chart.

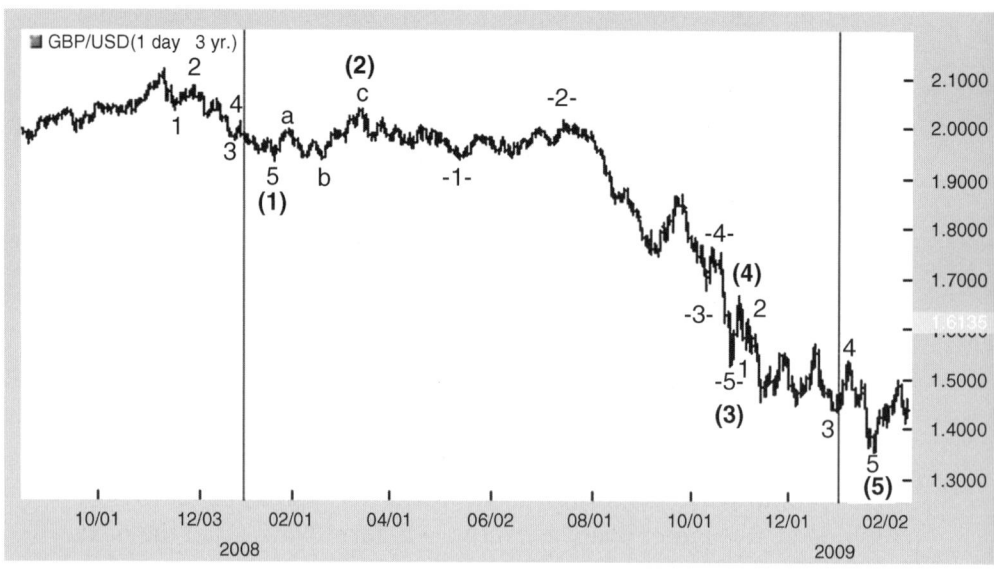

FIGURE 1.4 A Complex Impulsive Wave in GBPUSD
Source: FXtrek IntelliChart™ in collaboration with FX-Strategy.com Pro Charts™

Extended Impulsive Waves

Elliott also noted that impulsive waves had an occasional tendency to extend; he observed that there was more than a single set of impulsive waves in a trend (see Figure 1.5).

This is a simple concept, noting that the five waves constructing Wave (3) are made up of five waves of the same degree. This can perhaps be best described as saying that if this is a daily chart, then the five waves in Wave (3) are also visible and measurable in the daily chart rather than, say, the hourly chart. Of course, the impulsive waves 1, 3, and 5 will be composed of five waves themselves.

In addition to this, Elliott found that there were cases of multiple extensions (as shown in Figure 1.6).

Extended waves may occur in any of the three impulsive waves, but most commonly in a third-wave position which Elliott observed was generally the wave with the strongest risk of a powerful trending extension. Considering the often seen reversal which tends to begin with the market believing that another correction is developing—thus adding to positions in favor of the prior trend—it makes sense that the third wave is more often than not the stronger move as it begins with positions being unwound and fresh positions in the opposite direction being established.

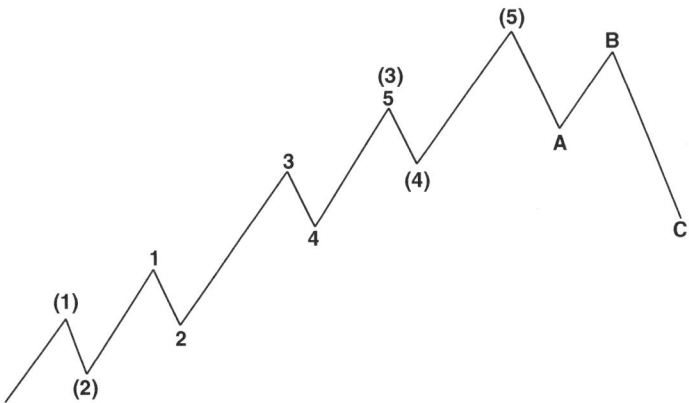

FIGURE 1.5 A Single Extended Impulsive Wave

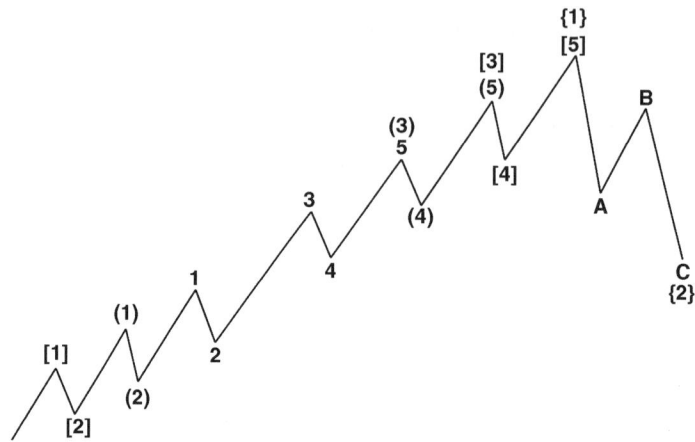

FIGURE 1.6 A Double Extended Impulsive Wave

Figure 1.7 displays an extended wave in the Wave (3) position. There is always the question of when should we know when an extended wave is likely to occur. Sometimes it springs upon us quite suddenly and we are left scrambling to understand what is happening. I have always suggested that if there is any time where we may

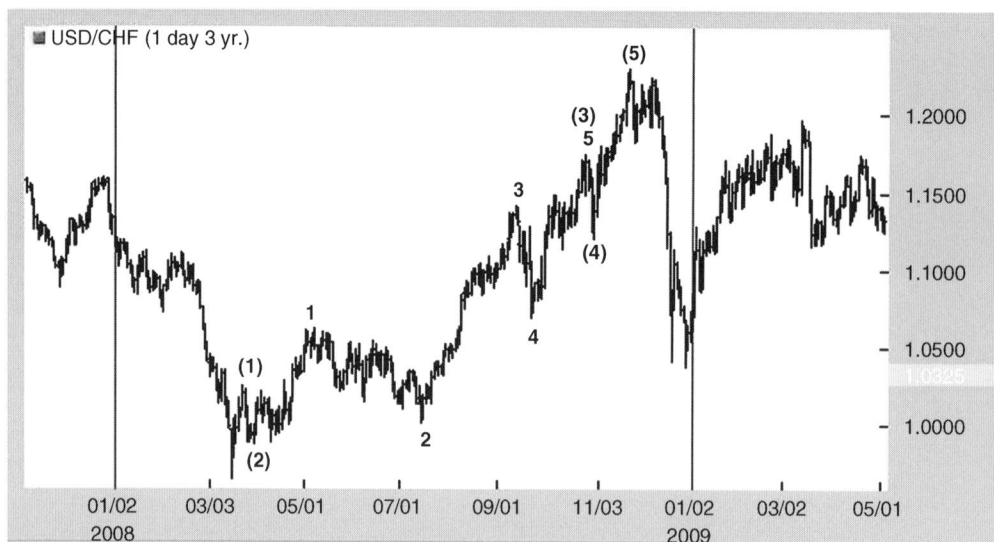

FIGURE 1.7 An Extended Wave in Daily USDCHF
Source: FXtrek IntelliChart™ in collaboration with FX-Strategy.com Pro Charts™

anticipate such a move then it must be that perhaps the final stalling area is one that can be determined from an extension of the prior wave structure. Perhaps we are looking at a five-wave move in Wave (C), and this has projections in a wave equality move around the end of Wave (5).

Later on I shall highlight why I now feel this is unlikely.

Wave 5 Position

Elliott noted a variety of ways a Wave 5 could develop. This of course included an extended Wave 5 that would look similar to Figure 1.8.

Again, the argument tends to be that our target is much higher, and since the normal extension ratios would not reach that target, we should be aware of the potential for an extended Wave (5).

Figure 1.9 displays a long rally in the weekly AUDJPY chart. Note that in this original Elliott method of counting, Wave (3) was extended and was followed by an extended Wave [5] of Wave (5). Clearly I disagree with this counting method, and will highlight this in Chapters 3 and 4.

Another potential Wave 5 is a Diagonal Triangle. Elliott noted that this has a different structure from a normal impulsive move,

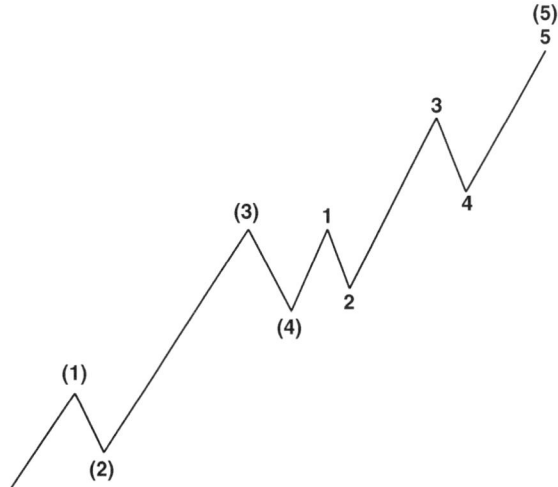

FIGURE 1.8 Extended Wave 5

8 HARMONIC ELLIOTT WAVE

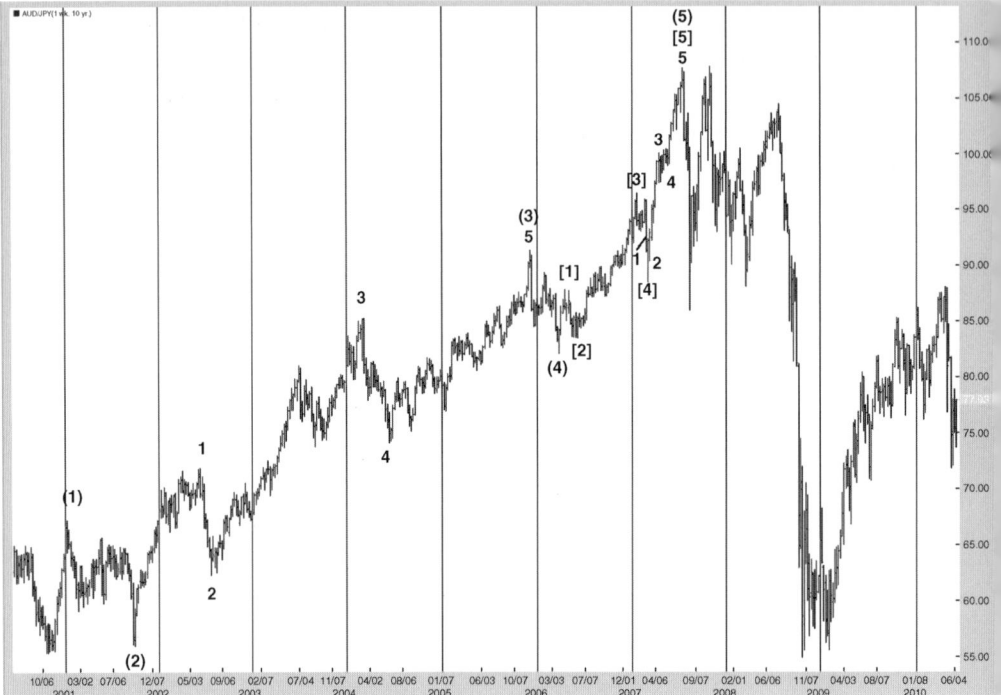

FIGURE 1.9 An Extended Wave in Weekly AUDJPY
Source: FXtrek IntelliChart™ in collaboration with FX-Strategy.com Pro Charts™

being constructed of five waves of three and commonly holding within a channel or within converging lines (as shown in Figure 1.10).

In traditional pattern analysis this is obviously nothing more than a wedge, but Elliott refined the expectations by detailing that there needs to be five waves, three in the direction of the underlying trend with two intervening corrective waves. In general, those that practice Elliott Wave tend to change the labeling to (i), (ii), (iii), and so on, to differentiate impulsive waves 1, 3, and 5 constructed of five waves with those constructed of three waves.

Figure 1.11 shows how a Diagonal Triangle Wave 5 wave rally would appear on a chart, the example being the five-minute EURUSD chart.

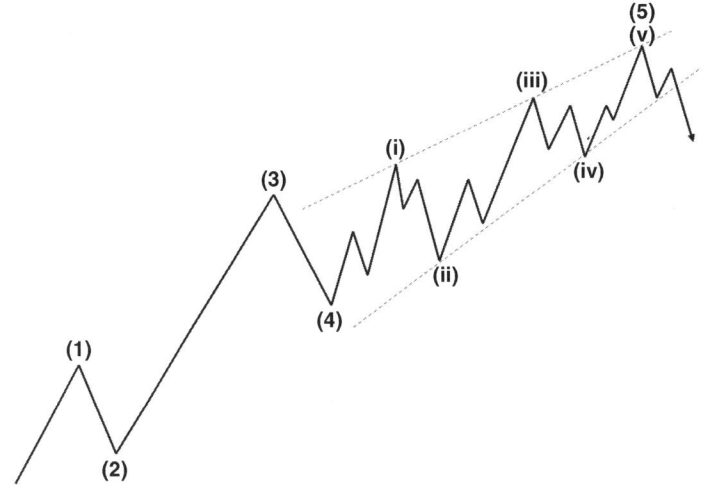

FIGURE 1.10 Diagonal Triangle Wave (5)

Elliott proposed that extended waves could appear in any of the three impulsive waves—that is, Waves 1, 3, or 5—but only one impulsive wave could be extended in any one sequence of five waves.

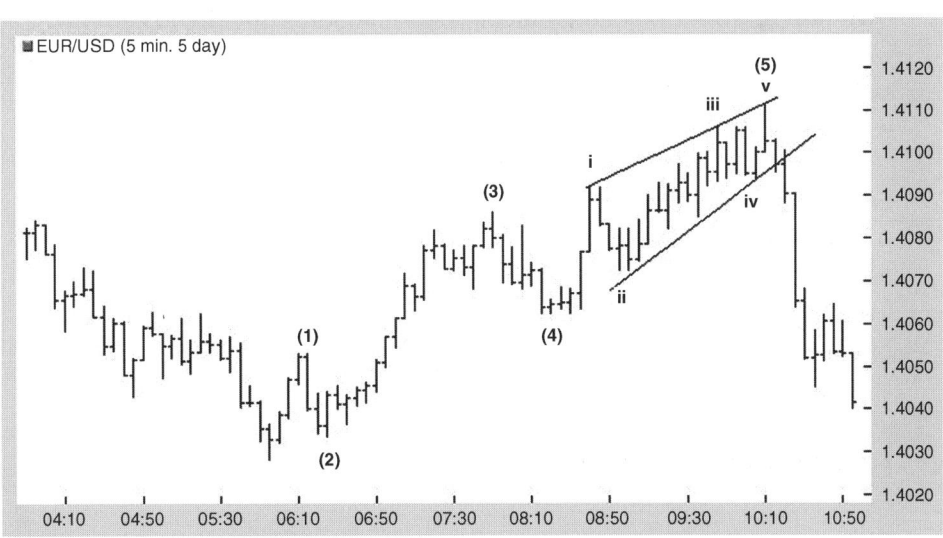

FIGURE 1.11 A Diagonal Wave (5) in the Five-Minute EURUSD Chart
Source: FXtrek IntelliChart™ in collaboration with FX-Strategy.com Pro Charts™

In my own findings I feel this is really a reflection of an alternative structure and was misunderstood. Later, through the use of detailed measurements of waves, I shall describe why I have come to this conclusion.

Failed Fifth Waves

Elliott noticed that on occasion Wave 5 fails to extend beyond the extreme of Wave 3 and generates a reversal directly (as shown in Figure 1.12).

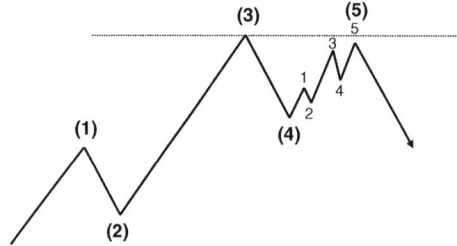

FIGURE 1.12 A Failed Fifth Wave

This has been in mainstream Elliott Wave counting, but from my own perception it is a convenient way to account for the loss of an extra anticipated move higher. I feel this actually indicates that the structure is incorrect. However, I shall discuss this later when explaining my findings.

Figure 1.13 displays two five-wave rallies, the first in Wave (A) with a distinct extended wave in Wave (3), while the second in Wave (C) has an extended Wave 5 of Wave (5). In Wave (5) the final Wave v of 5 appears to have developed as a failed fifth wave.

Again, I shall describe later in Chapter 4 why I feel this count is incorrect.

UNBREAKABLE RULES

Elliott detailed only three rules in the entirety of his findings, and all were confined to the actions of impulsive waves.

R. N. Elliott's Findings: Impulsive Waves

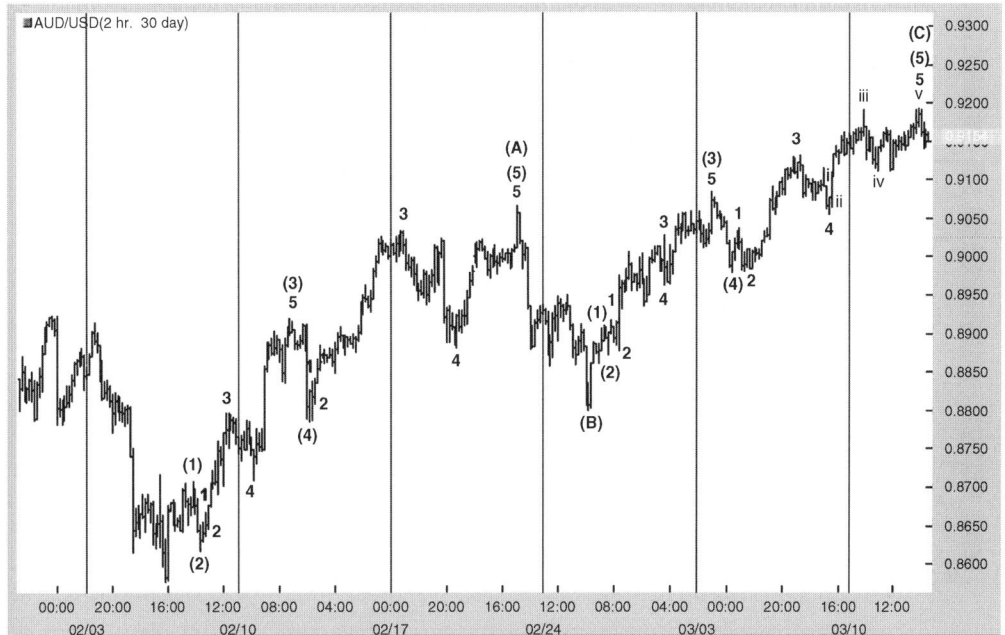

FIGURE 1.13 Two Sets of Five-Wave Rallies in AUDUSD
Source: FXtrek IntelliChart™ in collaboration with FX-Strategy.com Pro Charts™

Rule 1: Wave 2 can *never* retrace more than 100% of Wave 1.

This is quite logical. If we are talking about an impulsive wave representing the underlying trend, it would be illogical to have a retracement that breaks the basic definition of a trend as defined by classical technical analysis.

An uptrend is a sequence of higher highs and higher lows. Once that sequence is broken, the uptrend can be assumed to have ended. A downtrend is a sequence of lower lows and lower highs. Once that sequence is broken, the downtrend can be assumed to have ended.

Rule 2: Wave 3 is *never* the shortest of the three impulsive waves.

Elliott also noted that statistically Wave 3 is *generally* the longest, and of all extended waves it is Wave 3 that most commonly extends as this is where the market has realized that it has the wrong position, and exits from its prior trending position to enter into the anticipated new trend direction.

Rule 3: Wave 4 in an impulsive wave *never* retraces to a level below the peak of Wave 1 in an uptrend or above the trough of Wave 1 in a downtrend.

This rule basically highlights that during a trend that indicates a sustained movement in one direction, the extreme of Wave 4 would not be expected to retrace so deep as to overlap with the extreme of Wave 1.

ELLIOTT'S GUIDELINES

Elliott also noted some guidelines that he would not count as rules but noticed a high ratio of instances where these factors occurred. They are helpful hints in outlining high-probability outcomes in certain circumstances, ones I have found exceptionally useful in

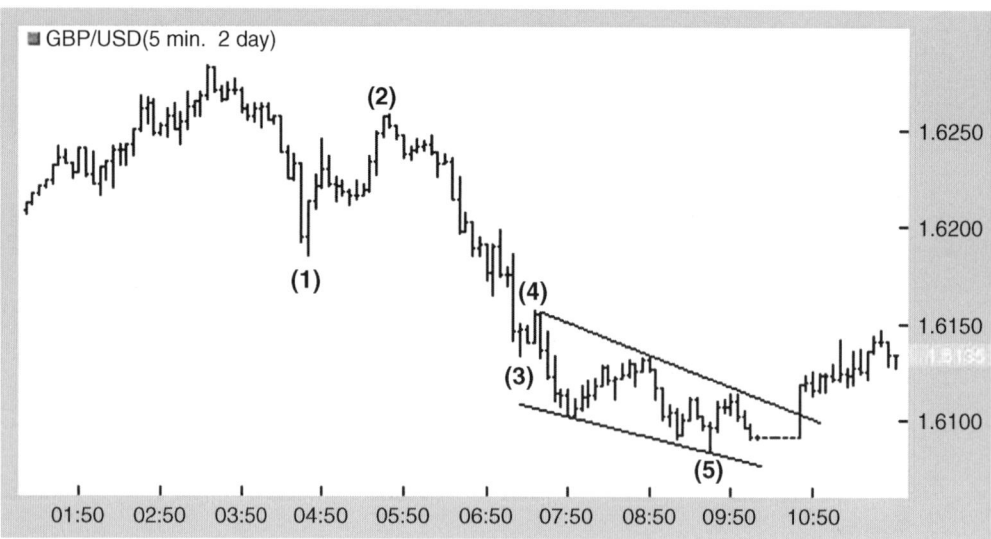

FIGURE 1.14 Deep Wave (2) and Shallow Wave (4) Demonstrating Alternation in Five-Minute GBPUSD
Source: FXtrek IntelliChart™ in collaboration with FX-Strategy.com Pro Charts™

my own analysis and which indeed blend in well with my own views on price structure.

Alternation

Elliott noticed a strong tendency for corrective waves within an impulsive structure to alternate in terms of depth and complexity. I shall cover corrective waves briefly at this point.

If Wave 2 develops in a simple manner (an ABC Zigzag move) then Wave 4 will tend to be complex (Triangle, Flat, Expanded Flat, or Triple Three). If Wave 2 develops in a complex manner then Wave 4 tends to be a simple ABC move.

In addition, alternation covers the depth of the retracements in Waves 2 and 4. If Wave 2 was shallow then Wave 4 will be deep, and vice versa (as shown in Figure 1.14).

In this example of a five-wave decline in the five-minute GBPUSD chart, Wave (2) retraced Wave (1) by 74.8%. Conversely, Wave (4) retraced only 18.4% before seeing a Diagonal Triangle decline in Wave (5).

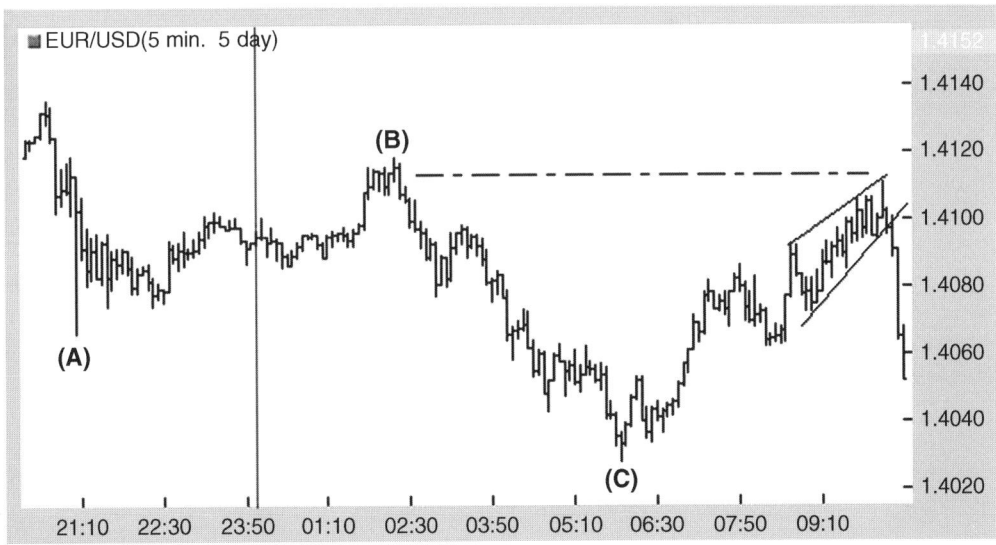

FIGURE 1.15 Following the Completion of an ABC Move Lower Price Retraces to the Prior Wave (B)
Source: FXtrek IntelliChart™ in collaboration with FX-Strategy.com Pro Charts™

B Waves

The second guideline Elliott noticed was that after the completion of a three-wave move there is a tendency for price to reverse to the area of the preceding Wave B (as shown in Figure 1.15). This may prove temporary or a long period depending on which part of the wave structure it occurred in.

This chart is one such example of an event that occurs so frequently that it provides an excellent first target in a retracement.

CHAPTER 2

R. N. Elliott's Findings: Corrective Waves

The corrective wave structure is probably the biggest headache for any Elliottician. The large variation in types of corrective structures is still rather overwhelming for even me following the completion of a five-wave move.

How deep will the retracement be? How long will it last and how complex will it be? There is a bewildering range of potential outcomes that can push a new analyst attempting to learn the principle into finding a more simple method of forecasting. While it can be a deterrent, I find the eventual benefits far outweigh the negatives, and the understanding of how structures develop actually aids the final recognition and awareness of not only when a correction is complete but also when an alternative structure is developing.

With the use of Fibonacci and harmonic ratios and a broad understanding of how these need to slot into the structure of the next higher degree, it is possible to piece together the developing clues as to what will happen next. I would therefore encourage all students of the principle to stick with it and remain determined to conquer the challenges; the benefits are substantial.

CORRECTIVE WAVES

Let's now have a look at corrective waves.

Zigzags

Zigzags (as shown in Figure 2.1) are the most basic and simple of all corrections. They comprise two counter-trending waves, Wave A and Wave C (that develop in five waves), which are divided by a three-wave structure (or combination of three-wave structures). Quite commonly Elliotticians will refer to these as 535 moves.

This type of move is quite simple to observe, and as long as the two impulsive waves—that is, Wave (A) and Wave (C)—can be identified through observing the five waves, it is unusual to get too confused.

Figure 2.2 shows how a three-wave correction in a Zigzag may look in USDJPY.

Following completion of a simple ABC correction we can expect the main trend to resume.

Complex Corrective Structures

From the initial description of corrective waves it should come as no surprise to learn that ABC patterns do not always complete a correction. There are several basic types of complex corrective structures which all commence with a simple ABC move. I shall outline some guidelines to highlight when you might be able to anticipate the

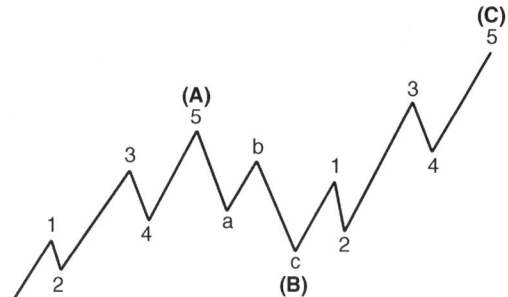

FIGURE 2.1 A Simple Zigzag Correction

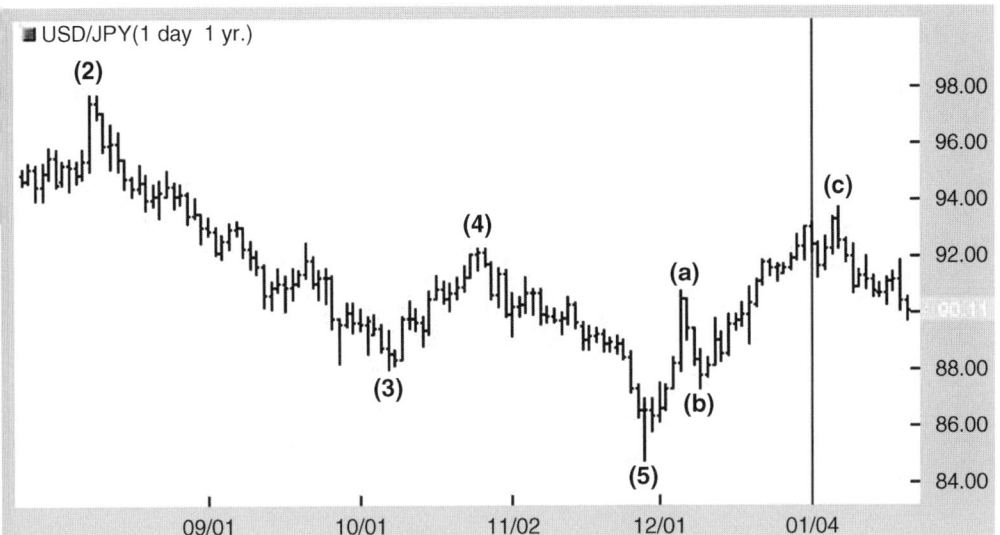

FIGURE 2.2 An ABC Correction Higher in Daily USDJPY
Source: FXtrek IntelliChart™ in collaboration with FX-Strategy.com Pro Charts™

development of a more complex correction later. For now I shall describe the basic types of complex corrective structures.

Double Zigzag To complicate matters, and probably more often than not, corrections do not end with just a simple ABC move. In the second variation, once an ABC move has been seen a correction is seen in what is then labeled Wave (x) and which is then followed by a second ABC move (see Figure 2.3). The Wave (x) will not normally break through the prior Wave (b), and will itself comprise three

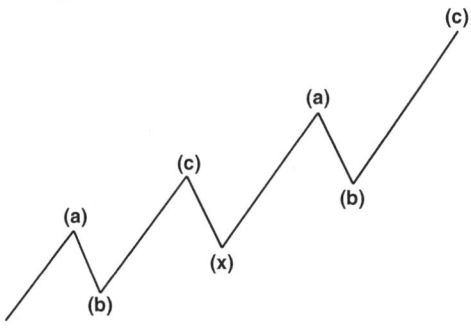

FIGURE 2.3 A Double Zigzag Higher

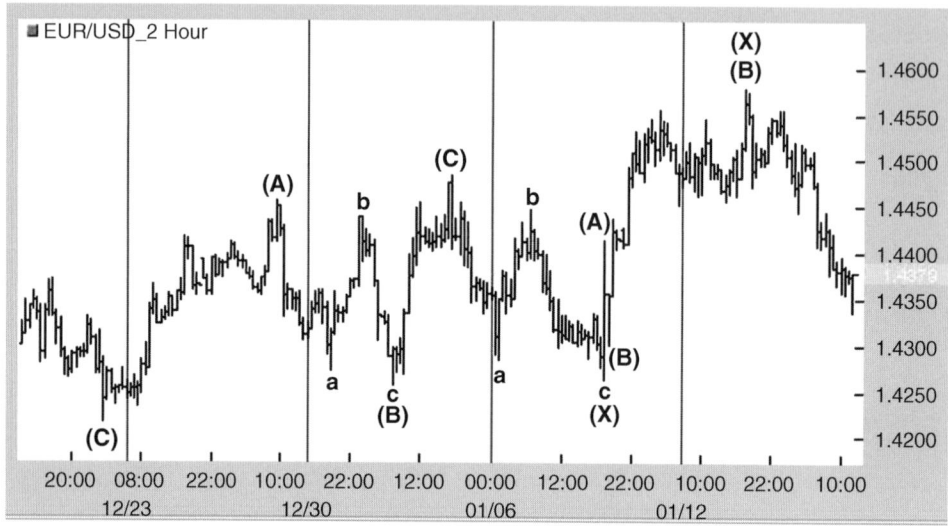

FIGURE 2.4 A Double Zigzag Higher in Two-Hour EURUSD
Source: FXtrek IntelliChart™ in collaboration with FX-Strategy.com Pro Charts™

waves or a combination of three waves in any of the corrective structures in this list.

Once the Double Zigzag is complete the underlying directional move will continue.

Figure 2.4 demonstrates how a Double Zigzag could develop.

This shows a two-hour EURUSD chart in which there are two ABC corrections higher and separated by a Wave (X). The two instances of a Wave (B) are constructed of a simple Zigzag structure. Also note how the Wave (X) declines close to the first Wave (B) but does not penetrate. Normally we can judge that the directional move is resuming by a break of the last Wave (B).

Triple Three The next example of a complex series of ABC corrections is simply another ABC move tagged on the end of a Double Zigzag. The third ABC structure is separated from the second by a second Wave (x). This is shown in Figures 2.5 and 2.6.

If I am to make an observation on these types of corrections I would say that I find Triple Threes the most common. I do not notice Double Zigzags that often or a simple ABC structure, except for those acting as a Wave (x).

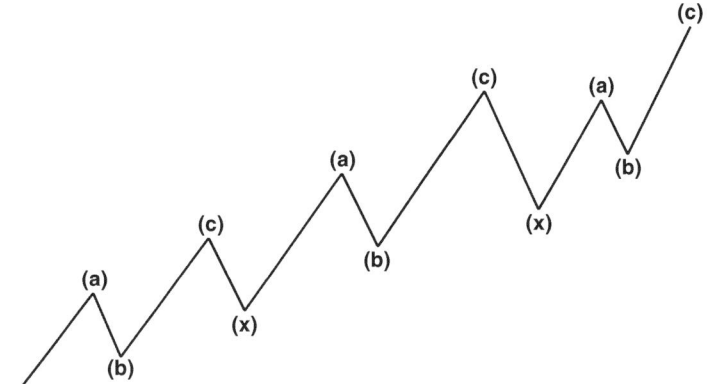

FIGURE 2.5 A Triple Three Higher

The corrective decline in EURUSD was particularly complicated. It comprised three ABC declines, each separated by an intervening Wave x. These tend to occur when the market has had a strong directional move which, on completion, leaves the market unconvinced of that move. Hence the tendency to attempt to look for the resumption of the underlying trend, only to have the early

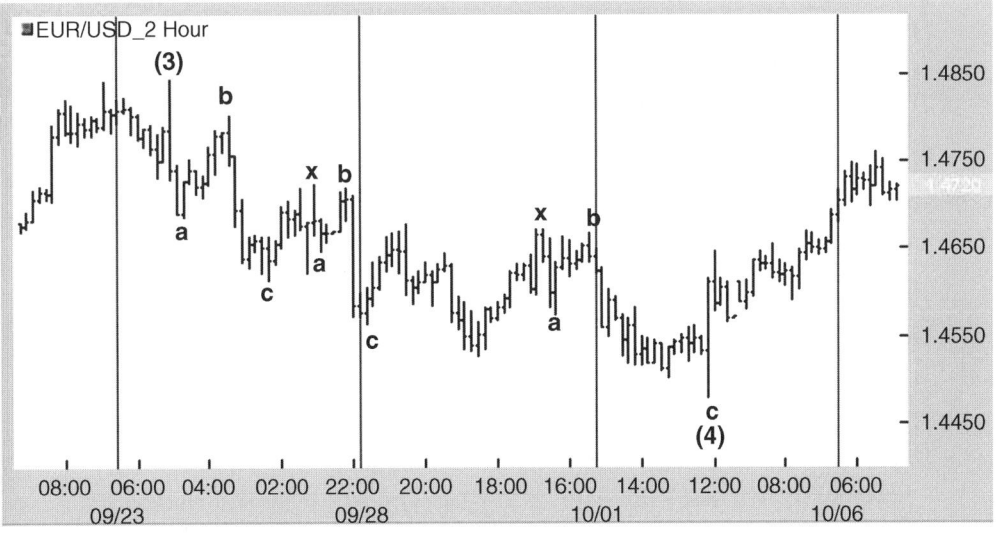

FIGURE 2.6 A Triple Three Lower in Two-Hour EURUSD
Source: FXtrek IntelliChart™ in collaboration with FX-Strategy.com Pro Charts™

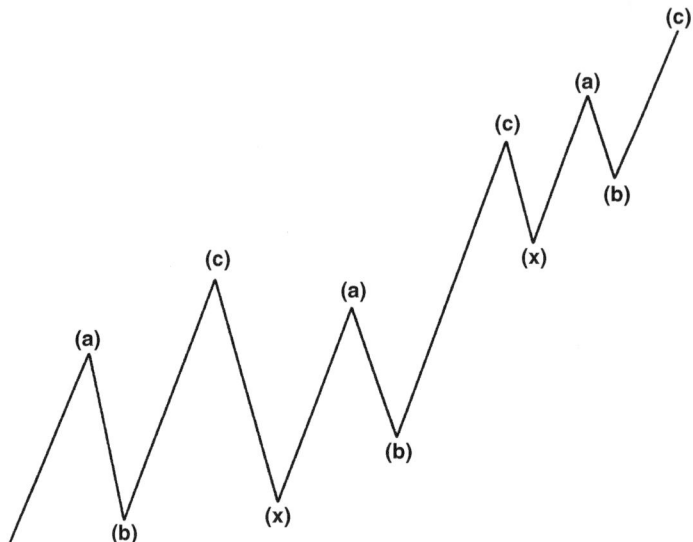

FIGURE 2.7 A Triple Three Higher with the First Wave (x) Retracing Close to the Prior Deep Wave (b)

resumption thwarted and followed by a further erratic correction. This then happens a second time.

The more positive note is that once there has been a Triple Three we can be confident that a Quadruple Three does not exist. Hence, if the completion of such a correction is correctly identified the resumption of the trend is a certain event.

There is a tendency for a deep Wave (x) following a deep Wave (b) (see Figure 2.7). This is a guideline only and does not occur in 100% of the cases, but the tendency is quite common in complex corrective structures. Following a deep Wave (b) the subsequent Wave (x) is also quite deep and can correct quite close to the prior Wave (b).

The deep Wave (b) can clearly occur either in the first or second Wave (b), which will both have a subsequent Wave (x) developing on the completion of the Wave (c). If one of the instances of Wave (b) happens to be deep then the Wave (x) can often be the same.

Figure 2.8 displays a pullback in Wave (B) that develops as a Triple Three. The first correction in Wave (b) is quite deep. Note that

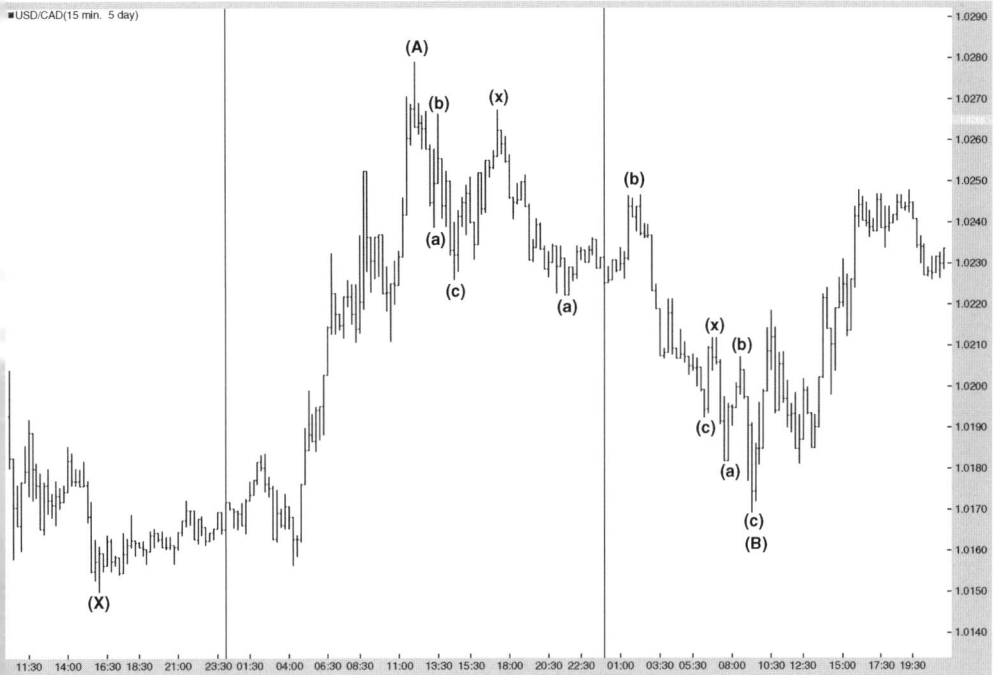

FIGURE 2.8 A Triple Three Lower in USDCAD with a Deep First Wave (x)
Source: FXtrek IntelliChart™ in collaboration with FX-Strategy.com Pro Charts™

following the completion of Wave (c) the Wave (x) retracement is also very deep, and in this case actually retraces above Wave (b). The third Wave (b) is also very deep. However, since there have been three sets of (a)(b)(c) structures in this decline and since Quadruple Threes do not exist, we can be confident that there will be no third instance of a Wave (x).

Other Complex Corrective Structures

Unfortunately the three types of corrections which comprise independent ABC structures do not encompass the entirety of the complex structures. To make the problem of recognizing corrections more difficult there are three other types that start with a simple Zigzag.

We have covered the situation when a correction develops as a Zigzag, which by definition is a three-wave move that is labeled ABC. It is quite common for this ABC move to actually become the first wave of a more complex structure. These additional structures are the Flat Correction, Expanded Flat Correction, and Triangle.

Flat Corrections A Flat Correction is very simply that the three legs of the correction—which I refer to as Wave Fa, Wave Fb, and Wave Fc—develop in a manner that the Fb retraces from the initial ABC correction (Wave Fa) back to the same area as the end of the trending move (Wave Fb). From that same area, price then moves back to the first corrective point at Wave Fa, but this develops in a five-wave move to complete Wave Fc (as shown in Figure 2.9).

Flat Corrections can occur at any corrective point in the wave structure. Thus, this could be Wave 2, Wave 4, Wave B, or even Wave X.

In the example in Figure 2.10, USDCHF rallied in five waves in Wave (A), in which Wave 4 was an ascending Triangle. This was followed by Wave Fa, a recovery to the peak at Wave 5, and a second decline in Wave Fc back to the same point as Wave Fa. This formed the correction in Wave (B).

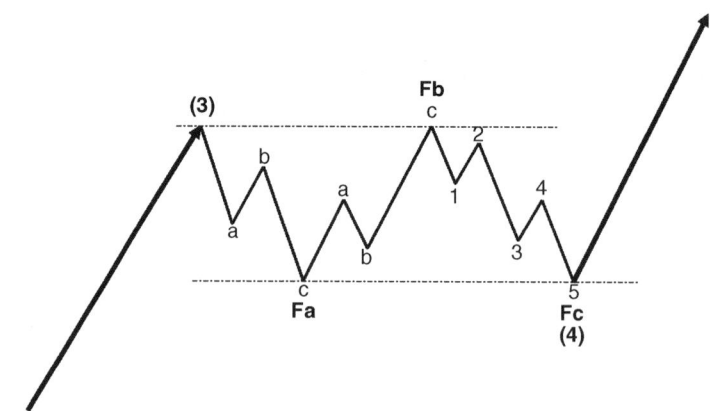

FIGURE 2.9 A Flat Correction

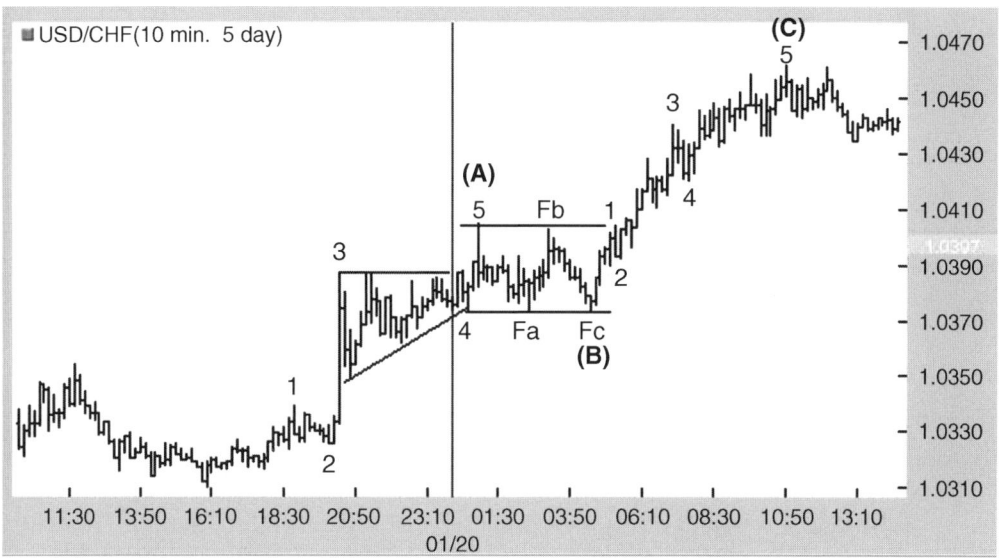

FIGURE 2.10 A Flat Correction within an ABC Rally in 10-minute USDCHF
Source: FXtrek IntelliChart™ in collaboration with FX-Strategy.com Pro Charts™

Expanded Flat Corrections In stronger trending moves the market sentiment is particularly bullish so that after an initial three-wave correction (to Wave efa) price resumes in the direction of the prior impulsive wave but *extends beyond* the end of the first move to Wave efb. This move also comes in three waves (or a more complex corrective structure) before reversing in Wave efc to the original area around Wave efa (see Figure 2.11). It can fall a little short of Wave efa or indeed overshoot a little.

Similar to Flat Corrections, the Expanded Flat can occur in any Wave 2, Wave 4, Wave B, or Wave X (see Figure 2.12).

Recalling the example of the Triple Three in Figure 2.6, there was a Wave x that actually saw the Wave b extending below the low of the last Wave c. It is not too easy to see the three-wave move in Wave efa but it is very clear in Wave efb. Finally price rallied back to a few points short of Wave efa before the final ABC structure developed and ended at 1.4480.

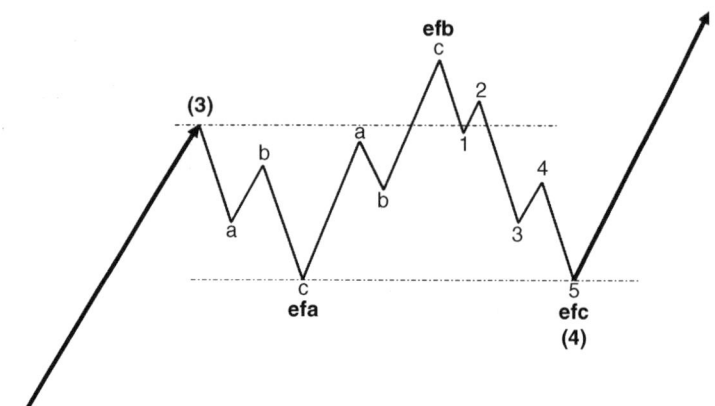

FIGURE 2.11 An Expanded Flat Correction

Triangles A final complex corrective structure is the Triangle. In contrast to classic technical analysis which has no structure for the Triangle, Elliott's version is strict in requiring five sets of ABC patterns and generally (but not always) with contracting peaks and troughs (as shown in Figure 2.13).

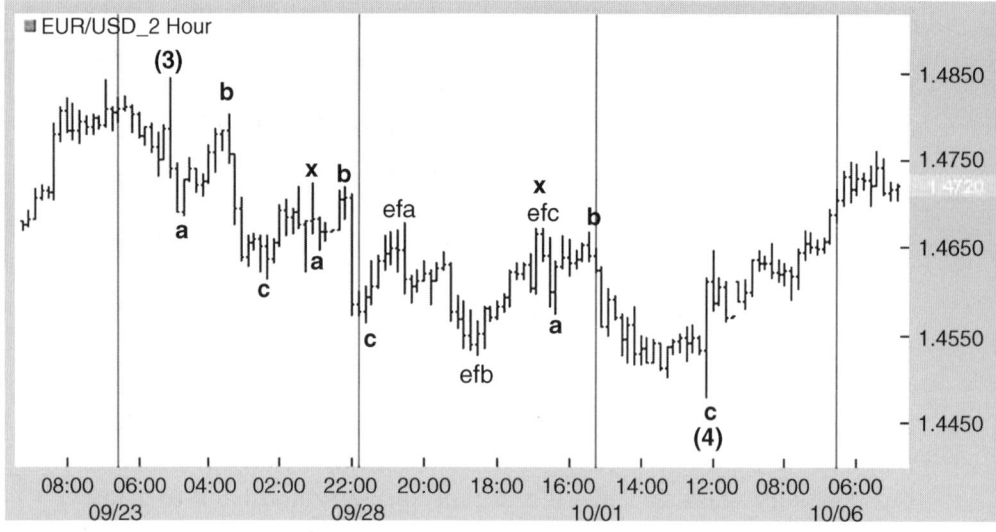

FIGURE 2.12 An Expanded Flat Correction in Wave x within a Triple Three Correction in EURUSD
Source: FXtrek IntelliChart™ in collaboration with FX-Strategy.com Pro Charts™

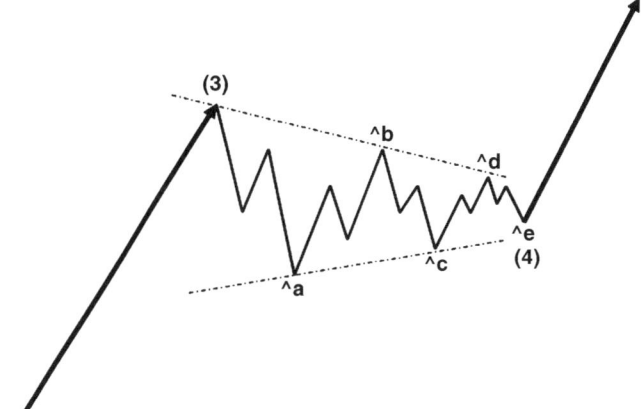

FIGURE 2.13 A Triangle Correction

Note that each leg of the Triangle comes in three waves or may come as a combination of three waves, as Double Zigzags or Triple Threes. The Wave b of each leg can also be any of the simple or complex corrective structures. They tend to be the most complex of all wave structures as they basically represent a conflict between bulls and bears, with neither camp being able to force an extension of their sentiment.

In Figure 2.14, price rallied in Wave (A) and then fell into a sideways consolidation within converging peaks and troughs. It is not always obvious that each leg of the Triangle develops in an ABC structure (or combination of three-wave moves), but these should be more obvious in the lower time-frame chart. Once the five legs are complete in Wave ^e, this completes Wave (B) and triggers an extension high in Wave (C).

Judging When a Complex Correction is More Likely to Occur Clearly the array of corrective structures can be quite dismaying and generates some uncertainties over just what may occur. Indeed corrections are a lot more complex due to the fact that more two-way views are being expressed by the market, possibly due to inconclusive economic releases or the market is awaiting such a release.

However, there are clues that are quite straightforward if these occur in particular areas of the wave structure. In Chapter 4,

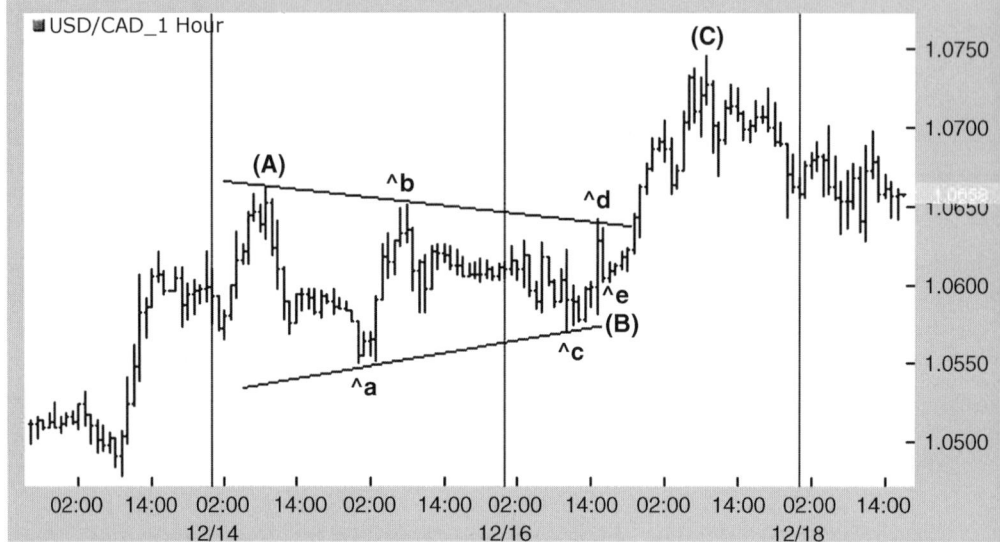

FIGURE 2.14 A Triangle within a Wave (B) Position in a Zigzag Higher in USDCAD
Source: FXtrek IntelliChart™ in collaboration with FX-Strategy.com Pro Charts™

I describe the use of Fibonacci and harmonic ratios to determine high-risk areas where corrections should end. For example, if we are looking at a correction in Wave 4 which has a high chance of providing a 50% retracement, if the first ABC move has retraced only 20% of the length of Wave 3 then there's a much greater chance of seeing a Double Zigzag or Triple Three. However, if the first ABC move retraces a full 50% then we must be alerted to the possibility of a Flat, Expanded Flat, or Triangle in the Wave 4 position.

We must also be aware of the structure of price development to confirm whether it is consistent with an impulsive structure (and measurement) or whether it is consistent with another three-wave move which will imply a corrective structure.

Further Examples of Complex Corrective Structures

One of the most frustrating elements of the entire Elliott Wave structure is the complexity with which corrective waves can develop. While straight Zigzags, Double Zigzags, and Triple Threes will always see the Waves A and C develop in five waves, Wave B and

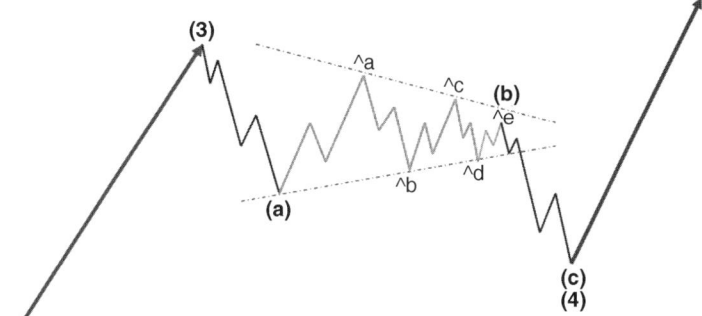

FIGURE 2.15 A Triangle within a Wave (b) Position within a Zigzag in Wave (4)

Wave X can produce a great deal of complexity. It is these corrections in the midst of a corrective structure that tend to stretch the limits of the imagination and possibly even belief. What are always key in identifying these are the wave relationships, and I'll cover these in Chapter 4. For now I shall merely note some of the different combinations of structure that are possible.

Figure 2.15 displays an example of a Zigzag in a Wave (4) position which has a Triangle in the Wave (b) position. Note the five waves lower, in Wave (a), suggests a Zigzag, Double Zigzag, or Triple Three. The contracting set of three-wave structures completes Wave (b) and then triggers a follow-through in Wave (c) to complete a Zigzag.

Figure 2.16 displays another example of a Zigzag in a Wave (4) position but this time it has the Wave (b) developing as a Triple Three. Note the five waves lower, in Wave (a), suggests a Zigzag, Double Zigzag, or Triple Three. Within the Triple Three, note that the second Wave x has developed in a Flat Correction to complete Wave (b). This is followed by an extension lower in Wave (c) to complete the Zigzag.

Figure 2.17 displays another example of a Zigzag in a Wave (4) position within which the Wave (b) also develops as a Zigzag. Note the five waves lower, in Wave (a), suggests a Zigzag, Double Zigzag, or Triple Three. This is followed by a five-wave rally in Wave [a] and an Expanded Flat Wave [b] before the five-wave rally in Wave [c] to complete Wave (b). This is followed by an extension lower in Wave (c) to complete the Zigzag.

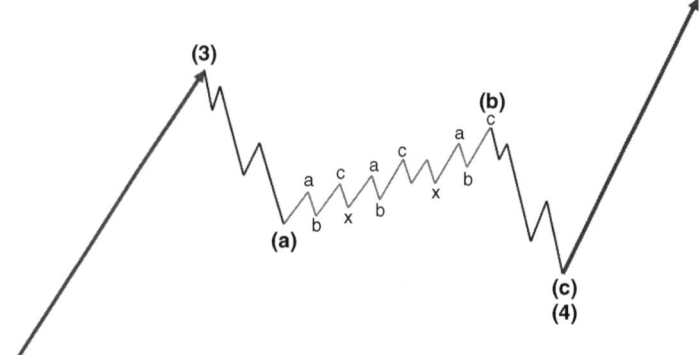

FIGURE 2.16 A Triple Three within a Wave (b) Position within a Zigzag in Wave (4)

On the assumption that Wave (2) was probably a brief correction, the guideline of alternation would warn of a potential complex correction in Figure 2.18. The initial Wave A in three waves would double that warning. At that point it would not be possible to know what would eventually develop. The three-wave rally back to the same peak as Wave (3) would suggest a Flat Correction. However, the decline also comes in three waves and thus we can begin to anticipate a far more complex structure. The rally from the second low at Wave Fb developed in five waves and thus completes a Flat Correction in

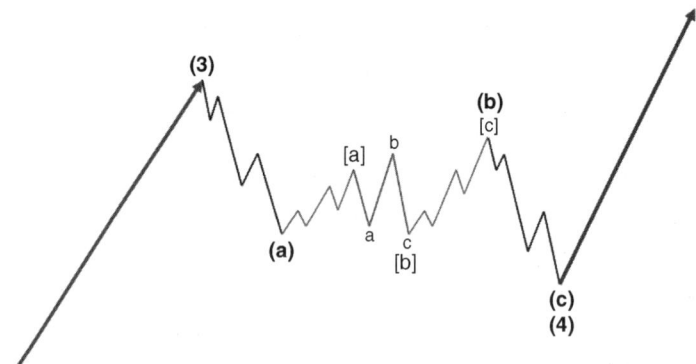

FIGURE 2.17 An Expanded Flat Wave [b] within a Zigzag in a Wave (b) Position within a Zigzag in Wave (4)

R. N. Elliott's Findings: Corrective Waves

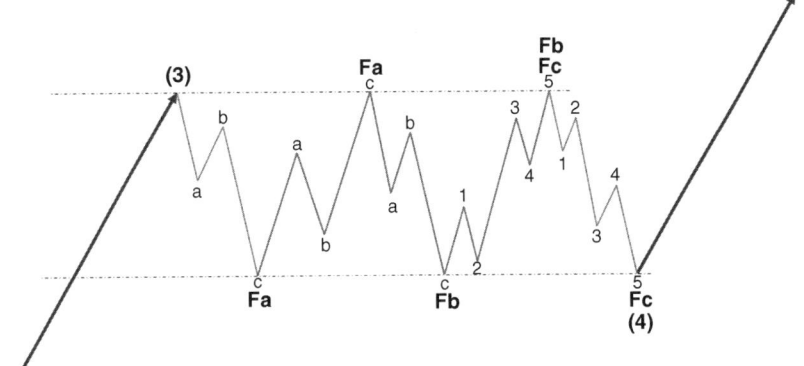

FIGURE 2.18 A Flat Correction in Wave Fb within a Flat Wave (4)

Wave Fb of the larger Flat Correction. It is then possible to anticipate a five-wave decline back to around the area close to the earlier two lows in Wave Fc to complete Wave (4).

In Figure 2.19 the move lower ended in a Wave (3) and was followed by a three-wave recovery. At this point it would not be possible to know which complex structure would develop. From the peak marked as

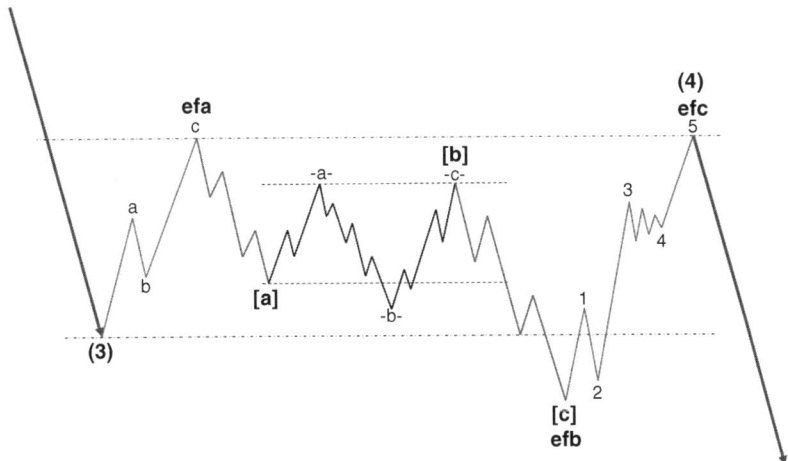

FIGURE 2.19 An Expanded Flat Wave (4) with an Expanded Flat Wave [b] in Wave efb

Wave efa there was a five-wave decline that fell short of the Wave (3) low. At this depth it would be reasonable to believe that this would not develop as a Triangle and thus the two alternatives would be a Flat Correction or Expanded Flat. The pullback came in three waves and then a decline in a Double Zigzag that ended below Wave [a]. Again, it would be necessary to judge whether there could be a third ABC structure to complete a Triple Three. However, the next move was a five-wave rally back to the area close to Wave [a]. Thus it suggests this was an Expanded Flat Wave [b]. The logical conclusion of this is still the possibility of a decline to the base of Wave (3) in a Flat Correction or a possible Expanded Flat. Measurements should be made of the five waves to see where the completion would be likely. Indeed, it became a larger Expanded Flat Wave efb, and thus a five-wave rally in Wave efc should be anticipated to complete Wave (4).

Figure 2.20 is an example of how a complex Triple Three in a Wave (4) position may develop. The first ABC structure is straightforward in a simple five-wave Wave (A), a deep three-wave Wave (B), and followed by a rally in Wave (C). Wave (X) then develops as an Expanded Flat. The second ABC structure develops with Wave [B] as a Triangle. The second Wave [X] develops as a Flat Correction, and then the Wave {B} of the third ABC structure develops as a choppy Double Zigzag.

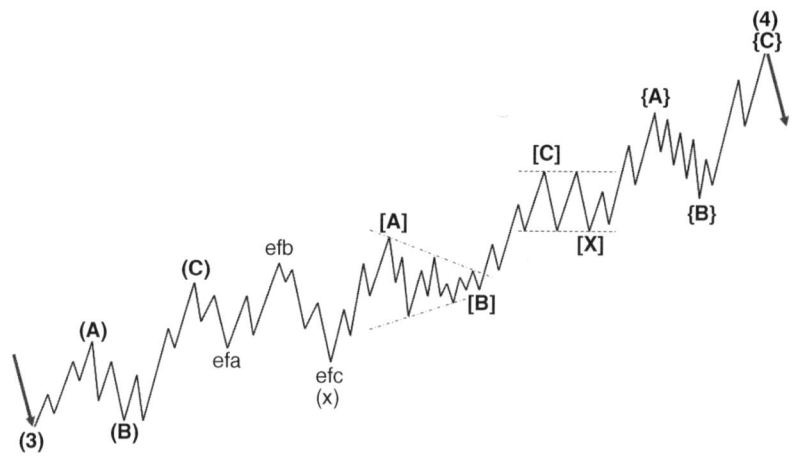

FIGURE 2.20 A complex Triple Three in a Wave (4) Position

R. N. Elliott's Findings: Corrective Waves   **31**

The following charts provide a few examples of how complicated corrections can become, specifically in corrections within the corrections.

Figure 2.21 displays a bullish correction in the hourly EURUSD. The pullback in Wave (b) was very deep, and it is possible that if not measured carefully the low marked Wave -a- may have been assumed to be Wave (b). Failure to break above the Wave (a) peak then generated a Wave -c- that may have even caused doubts whether Wave (5) had already begun. However, the subsequent rally was very approximately a wave equality projection to complete Wave (c). Again, at this point the correction has occurred in three waves and the consideration of a complex correction would have had to be made. The issue here is to be aware of the depth of retracement that is implied by alternation in Wave (4). There was another deeply swinging

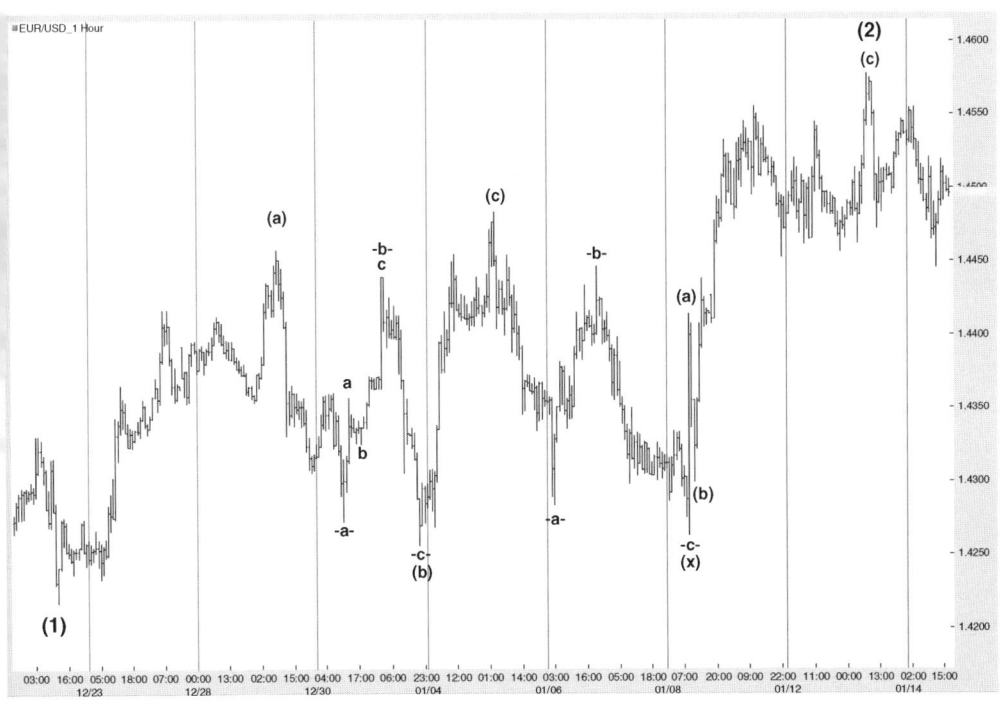

FIGURE 2.21 A Double Zigzag in a Wave (2) Position in Hourly EURUSD
Source: FXtrek IntelliChart™ in collaboration with FX-Strategy.com Pro Charts™

Zigzag in Wave (x) which was followed by the second three-wave rally to complete a Double Zigzag and also the Wave (4).

Figure 2.22 is an example of an Expanded Flat Correction in the two-hour GBPUSD market. Price had been declining quite sharply and completed the end of a Wave (3), from where it began a shaky recovery. The first two waves higher (labeled Wave (i) and Wave (ii)) may well have been mistaken as an ABC recovery, and assuming the expectation was for a deeper correction the analysis could have implied a Double Zigzag or Triple Three. In fact, there was a third move higher and then deeper correction, and thus it appears that these five waves higher developed in a Diagonal Triangle (wedge) pattern to complete Wave (a). This was followed by a Wave (b) and Wave (c).

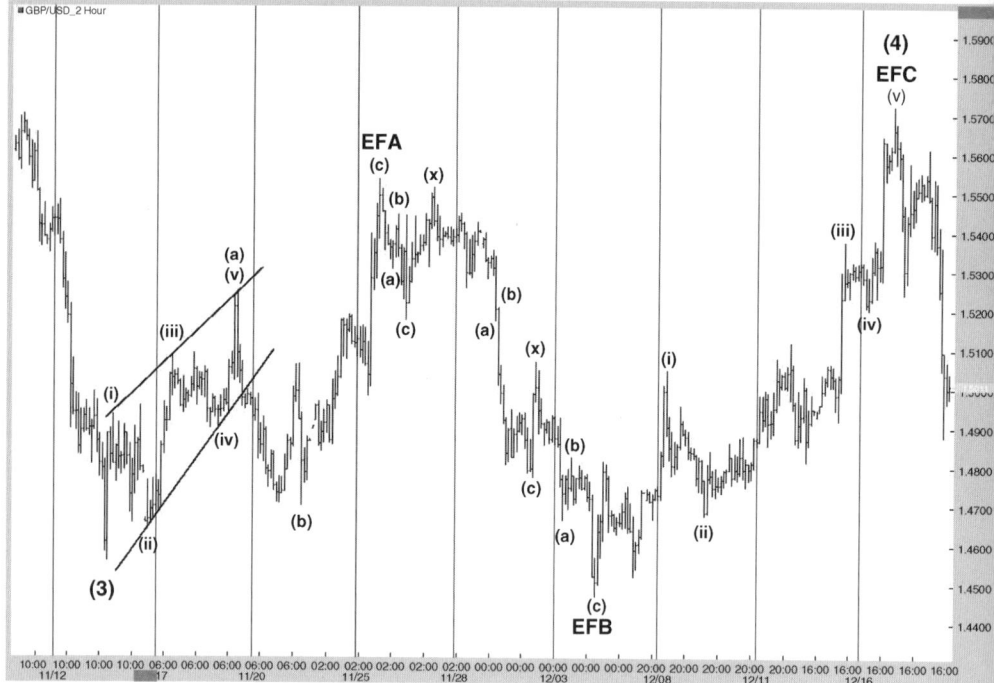

FIGURE 2.22 An Expanded Flat Wave (4) in Two-Hour GBPUSD
Source: FXtrek IntelliChart™ in collaboration with FX-Strategy.com Pro Charts™

R. N. Elliott's Findings: Corrective Waves

At this point the decision would need to be made whether this indeed completed Wave (4) or was part of a complex correction. Consideration of the structure in Wave (2) should be given in respect to alternation to aid in the decision-making process.

Price then declined very clearly in a more corrective manner, which ended just below the Wave (3) low and then reversed higher. At this point the analysis would highlight the potential for an Expanded Flat Correction. Price then rallied in a Diagonal Triangle Wave (c) to complete Wave EFC and therefore Wave (4).

Figure 2.23 provides an example of a long Triangle that lasted around six months in USDCAD and included a variety of corrective structures. Wave ^A declined in a simple Zigzag to warn of a potential complex correction. However, the Wave (b) developed in an Expanded Flat Correction. In Wave ^B the Wave (b) developed

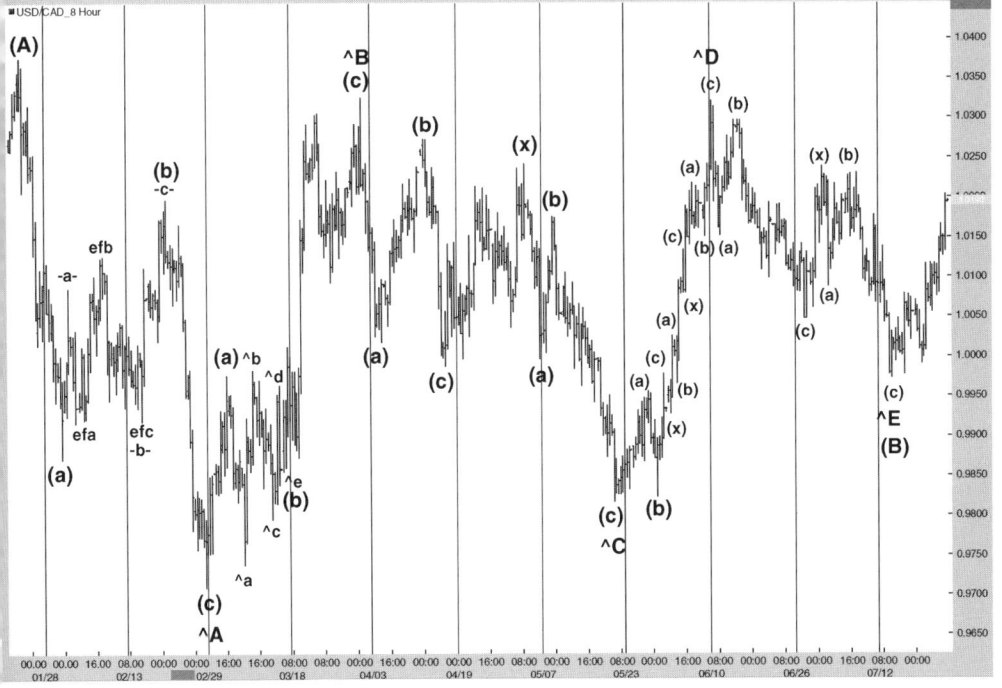

FIGURE 2.23 A Triangle in a Wave (B) Position in Eight-Hour USDCAD
Source: FXtrek IntelliChart™ in collaboration with FX-Strategy.com Pro Charts™

as a Triangle and Wave ^C as a Double Zigzag. Wave ^D developed as a Triple Three and finally Wave ^E as a Double Zigzag.

This type of move can cause a lot of frustration in the market as very clearly highs and lows are broken but without any significant follow through. This in itself is a symptom of a corrective structure, and again it will be important to be aware of the period of time it took for Wave (A) to complete and judge the implication for the length of Wave (B). Following the first leg of three waves this would have pointed to a complex correction, and then judgment will need to be made in determining whether the degree of correction was sufficient to retrace Wave (A). If it was sufficient it would support the probability of this being a Flat, Expanded Flat, or Triple Three.

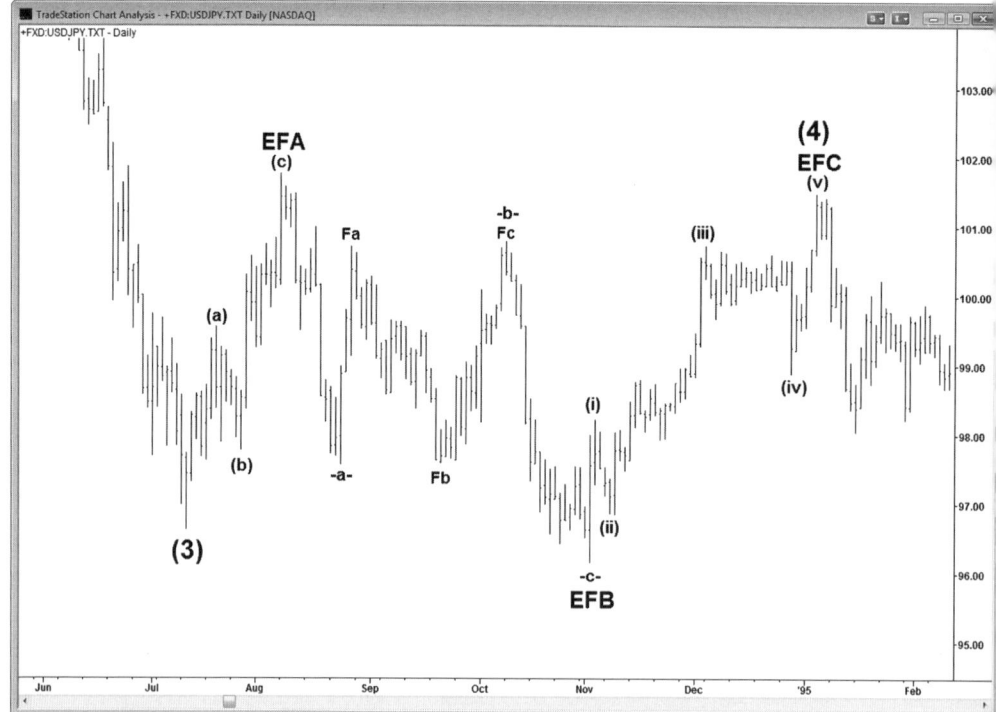

FIGURE 2.24 An Expanded Flat in a Wave (4) Position in Daily USDJPY
Source: Created with TradeStation. ©TradeStation Technologies, Inc. All rights reserved.

R. N. Elliott's Findings: Corrective Waves

Figure 2.24 is another example of an Expanded Flat. I included this example in my first book, *Integrated Technical Analysis*, and find this an excellent example of how complicated corrections can be.

Price had been declining to complete Wave (3) and then began the correction in Wave (4). The first three-wave recovery was deep enough to satisfy the pullback in terms of extent but not in duration. Therefore a complex correction could be anticipated. The next move lower formed a new Wave -a- and was followed by a correction. This may have been assumed to be Wave -b-, which would have implied that Wave -c- lower would develop. However, this decline stalled at the same area as Wave -a- and corrected to just above the pullback high. This formed a Flat Correction in Wave -b-. Thus the next decision to be made is whether the Wave -c- will stall just ahead of the Wave (3) low and become the second leg of a Triangle at the Wave (3) low and become a larger Flat Correction or extend beyond the Wave (3) low to become Wave EFB in an Expanded Flat.

In fact the latter occurred. From that low, price rallied in five waves to just below the Wave EFA high to complete Wave (4) and thus extend losses in Wave (5).

CHAPTER 3

Impulsive Wave Modification

BACKGROUND

After reading my first book on Elliott Wave it took me a long time to feel comfortable when using it for forecasting. The basic concept of wave development is quite simple, but when faced with the daunting task of actually recognizing waves among all the apparently disjointed and erratic movements seen in a chart it is all too easy to make mistakes.

Some leading Elliotticians talk elegantly on the use of Fibonacci ratios, which are calculated from a simple sequence of numbers and which appear not only in nature but also in financial markets. They detail how market retracements and extensions develop in line with Fibonacci ratios, implying that their analysis blends harmoniously with the ratios. However, when you see their analysis there appears to be few occasions where there are any relationships. To be fair, some believe that the ratios are secondary to the actual wave structure and concentrate on ensuring that the rules are followed and they identify correct five-wave movements.

In my early days I followed what was probably the normal progression of any analyst learning to apply Elliott Wave. I would look for projections of 161.8%, but when they didn't develop I began to look at the waves and think, "Well, this looks about right."

Over time I began to be able to provide relatively acceptable forecasts, but I was never fully satisfied. There were just too many errors in stalling points, depths of corrections, and wave extensions that all too often fell short or exceeded the accepted Fibonacci projections.

After a spell away from direct involvement with trading and forecasting I began my own service, but still found these issues of identifying sufficiently accurate stalling points detracted from the success of the forecasting. Quite often I would find there was a wave missing at Wave 5.

Given that I believe quite strongly in the use of natural order ratios in both retracements and wave projections, I would spend a lot of time working out which waves were related. It was through this process that I thought I noticed a "Special Wave A" move that Robert Prechter noted in 1986. He observed that a Diagonal Triangle wave development, which is normally associated with an extended Wave 5, was occasionally seen in a Wave A position (see Figure 3.1).

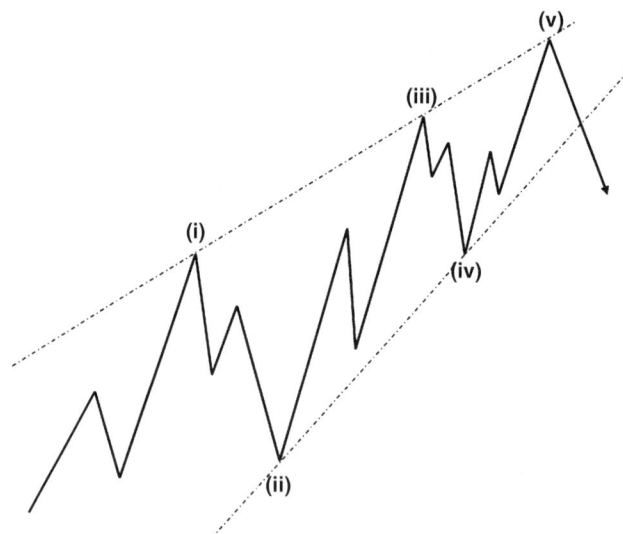

FIGURE 3.1 Prechter's Special Wave A Developing in Five Sets of Three Waves

Impulsive Wave Modification 39

However, what I was facing was a five-wave move that developed in a similar manner to a Diagonal Triangle, in which Waves (i), (iii), and (v) all developed in three waves and not five. This implied that any individual five-wave move could only develop in a Wave A position or in a Wave C position. In the next higher degree, this ABC sequence actually formed one section of a larger five-wave sequence all constructed of three waves.

If I attempted to apply Fibonacci relationships to the standard count, that would treat these as an example of an extending wave (see Figure 3.3) and everything fell flat. There were no relationships. When I used the three-wave structure for Waves (i), (iii), and (v), the wave relationships were perfect—and there was no missing wave at completion.

As I went through my daily ritual of tapping out various potential waves and finding relationships, I suddenly found myself using this alternative all the time. The projections and retracements began to become consistently accurate.

Figure 3.2 displays how the modified impulsive wave now appears. Note that each Wave a and Wave c is constructed of five

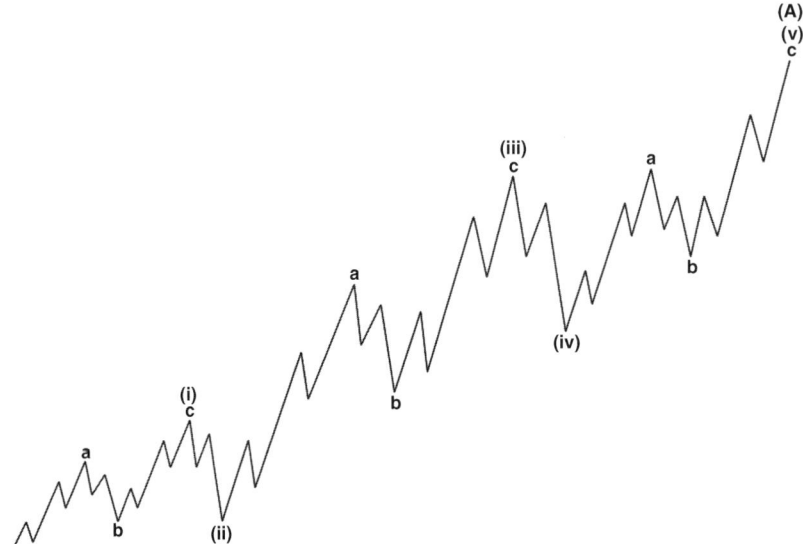

FIGURE 3.2 A Modified Impulsive Wave

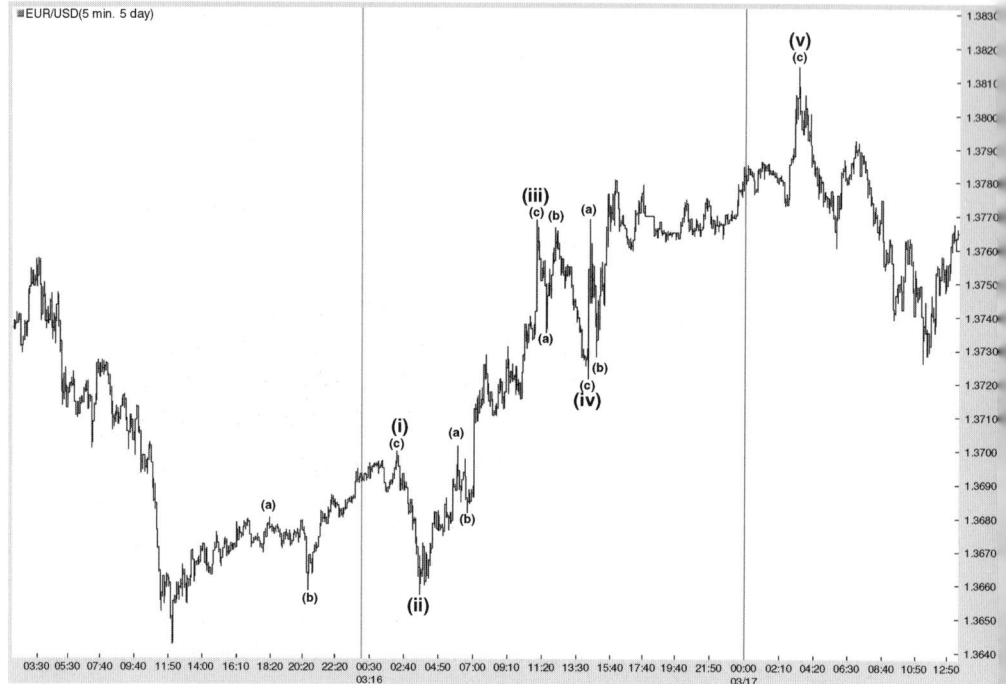

FIGURE 3.3 Modified Structure in Five-Minute Chart of EURUSD
Source: FXtrek IntelliChart™ in collaboration with FX-Strategy.com Pro Charts™

waves as Elliott originally proposed. As opposed to the five-wave impulsive move in Elliott's original version that could form a Wave 1, Wave 3, Wave 5, Wave A, or Wave C, the modified version can only form Wave A or Wave C.

Figure 3.3 displays this modified structure in the five-minute chart of EURUSD. All the waves had very close adherence to common wave relationships and this five-wave sequence was the culmination of a rally from 1.3442. Thus it cannot be considered as a Triple Three. An alternative count of an extended impulsive wave in Elliott's original structure is also impossible since the correction in Wave (ii) dipped one point below the initial correction labeled as Wave (b) within Wave (i). I shall cover this example in Chapter 4 to highlight the wave relationships.

Impulsive Wave Modification 41

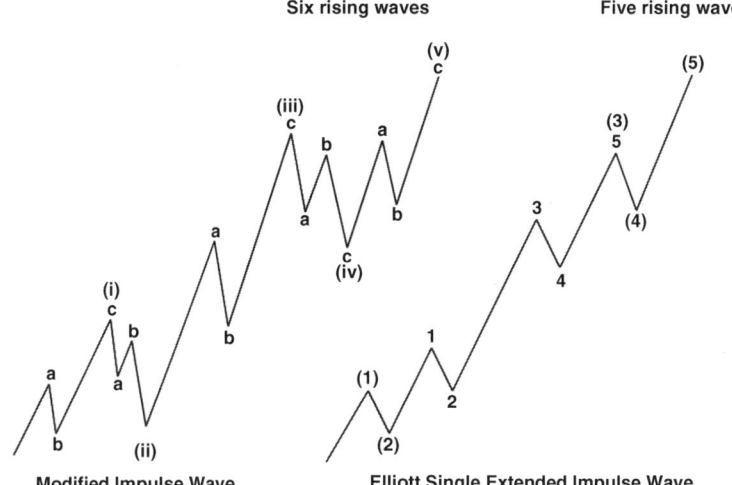

FIGURE 3.4 Comparison of the Modified Rally versus a Single Extended Elliott Rally

While a few Elliotticians with whom I have discussed the modifications have shown some shock, and in most cases disbelief, this is not such a radical modification. Firstly, it merely represents what Robert Prechter noted, but in special instances of a Wave A. Secondly, it actually adheres to the Dow Theory which recognizes a three-wave development in price. However, it does change the number of rising waves. In a simple five-wave rally in Elliott's structure there are three impulsive moves higher. In a single extended rally there are five impulsive moves higher, while in a double extended rally there are seven impulsive moves higher. In my modification there are a standard six impulsive moves higher (as shown in Figure 3.4).

Implications in Wave Relationships

As has been mentioned on several occasions, the basis quoted by leading Elliott Wave followers is that market movements follow natural ratios and therefore the sequence of waves in a structure should reflect this principle of relationships.

For the original Elliott structure the commonly quoted relationships are Fibonacci-based. I will not list these in this chapter as I will lay down the foundation and application of ratios in the next chapter. At this point I will merely list the waves that should be related:

Elliott's Single Extended Impulsive Wave   Wave (2) should be related to Wave (1).
   Wave 2 should be related to Wave 1.
   Wave 3 should be related to Wave 1.
   Wave 4 should be related to Wave 3.
   Wave 5 should be related to a ratio of the beginning of Wave 1 to the end of Wave 3.
   Wave (3) should be related to Wave (1).
   Note: Therefore the target in Wave 5 should end at a projection of Wave (1).
   Wave (4) should be related to Wave (3).
   Wave (5) should be related to a ratio of the beginning of Wave (1) to the end of Wave (3).

The Modified Impulsive Wave   Wave c in Wave (i) should be related to Wave a.
   Wave (ii) should be related to Wave (i).
   Wave (iii) should be related to Wave (i).
   Within Wave (iii), Wave c should be related to Wave a and match the target in Wave (iii).
   Wave (iv) should be related to Wave (iii).
   Wave (v) should be related to a ratio of the beginning of Wave (i) to the end of Wave (iii).
   Within Wave (v), Wave c should be related to Wave a and match the target in Wave (v).
   There is little difference between the two, as all subsequent waves must be related to the prior Wave(s) in the sequence. However, what you will find in general is that many Elliotticians will hail the natural Fibonacci element to the wave structure and how it is therefore a natural development of waves, but will rarely actually observe them. Effectively it makes forecasting a hit-or-miss affair. This was something I could never accept.

Impulsive Wave Modification

I will not state that there are perfect relationships in all circumstances, but in general I find them very common and this provides an excellent tool for forecasting and generating more accurate support and resistance levels. I shall present this in more detail in Chapter 4.

COMMON WAVE CHARACTERISTICS OF THE MODIFIED IMPULSIVE WAVE

Over the years I have noted several different characteristics that appear in the modified structure. I shall highlight the most common in preparation for the charts that will follow the description of the Fibonacci and harmonic ratios that commonly occur.

Extended Waves

In the modified structure, extended waves do not occur in the manner in which Elliott proposed in his structure. From my extensive observations I have not seen an equivalent to an extended Wave 1. My opinion is that the concept of extended waves developed because of the factor I am addressing in this book. The first Wave (a) and Wave (c) develop in five waves (even though the Waves (i), (iii), and (v) comprise three waves) and would therefore have looked as if waves were developing in a (1), (2), 1, 2, 3, so on, manner. Considering Wave (a) and Wave (c) of Wave (iii) also comprise five waves, that will have appeared to be a continuation of the extended sequence.

Figure 3.5 is a representation of how I believe R. N. Elliott may have mistaken the manner in which the impulsive structure develops by classifying the Waves (a) and (b) as individual five-wave moves. Since each of the Waves (a) and (c) develop in five waves they could easily be mistaken as separate waves as described by R. N. Elliott. The key point to the difference between Waves (i) and (iii) compared to Wave (v) is that *invariably* Wave (a) of Wave (v) ends lower than the Wave (iii), whereas in Waves (i) and (iii) the Wave (a) is above

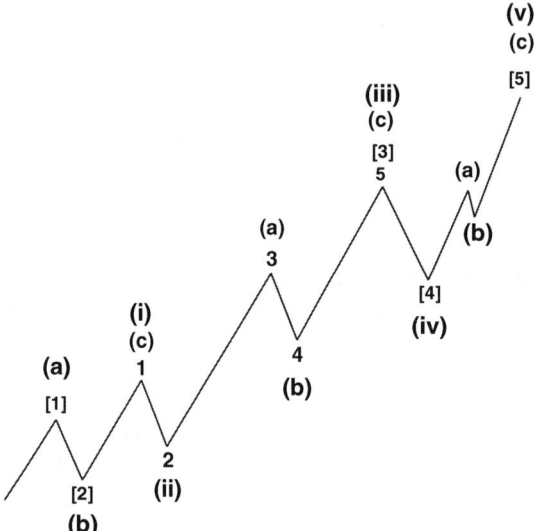

FIGURE 3.5 Labeling of the Modified Rally versus a Single Extended Elliott Rally

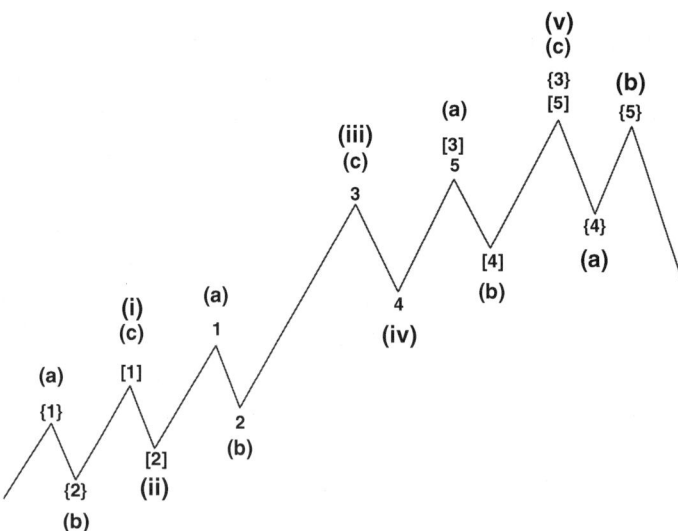

FIGURE 3.6 Labeling of the Modified Rally versus a Double Extended Elliott Rally

Impulsive Wave Modification

the prior swing (wave) high. Thus it could easily be considered that Wave (v) was labeled as Wave {5}.

Now consider a double extension in Wave 3 (as shown in Figure 3.6).

Figure 3.6 is one representation of how a double extended wave could be labeled. I have never noted any occasion where a failed fifth wave has occurred. In this example the Wave (a) of Wave (v) did end above the prior Wave (iii) and this has caused what appears to be a double extension of Wave 3. However, Wave {5} is a failed fifth. In the modified structure Wave {4} is actually Wave (a) of the new move lower and Wave {5} is Wave (b).

Another possible confusion that can cause the apparent extended wave structure is the development of a deep Wave b of Wave iii. For example, in Figure 3.6 the Wave (c) of Wave (iii) could develop with a deep Wave b of Wave iii. I cover this situation a little later in this chapter; it will be seen how this appears to be an additional wave that could have been assumed to be part of an extension.

I have taken an example of a rally in the hourly chart of the GBPUSD market in Figure 3.7 and provided a possible wave count in Figure 3.8 that would be used within a traditional Elliott Wave five-wave structure, although the high at 1.5484 has only been counted as the end of Wave {3}. There are probably other different counts that could have been employed, the problem being that it is mostly subjective and there is implied "permission" to arrange the count to suit the fact that such a rally is obviously a five-wave move which has extended. No real attention is given to wave relationships at this stage and more attention is given to fitting in a wave count that suits the analyst's expectations. I could never quite accept this form of Elliott Wave as a forecasting tool, as not only does it tend to cause too many changes in view but it also makes forecasting reversal points more a matter of chance.

Now let's look at the harmonic version of this rally.

As I will demonstrate in Chapter 4, all ratios between Wave (c) and Wave (a) and their corresponding Waves (i), (iii), and (v) are in harmony, as is the attention to the alternation of Wave (ii) and Wave (iv). I will not suggest that at every stage the individual structural development could have been anticipated, but with due diligence

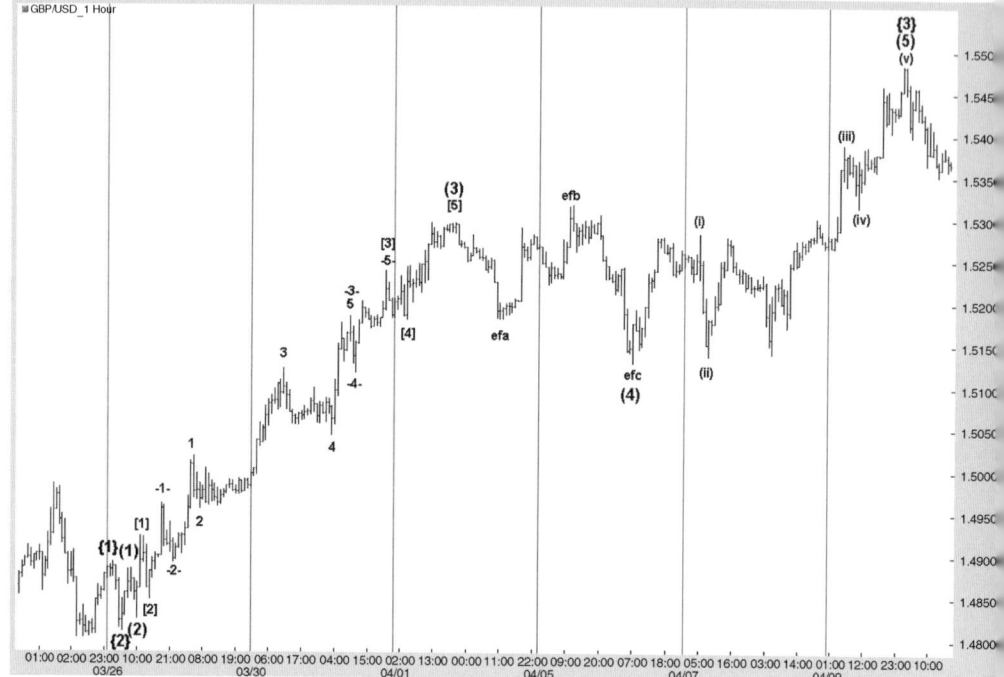

FIGURE 3.7 An Example of how a Multiple Extended Rally in GBPUSD may be Labeled
Source: FXtrek IntelliChart™ in collaboration with FX-Strategy.com Pro Charts™

and attention to matching ratios there would have been plenty of opportunities to identify the waves in retrospect. While this may sound no different from the original structure Elliott described, it is in fact quite different. The use of requiring ratios to develop in harmony across the wave structure brings a higher level of certainty to the correct structure and therefore greater confidence in understanding what move is required next to confirm. It will also confirm the structure and approximate extent of the forthcoming waves.

Development of Extensions in the Harmonic Structure

In the harmonic structure there is basically little difference in the structure between a standard five-wave move and an extended five-wave move. Both are constructed of five waves, all developing in

Impulsive Wave Modification

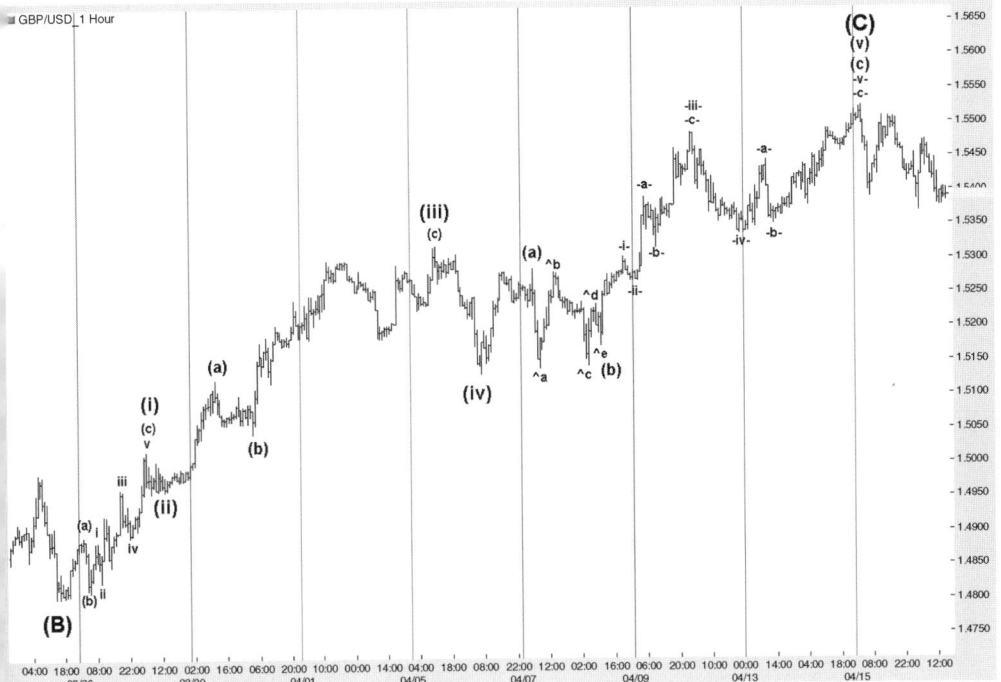

FIGURE 3.8 The Same Rally as in Figure 3.7 but with a Harmonic Wave Count Applied
Source: FXtrek IntelliChart™ in collaboration with FX-Strategy.com Pro Charts™

three waves. However, quite clearly some trends develop more aggressively than others, and it is worth noting the difference.

Figure 3.9 displays two five-wave rallies. On the left, labeled as Wave -i- to Wave -v-, it can be seen that the rally is not really aggressive but develops in the harmonic manner. On the right the rally begins in a very similar manner. However, the equivalent to Wave a, Wave b in Wave -iii- plus the Waves abc in Wave -v- actually develop in their own five waves to form Wave (a) of Wave (iii). This is then followed by a pullback in Wave (b) and again another five waves in Wave (c) of Wave (iii). It is then that Waves (iv) and (v) develop.

The key to identifying this type of extension is that what is a five-wave Wave a on the left will develop in three waves on the right. In addition, the wave relationships in Wave i through Wave v will demonstrate harmonic ratios. In particular this will become evident

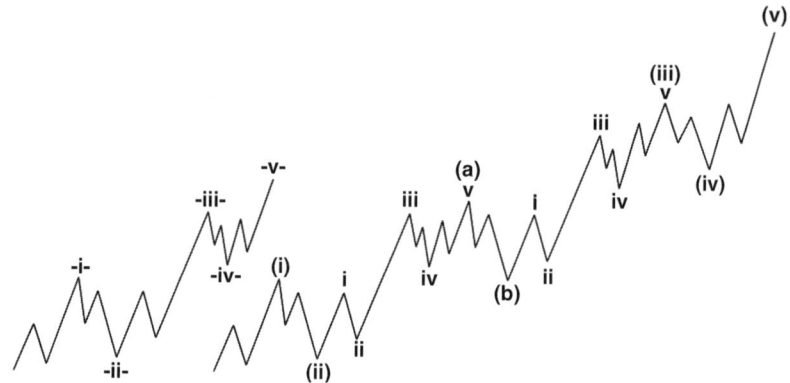

FIGURE 3.9 A Standard Five-Wave Rally on the Left Compared to an Extended Rally on the Right

since the extension in Wave v will be a projection of the rally from Wave (ii) and not from the very start of the rally. The extension in Wave (iii) will also be a projection of Wave (i).

Figure 3.10 displays an example of a five-wave decline in the five-minute USDCHF market in which the Wave -a- and Wave -c- of Wave -iii- developed as if they were in the same wave degree as Wave -i-, -ii-, and -v-. Within both of these declines a five-wave structure can be seen. Once again I will highlight the wave relationships in Chapter 4.

As a second example of how extended waves develop in the harmonic structure I have offered part of the decline in EURUSD. While yet to be confirmed, I had counted this as the Wave (c) of Wave (iii) lower and therefore also had implied targets from the projections in Wave (i) and of Wave (a) of Wave (iii).

Figure 3.11 displays a five-wave decline in EURUSD to the 1.1877 low. The nature of the construction of Wave (i), (iii), and (v) being in three waves is very clear, while the Wave (a)'s and Wave (c)'s are all clearly developing in more direct structures that are actually five-wave moves. All the waves had excellent relationships, with only the Wave (v) stalling short of normal projections but it actually met long-term projections in Wave (iii) and the projection of Wave (a). I shall cover the relationships in Chapter 4.

Impulsive Wave Modification

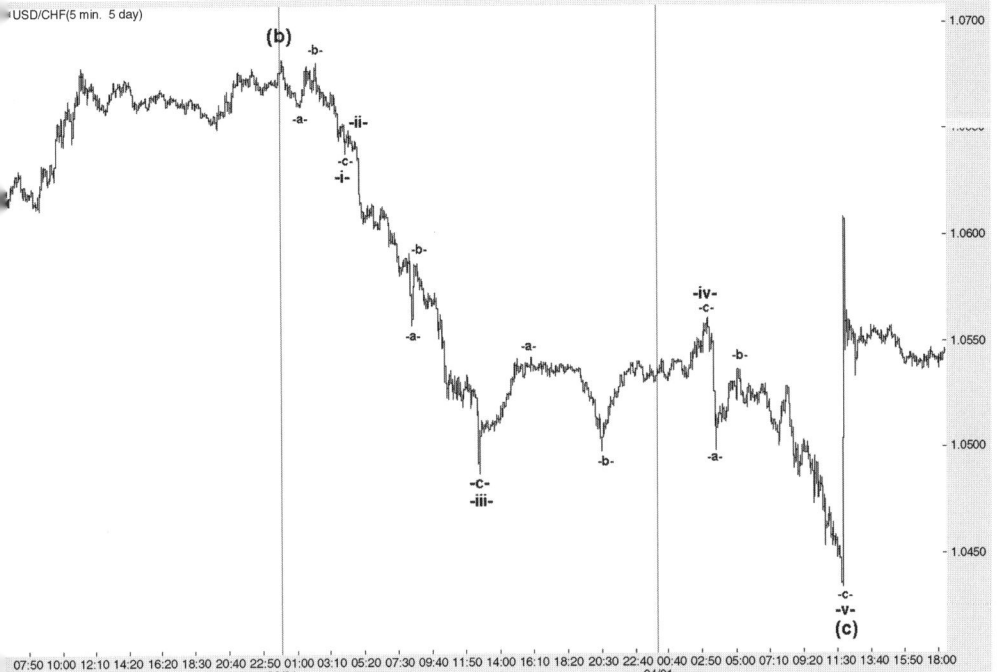

FIGURE 3.10 A Five-Wave Decline in Five-Minute USDCHF with an Effective Extended Wave -iii-
Source: FXtrek IntelliChart™ in collaboration with FX-Strategy.com Pro Charts™

Extended Fifth Waves

Similar to extended third waves, extensions in fifth waves do not require a change in the basic structure but merely reflect a longer than normal distance covered by the (a)(b)(c) structure. In my experience I tend to find these more to be aggressive and sudden moves rather than the more steady development seen in third waves.

Figure 3.12 displays how this would look in a bullish structure. Note the normal development of the first four waves. They will usually contain an element of alternation and the normal projections expected in such a structure. However, the Wave (v) develops more robustly and extends by more than the distance from the start of Wave (i) to the end of Wave (iii).

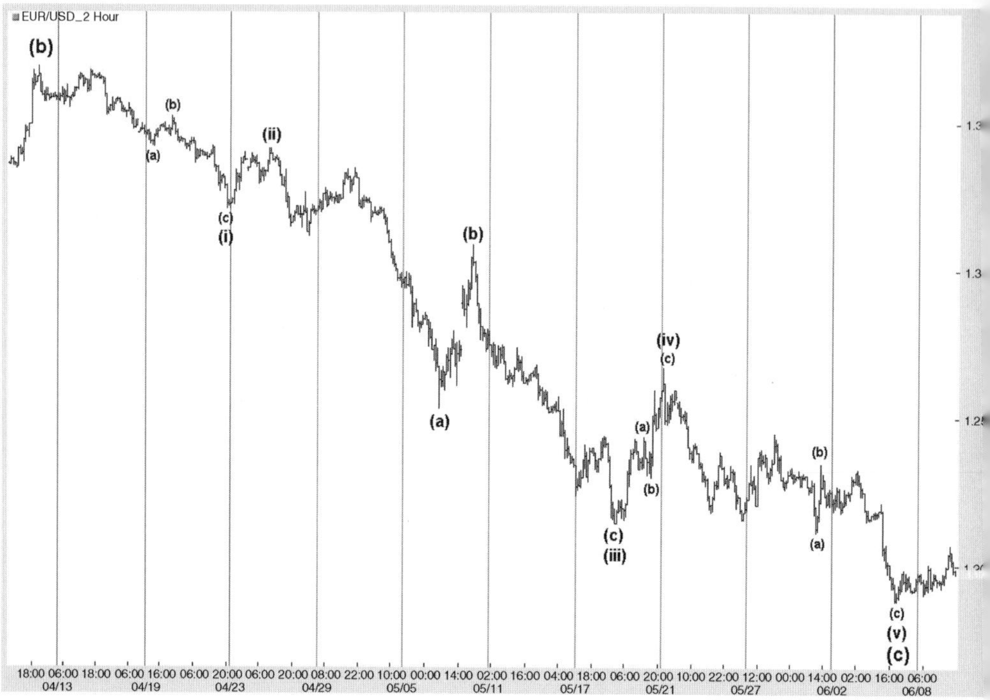

FIGURE 3.11 A Five-Wave Decline in Hourly EURUSD with an Effective Extended Wave (iii)
Source: FXtrek IntelliChart™ in collaboration with FX-Strategy.com Pro Charts™

FIGURE 3.12 Development of an Extended Wave (v)

Impulsive Wave Modification

In these circumstances such a move tends to cause market analysts to expect the trend to continue. In the middle of the shock of such a move it is difficult to be 100% certain of the analysis as such a sharp move momentum often remains over-extended without a divergence.

Figure 3.13 displays a three-wave decline in Wave (v) in the five-minute chart of USDCHF. Within Wave (c) the Wave -v- extended and was more than the decline from Wave (b) to the bottom of Wave -iii-.

While I will cover the wave relationships in Chapter 4, the important clues to identify the potential for an extended fifth wave come from the rest of the structural development. The harmonic structure will provide common extensions in both Wave (v) and in Wave (c) of Wave (v). If this is also the end of a Wave (C) of one higher

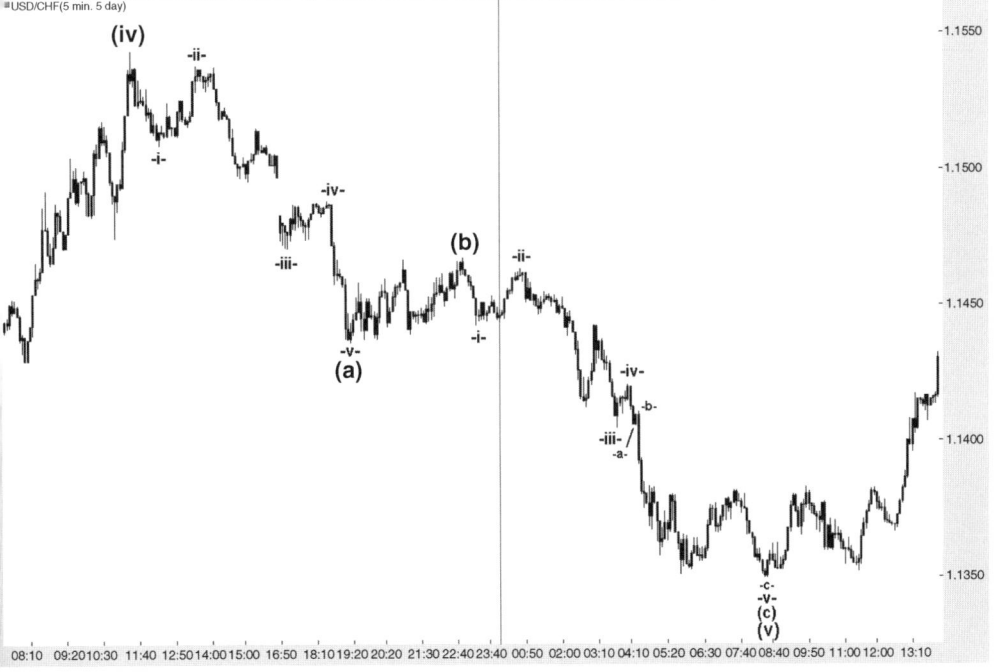

FIGURE 3.13 A Three-Wave Decline in Five-Minute USDCHF with an Extended Wave -v- of Wave (c)
Source: FXtrek IntelliChart™ in collaboration with FX-Strategy.com Pro Charts™

degree there will be targets for this too. The key is to identify the high-risk areas that are implied by all projected target measurements.

Modified Impulsive Wave Compared to a Triple Three

Figure 3.14 displays both the modified structure together with a Triple Three. In terms of development in the sequence of three-wave structures they are actually identical. Both comprise five sets of three waves. Clearly this raises a great deal of issues in recognizing one from the other, a basic conflict in being able to recognize when an impulsive (trending) move is developing versus a correction.

Identifying the Difference Between a Modified Impulsive Wave and a Triple Three
On the occasions I have mentioned my findings to others, a frequent question is how to spot the difference between a modified impulsive wave and Triple Three. While there will always be occasions when it is harder to follow a structure, in the majority of instances they are quite simple to identify. There are several key issues to note. While there is no single 100% solution for this, there are guidelines that identify the difference in the majority of cases:

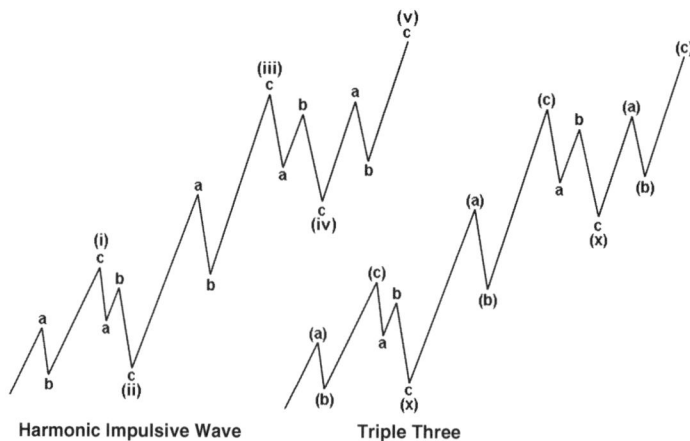

FIGURE 3.14 Comparison of the Modified Impulsive Versus a Triple Three

Impulsive Wave Modification

Triple Threes must develop as a corrective wave: Wave (b), Wave (ii), Wave (iv), or Wave (x). Therefore reference to the structure of the next higher wave degree is of utmost importance.

While Waves (ii), (iii), (iv), and (v) have relationships with each other, the three groups of ABC waves in a Triple Three rarely have relationships between them.

While even impulsive waves can get quite complex, it is far more common for Triple Threes to display a high level of complex structures.

I shall provide one example of how this should be watched.

Figure 3.15 displays the hourly market in EURJPY in which there appears to be a five-wave rally from 121.05 to 127.89. This is followed by a decline in three waves. At this point with the correction being in three waves we cannot be certain whether this is a complete Wave (B) or Wave cxa of a complex correction.

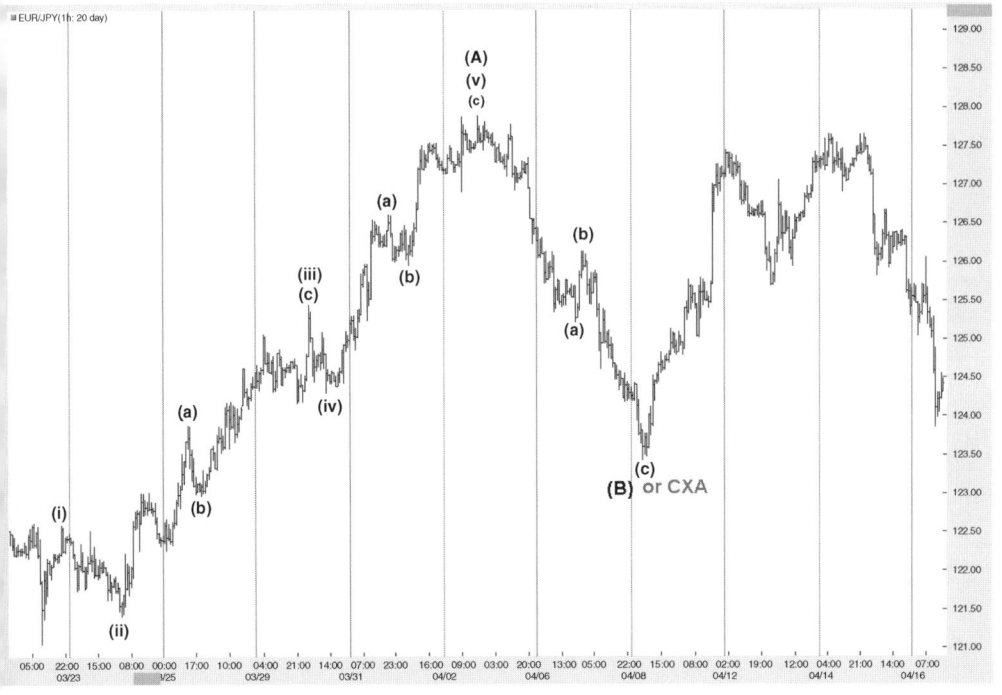

FIGURE 3.15 A Five-Wave Rally Labeled Wave (A) Followed by a Three-Wave Decline
Source: FXtrek IntelliChart™ in collaboration with FX-Strategy.com Pro Charts™

Therefore, as the rally from the 123.42 low develops it will be important to watch for evidence of either the development of an impulsive structure or a corrective structure that could develop as a Triangle, Flat Correction, or Expanded Flat Correction.

Figure 3.16 displays the rally seen from the Wave (B) (or Wave CXA) low. While it would be simple to say that all wave structures are obvious from the wave relationships, it is not uncommon for there to be a degree of uncertainty where there are perhaps two projections of Wave -a- that match with subsequent peaks.

However, in the case that this rally will become a larger Wave (C) and will therefore end above 127.89, the Wave (i) must be of a suitable degree that would imply a strong wave (iii) projection should end close to or preferably above 127.89. In this example there was a very close relationship between the first Wave -a- and the Wave -c- so that we could consider labeling this peak as a potential Wave (i).

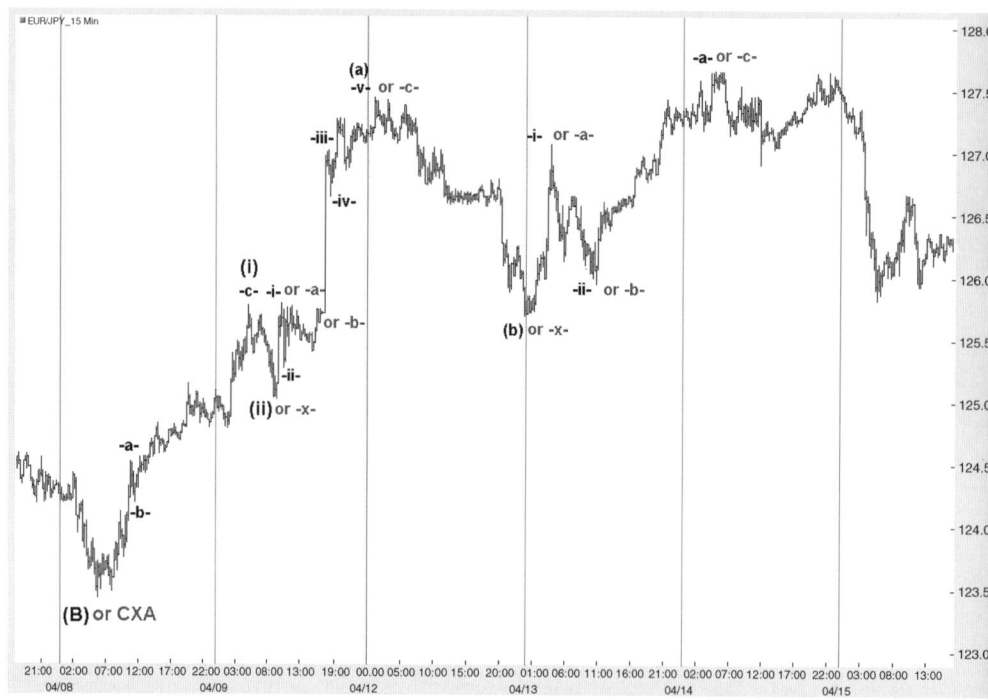

FIGURE 3.16 Breaking Down the Rally from Wave (B) to Identify the Structure
Source: FXtrek IntelliChart™ in collaboration with FX-Strategy.com Pro Charts™

Impulsive Wave Modification

The correction was very shallow, stalling just above the prior swing low that would be Wave iv of Wave -c-. The move to new highs would imply that Wave (a) of Wave (iii) or a second ABC move is developing. This rally was quite ambiguous, with the impulsive structure having a truncated Wave -v-, while for the -a-, -b-, -c- move to hold more accurate projections the Wave -b- must be considered to have developed in an ascending Triangle.

Therefore, at this stage the apparent cleaner look would favor a rally in Wave (a) of Wave (iii). However, the truncated Wave -v- and the better relationship between the alternative Wave -c- to Wave -a- provided an uncertainty to the entire structure. This implies that close scrutiny of the following rally to identify whether this will be a five-wave move in Wave (c) or a three-wave move in a third -a-, -b-, -c- to complete a Triple Three must be undertaken. This latter alternative will imply that the pattern will probably be a Flat Correction with a final stalling point close to the 127.89 high or an Expanded Flat Correction that adheres to common expansion ratios.

The depth of the decline from the (potential) Wave (a) high was exceptionally deep. This could still hold within an impulsive rally as Wave (ii) was exceptionally shallow, so there was potential for this to be a deep Wave (b).

From this point there must be a clear distinction to establish whether a Wave (c) will develop to complete Wave (iii) or whether there will be a third -a-, -b-, -c- move. Price recovered sharply and then saw a deep pullback. (The rally is labeled Wave -i- or Wave -a- and the correction as Wave -ii- or Wave -b-.) Attempt should be made to establish whether the rally developed in five waves or three. Looking at the rally from the Wave (b) or Wave -x- low there is a sharp initial move followed by a brief correction and then a stronger follow-through to a peak that is labeled Wave -i- or Wave -a-. It certainly looks like three waves in this time frame (15 minutes) but what appears to be Wave (c) is so sharp it could hide the true nature of the structure.

If it remains unclear then the labeling should continue to be "Wave -i-" or "Wave -a-" and the subsequent rally should be observed. The confusion will be that a five-wave rally will be expected in both alternatives, either as Wave -a- of Wave -iii- or in a Wave -c-. The end of this rally moved to a marginal new high but below the high in Wave (A) in Figure 3.15 at 127.89.

From this point there are two alternatives. Either the decline will be a correction in Wave -b- of Wave -iii- or the implication of a retracement of more than 50% of the Wave -a- will suggest the rally is complete and it can be safely assumed that this had been a Triple Three, and therefore a return to the Wave (B) low will occur in a possible Flat correction.

This example reflects an uncertain outcome as the structural development from the Wave (B) low was unclear. However, in the majority of cases it is normally possible to note one of several factors that will reveal the true nature of the move:

Not only was the assumed Wave (ii) shallow but also Wave (b) of Wave (iii) and Wave (iv). Occurrences of limited pullbacks point to the structure more likely being a Triple Three.

The relationships between the three ABC moves (that is, the anticipated Waves (i), (iii), and (v)) were not harmonic, which again suggests this is more likely to be a Triple Three.

The projection in the anticipated Wave (iii) would not be deep enough to satisfy a Wave (v) that would match with a projection in the Wave (C) of the higher degree.

Elliott's Rule Concerning the Overlap of Wave 1 and Wave 4

As one of Elliott's unbreakable rules he stated that the correction in Wave 4 should never penetrate the extreme of Wave 1. In my findings I do not really see any evidence of this, and whether or not the extremes of Wave (i) and Wave (iv) overlap really depends on whether the Wave (iii) has been a normal projection or a strong projection. While I will cover the degrees of projections in Chapter 4, for now I will merely point to Wave (iii) projections of between 161.8% and 194.43% as being normal with projections of 223.6% or higher being strong projections. It is probably fairly obvious that the stronger the Wave (iii) the less chance there is of the Wave (iv) retracement being able to reach the extreme of Wave (i).

Furthermore, since instances of Wave (iii) will only occur in a Wave (a) or Wave (c), which in turn appear in both impulsive five-wave

Impulsive Wave Modification

moves as well as corrective structures, the most common occurrences of overlap are in corrective structures. Extending this concept, it is also logical that since a Wave (iii) in an impulsive (trending) move has the greatest occurrence of strong projections the instances of overlap are least. In Waves (i) and (v), overlaps are more common.

Figure 3.17 displays an (a)(b)(c) rally in a Wave (b) of the next higher degree. Note in Wave (a) the peak of Wave -i- is not touched by the low of Wave -iv-. However, in Wave (c) the low in Wave [iv] does overlap the peak in Wave [i]. This does not necessarily mean that overlaps are seen only in Wave (c). They can happen in either Wave (a) or Wave (c). What is more important to understand is that the overlap occurred in a corrective structure of the next higher degree and not a true impulsive, trending move.

Figure 3.18 displays a decline in Wave efc of an Expanded Flat Wave (iv) in USDCAD. In this example, the extremes of Wave -i- and Wave -iv- are not close at all.

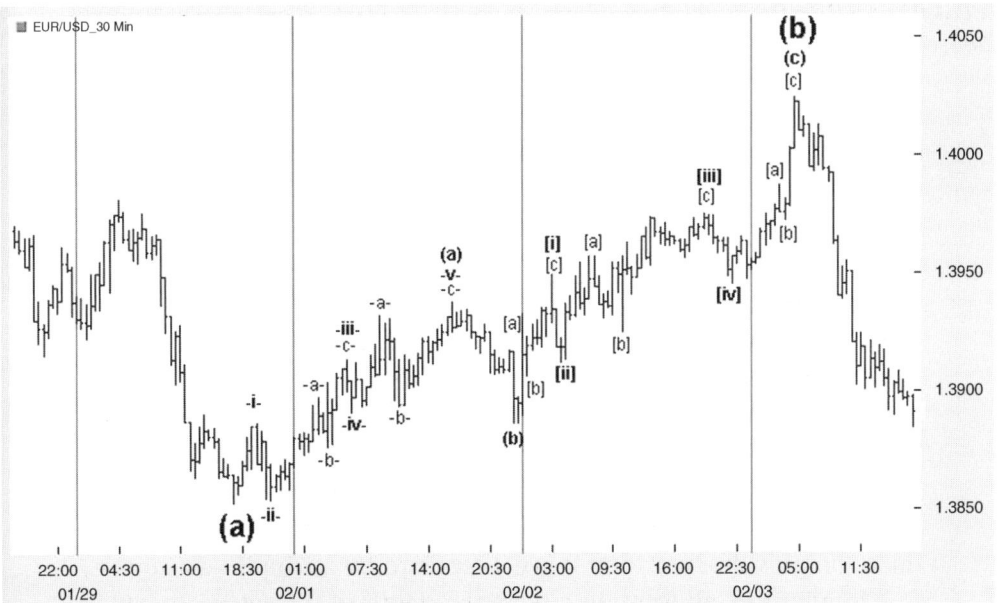

FIGURE 3.17 Zigzag Higher in 30-Minute EURUSD with Overlap in Wave [i] and Wave [iv]
Source: FXtrek IntelliChart™ in collaboration with FX-Strategy.com Pro Charts™

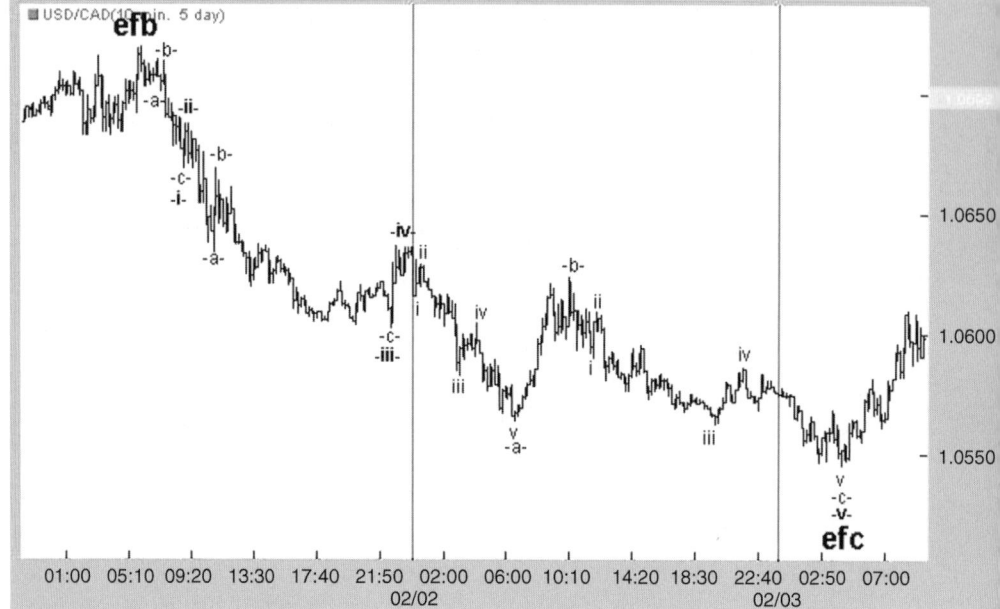

FIGURE 3.18 A Decline in Wave efc in 10-Minute USDCAD to Complete what was a Wave (iv)
Source: FXtrek IntelliChart™ in collaboration with FX-Strategy.com Pro Charts™

Note: The two examples will be used in Chapter 4 to confirm the remarkably accurate relationships between all related waves.

Alternation

Elliott's guideline on the alternation between Wave 2 and Wave 4 holds true in the modified structure. However, it does raise one additional complication. To recap on Elliott's guideline, Elliott noticed a strong tendency for corrective waves within an impulsive structure to alternate in terms of depth and complexity. If Wave 2 develops in a simple manner (an ABC Zigzag move) then Wave 4 will tend to be complex (Triangle, Flat, Expanded Flat, or Triple Three). If Wave 2 develops in a complex manner then Wave 4 tends to be a simple ABC move.

In addition, alternation covers the depth of the retracements in Waves 2 and 4. If Wave 2 was shallow then Wave 4 will be deep, and vice versa.

Impulsive Wave Modification

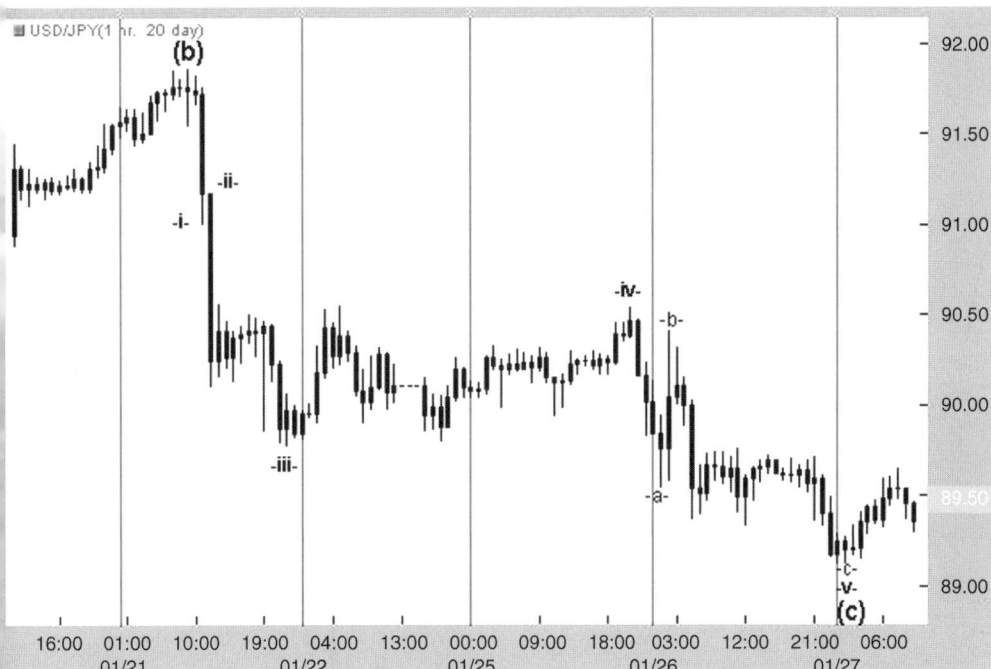

FIGURE 3.19 A Five-Wave Decline in Wave (c) in USDJPY which has Wave -i- and Wave -iv- Alternating
Source: FXtrek IntelliChart™ in collaboration with FX-Strategy.com Pro Charts™

Figure 3.19 displays a five-wave decline in a Wave (c) in the hourly USDJPY. Note how Wave -ii- was almost non-existent. In fact, the extension in Wave -iii- held a moderately good relationship with Wave -i- and the correction in Wave -iv- is clearly a deep and long correction. This also held what is a very common relationship in a deep Wave -iv-, and will be covered in Chapter 5.

Deep Wave (b) of Wave (iii)

This type of alternation is what we have come to expect from Elliott's guideline. The added complication comes from the fact that Wave (iii) develops in three waves. Contrary to the widely held belief that Wave 3 is normally the most aggressive wave, and in a strong trend this does remain the same even in the modified

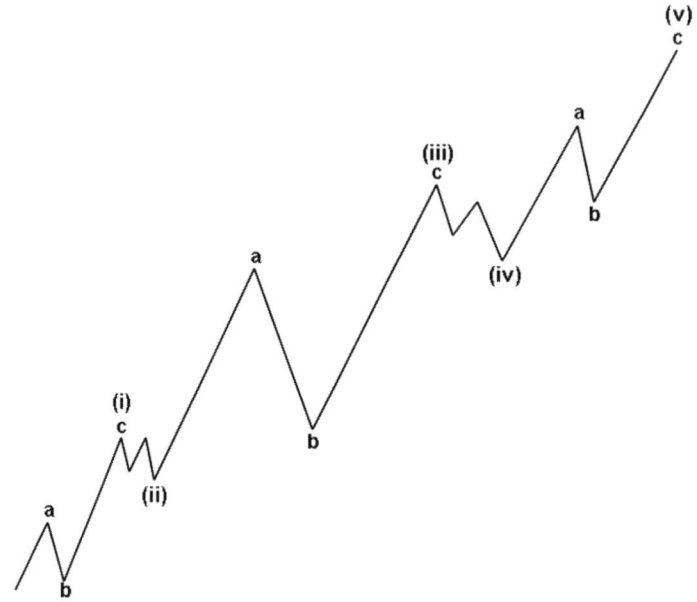

FIGURE 3.20 Shallow Wave (ii) and Wave (iv) but a Deep Wave b of Wave (iii)

structure, I have found that in some instances Wave (b) of Wave (iii) can retrace very deeply, as shown in Figure 3.20.

This particular version of alternation doesn't occur that frequently. In foreign exchange, for example, I note this tends to occur more frequently in JPY crosses such as EURJPY and GBPJPY where there are clearly trades being made in the two individual currency pairs that make up the cross as well as the trades in the cross itself.

At first glance it may actually look as if price has rallied to Wave a in a five-wave move and is casually counted as a Wave (a). However, the key to confirming this type of move is in the wave relationships. Clearly Wave (iii) must be a projection of Wave (i) and also a projection of Wave c in Wave (iii). To confirm this, the completion in Wave (v) must also be a projection of the distance from the beginning of Wave (i) to the end of Wave (iii) and projected from the extreme in Wave (iv).

Figure 3.21 displays an example of a deep Wave -b- wave within a Wave -iii- rally which occurred as I was preparing this section. I will

Impulsive Wave Modification

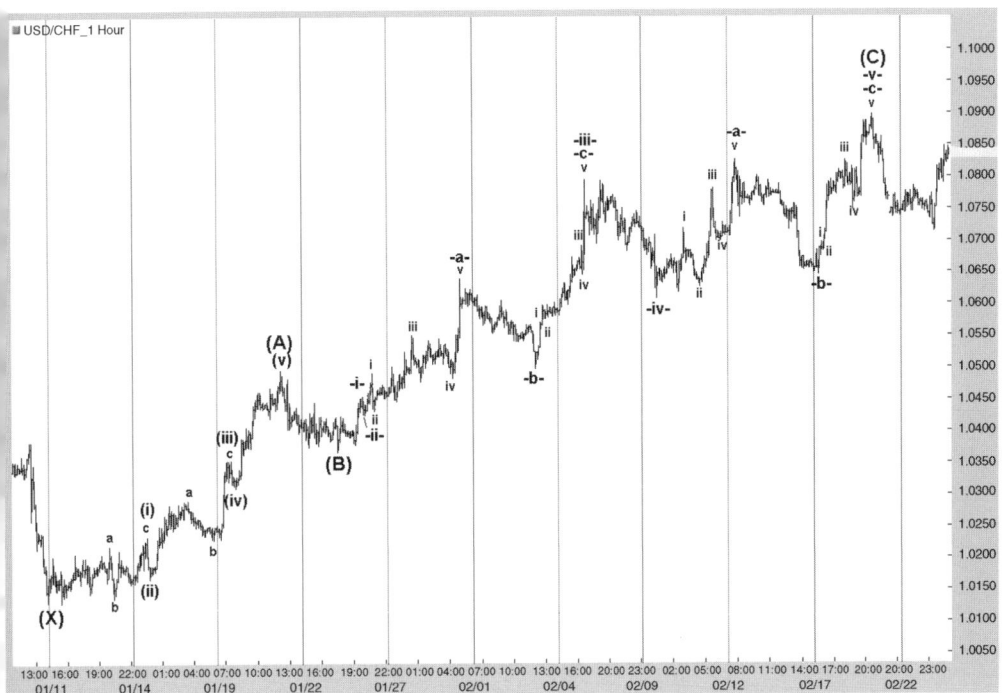

FIGURE 3.21 Deep Wave -b- within Wave -iii- of Wave (C) Higher in USDCHF
Source: FXtrek IntelliChart™ in collaboration with FX-Strategy.com Pro Charts™

detail the measurements in Chapter 4, which details examples of the type of wave development that can be seen and supports these with wave relationships to confirm their validity. However, suffice it to mention at this point that the relationship of Wave -c- to Wave -a- was not only very accurate but also matched with a projection in Wave -iii-.

The three waves in Wave -i- are simple to recognize but it was the Wave -iii- that became very complicated. In these cases it is almost impossible to forecast how the wave will develop, and only by taking detailed measurements did I actually confirm that a five-wave decline did in fact occur. A series of potential target projections can be generated from the prior wave and it is then necessary to ensure that the wave developed with a structure relevant for its position.

The fact that Wave -ii- was quite shallow and brief would raise the potential for a more complex Wave -iii- due to the guideline of alternation. That is, we would know that alternation could provide a deep Wave -b-. Again, having seen Wave -i- and Wave -ii- complete, we could generate a series of potential targets in Wave -iii- and keep in mind the targets for Wave (A).

Figure 3.22 displays the rally in Wave -a- of Wave -v- in USDCHF shown in Figure 3.21, as an example of how alternation can occur in a different way.

It can be seen that Wave i developed in three waves and was followed by a very deep Wave ii that ended just above the Wave b of Wave i. In the subsequent follow-through higher in Wave iii we can

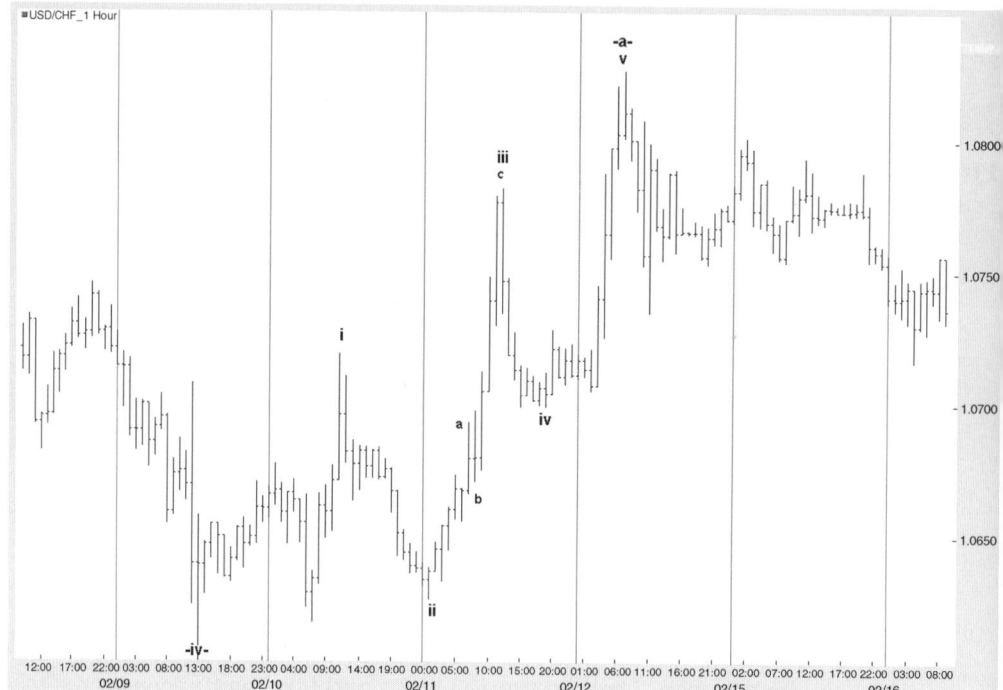

FIGURE 3.22 Shallow Wave b Following a Deep Wave ii within Wave -a- Higher
Source: FXtrek IntelliChart™ in collaboration with FX-Strategy.com Pro Charts™

Impulsive Wave Modification

note a very brief and shallow Wave b. This offers an example of how a deep Wave ii can generate a brief pullback in Wave b of Wave iii. Interestingly, the Wave iv was also very deep, even overlapping with the peak in Wave i. However, once again, all the wave relationships followed normal ratios and offered targets for Wave iii and Wave v.

Again, I shall include this example when providing greater detail of using ratios in Chapter 4.

Another example of a deep Wave (b) is shown in Figure 3.23, which also provided earlier an example of an extended wave. This correction was a quite steep 61.8%, but did then provide the same target as the projection in Wave (iii). Equally, both Wave (ii) and Wave (iv) were limited.

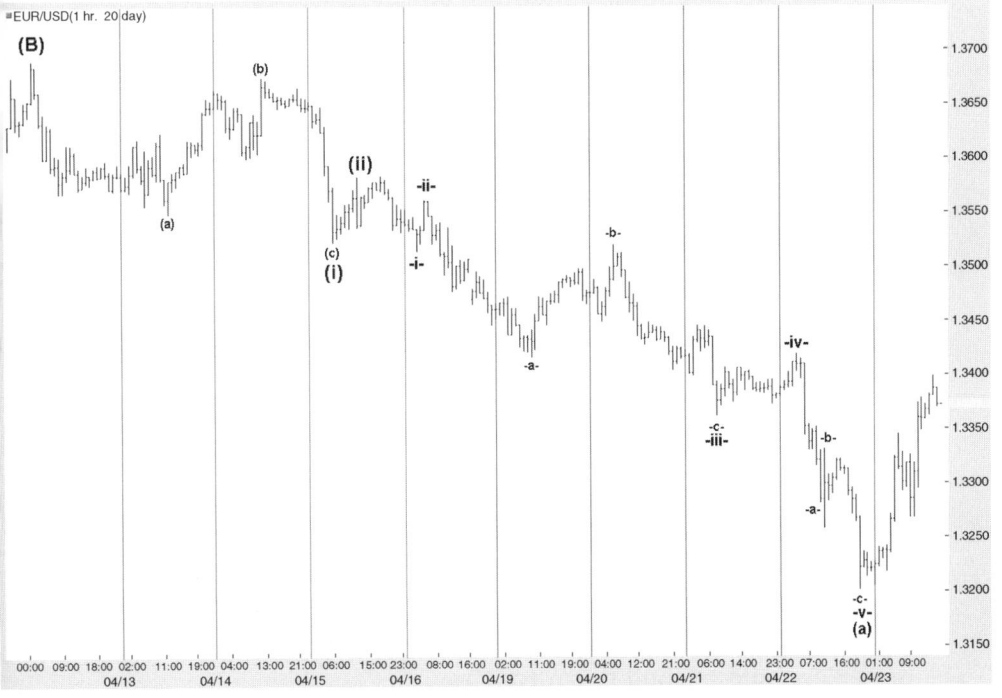

FIGURE 3.23 A Five-Wave Decline in Hourly EURUSD with a Deep Wave (b) in Wave (iii)
Source: FXtrek IntelliChart™ in collaboration with FX-Strategy.com Pro Charts™

Wave (iv) Retracements with Reference to Wave (b) of Wave (iii)

Rather like the Elliott rule that Wave 4 and Wave 1 extremes cannot overlap with the exception of Diagonal Triangles, I note that Wave (iv) will never retrace above the Wave (b) correction in a downward wave or below the Wave (b) correction in an upward wave. Indeed, not only will they not overlap, the Wave (iv) will also rarely move even close to the Wave (b).

This may seem obvious but has particular use in circumstances where Wave (ii) has been brief, Wave (a) very deep, and with an equally shallow Wave (b). In these circumstances a deep Wave (iv) would be implied under normal alternation guidelines but then generate a Wave (iv) beyond the Wave (b). I have never seen Wave (iv) move beyond the Wave (b).

This is also important as during confusing wave counts this event would automatically nullify the impulsive wave or alternatively suggest the waves are placed incorrectly.

Figure 3.24 displays a decline in Wave (c) in the five-minute USDCHF market. Wave -iv- stalled just short of a 50% retracement of Wave -iii-.

Elliott's Guideline on a Retest of a Wave (b) after Completion of a Three-Wave Move

Given that I have discovered that the impulsive waves 1, 3, and 5 actually comprise three waves and not five, this guideline can become a key pivotal forecaster in your analysis. However, I have noticed different reactions after the completion of each three-wave impulsive wave.

The retracement after Wave (i) may see the Wave (b) hold and sometimes not. In most cases it will be retested, but if Wave (ii) is a Triple Three then it will be quite common for the retracement to be quite deep and beyond the Wave (b).

The retracement after Wave (iii) will never fully test the Wave (b). Occasionally it comes close, but will not move particularly

Impulsive Wave Modification

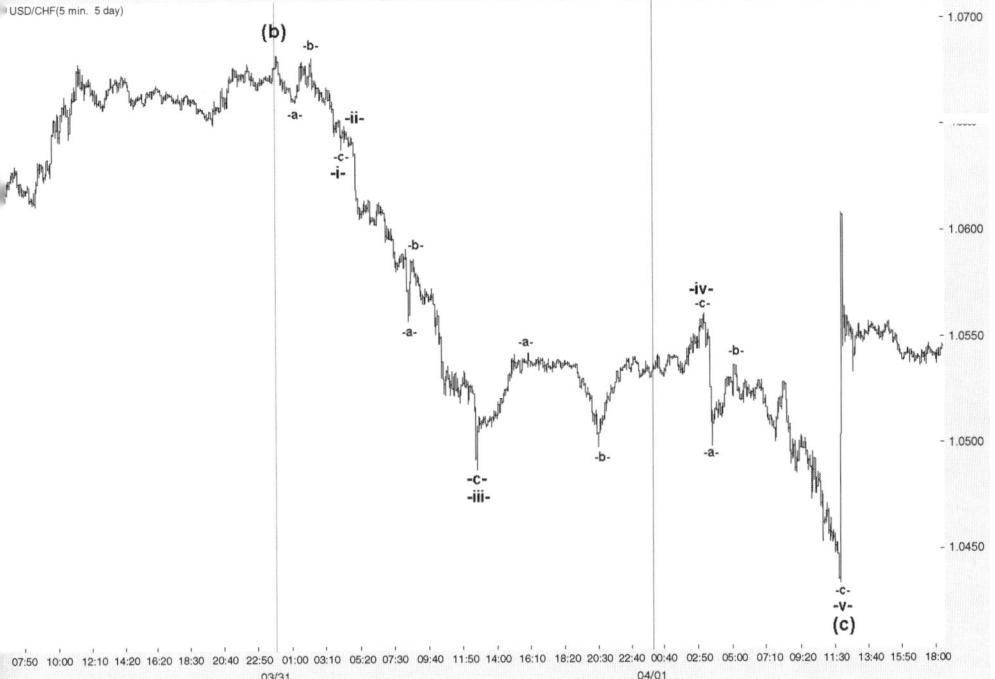

FIGURE 3.24 Wave -iv- Should not Reach the Prior Wave -b- of Wave -iii-
Source: FXtrek IntelliChart™ in collaboration with FX-Strategy.com Pro Charts™

close to the extreme. Even after the completion of Wave (v) and there has been a reversal, it is rare for the extreme of Wave (b) of Wave (iii) to provide any lasting reaction unless it is clearly a key swing high/low within the trend.

The retracement after Wave (v) almost always moves directly to the Wave (b). More than in any other position this can be relied upon in the vast majority of cases.

In the example in Figure 3.25 in the hourly USDCHF market we had a long move higher that came in three waves, this being the fifth wave of Wave (C). Within the Wave (v) the rally came in three waves, with Wave (b) just below 1.0600. After completion of Wave (v), price declined to the span of the Wave (b) and corrected higher. In fact this pullback reached higher to 1.0719. If we observe this market in a lower time frame, perhaps the five-minute chart, we should also be

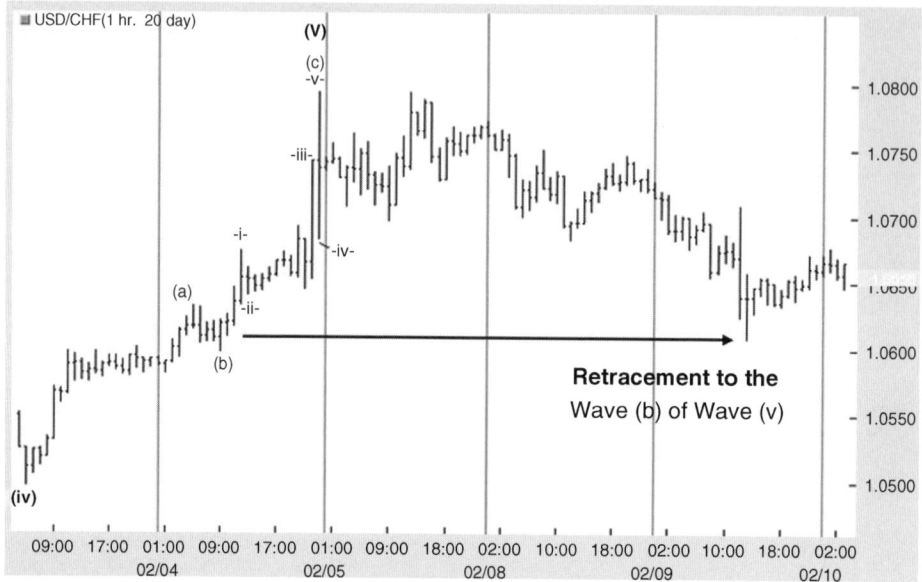

FIGURE 3.25 A Return to the Prior Wave (b) of Wave (v) after the Completion of the Wave (v)
Source: FXtrek IntelliChart™ in collaboration with FX-Strategy.com Pro Charts™

able to spot the Wave -b- of Wave -v-, which should have been the first target in the retracement.

An example of this type of move is shown in Figure 3.26, which shows the decline in Wave efc in USDCAD shown in Figure 3.18.

Following the perfect move lower in five waves it can be seen that price quickly retraced to the Wave -b- of Wave -v-, corrected lower, and then rallied toward the peak of Wave (b) of Wave (v). This type of reaction is extremely powerful and occurs very regularly, and can set up the reversal structure very well.

Viewing Waves Without Making Measurements

Many Ellioticians I speak to tend to comment that they don't follow Elliott Wave intensely but do observe wave development by eyeballing the chart to identify three-wave or five-wave sequences. However, this methodology can lead to quite misleading forecasts and expectations.

Impulsive Wave Modification

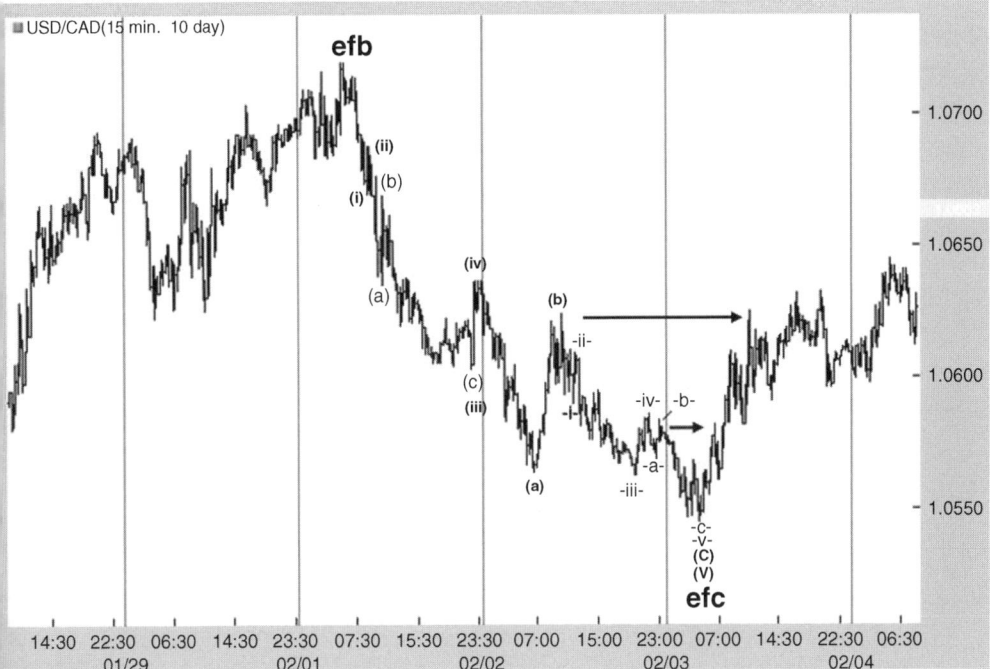

FIGURE 3.26 A Return to the Prior Wave -b- and Wave (b) of Wave (v) after the Completion of the Wave (v)
Source: FXtrek IntelliChart™ in collaboration with FX-Strategy.com Pro Charts™

In Elliott's structure a five-wave move will imply that price has completed one of Wave 1, Wave 3, Wave 5, Wave A, or Wave C. These all have different implications for what we expect the next development to be:

Wave 1: A correction in Wave 2 of between 14.6% and 100% followed by Wave 3.

Wave 3: A correction in Wave 4 of between 14.6% and 50% followed by Wave 5.

Wave 5: A complete reversal and correction to that five-wave move.

Wave A: A correction in Wave B of between 14.6% and 100% followed by Wave C.

Wave C: A correction in Wave X or the resumption of an impulsive wave in the next higher degree.

However, as I have already described, a deep Wave (b) in Wave (iii) can cause the structure to look totally unlike a five-wave move. The importance now of understanding that such an event can occur forewarns that eyeballing a chart simply does not work all the time.

Take the following situation in the 15-minute market of USD-CAD, which was forming a correction higher in Wave (iv). It had already completed one (a)(b)(c) correction, then saw the pullback in Wave (x), to be followed by a second (a)(b)(c) rally. However, note in Wave (b) that the Wave -b- of Wave -iii- had a deep retracement of 66.7%.

In Figure 3.27, all wave relationships adhered to normal Fibonacci or harmonic ratios that are explored more fully in Chapter 4. Not only did the (a)(b)(c) waves conform to these ratios but the

FIGURE 3.27 A Deep Wave -b- in Wave -iii- Higher in Wave (c) in 15-minute USDCAD
Source: FXtrek IntelliChart™ in collaboration with FX-Strategy.com Pro Charts™

Impulsive Wave Modification

waves of lower degree also produced targets relevant to the structure of larger degree, which cements the structure rather than leaving it to just observing the major highs and lows.

If an analyst or trader merely eyeballed the rally in Wave (c) the assumption will be that it possibly developed in two sets of three waves, or possibly that the Wave (c) peak was actually Wave 3 of an extension in Wave (3).

CHAPTER 4

Projection and Retracement Ratios

BACKGROUND

The power of Elliott Wave comes into its own when retracement and projection ratios are employed to generate targets for the anticipated moves implied by the wave structure. Commonly Fibonacci ratios are used, but I have found that harmonic ratios derived from the square root of two are also a very useful tool to have at your disposal.

I have always been intrigued by the natural beauty of Fibonacci ratios and the manner they slot nicely into the bindings of life. Indeed, these ratios are the key factors in qualifying the modifications to the impulsive wave structure. Given the often-quoted statement that markets adhere to these ratios, I stand by the impulsive modifications through the repetitive nature of certain ratios in various parts of the wave structure. It was these which convinced me that the original impulsive structure offered by R. N. Elliott is actually incorrect.

Let me first introduce Fibonacci, for any reader who is encountering this for the first time.

Fibonacci

Leonardo Pisano Bogollo (c. 1170–c. 1250), also known as Leonardo Fibonacci, was an Italian mathematician and is considered by many to have been one of the most talented western mathematicians of the Middle Ages. As a boy he studied the Hindu-Arabic numeral system, which was easier to use than Roman numerals.

In 1202, he published his findings in his book *Liber Abaci*, and introduced the number sequence that was known to Indian mathematicians as early as the 6th century. Later it became known as the Fibonacci sequence. In the Fibonacci sequence of numbers, each number is the sum of the previous two numbers, starting with 0 and 1. Thus the sequence begins:

0, 1, 1, 2, 3, 5, 8, 13, 21, 34, 55, 89, 144, 233, 377, 610, etc.

0	
1	
1	100.0000%
2	200.0000%
3	150.0000%
5	166.6667%
8	160.0000%
13	162.5000%
21	161.5385%
34	161.9048%
55	161.7647%
89	161.8182%
144	161.7978%
233	161.8056%
377	161.8026%
610	161.8037%
987	161.8033%
1,597	161.8034%
2,584	161.8034%
4,181	161.8034%
6,765	161.8034%

FIGURE 4.1 Division by the Following Number

Projection and Retracement Ratios

At first glance it seems an innocuous sequence, but as we will see, it holds quite extraordinary properties. By dividing one number in the sequence by the next, the results shown in Figure 4.1 occur.

Note that the first few numbers begin with common fractions:

$$1 \quad 1/2 \quad 2/3 \quad 3/5$$

However, after 10 numbers we can see that the result remains at 61.80%.

By dividing one number in the sequence by the preceding number we have a similar development which sees the result remaining at 161.8% (as shown in Figure 4.2).

This is the golden ratio, which is found in nature and in classical architecture, including the Egyptian pyramids and some Greek structures such as the Acropolis and Parthenon.

This can be developed further by dividing numbers two apart, three apart, and so on in the sequence (as shown in Figure 4.3).

Thus a series of ratios can be generated both below and above 100% (also as shown in Figure 4.3).

0	
1	
1	100.0000%
2	200.0000%
3	150.0000%
5	166.6667%
8	160.0000%
13	162.5000%
21	161.5385%
34	161.9048%
55	161.7647%
89	161.8182%
144	161.7978%
233	161.8056%
377	161.8026%
610	161.8037%
987	161.8033%
1,597	161.8034%
2,584	161.8034%
4,181	161.8034%
6,765	161.8034%

FIGURE 4.2 Division by the Preceding Number

	1	2	3	4	5	6
0						
1						
1	100.0000%					
2	200.0000%	200.0000%				
3	150.0000%	300.0000%	300.0000%			
5	166.6667%	250.0000%	500.0000%	500.0000%		
8	160.0000%	266.6667%	400.0000%	800.0000%	800.0000%	
13	162.5000%	260.0000%	433.3333%	650.0000%	1300.0000%	1300.0000%
21	161.5385%	262.5000%	420.0000%	700.0000%	1050.0000%	2100.0000%
34	161.9048%	261.5385%	425.0000%	680.0000%	1133.3333%	1700.0000%
55	161.7647%	261.9048%	423.0769%	687.5000%	1100.0000%	1833.3333%
89	161.8182%	261.7647%	423.8095%	684.6154%	1112.5000%	1780.0000%
144	161.7978%	261.8182%	423.5294%	685.7143%	1107.6923%	1800.0000%
233	161.8056%	261.7978%	423.6364%	685.2941%	1109.5238%	1792.3077%
377	161.8026%	261.8056%	423.5955%	685.4545%	1108.8235%	1795.2381%
610	161.8037%	261.8026%	423.6111%	685.3933%	1109.0909%	1794.1176%
987	161.8033%	261.8037%	423.6052%	685.4167%	1108.9888%	1794.5455%
1,597	161.8034%	261.8033%	423.6074%	685.4077%	1109.0278%	1794.3820%
2,584	161.8034%	261.8034%	423.6066%	685.4111%	1109.0129%	1794.4444%
4,181	161.8034%	261.8034%	423.6069%	685.4098%	1109.0186%	1794.4206%
6,765	161.8034%	261.8034%	423.6068%	685.4103%	1109.0164%	1794.4297%
10,946	161.8034%	261.8034%	423.6068%	685.4101%	1109.0172%	1794.4262%
17,711	161.8034%	261.8034%	423.6068%	685.4102%	1109.0169%	1794.4276%
28,657	161.8034%	261.8034%	423.6068%	685.4102%	1109.0170%	1794.4271%
46,368	161.8034%	261.8034%	423.6068%	685.4102%	1109.0170%	1794.4272%
75,025	161.8034%	261.8034%	423.6068%	685.4102%	1109.0170%	1794.4272%
121,393	161.8034%	261.8034%	423.6068%	685.4102%	1109.0170%	1794.4272%
196,418	161.8034%	261.8034%	423.6068%	685.4102%	1109.0170%	1794.4272%
317,811	161.8034%	261.8034%	423.6068%	685.4102%	1109.0170%	1794.4272%
514,229	161.8034%	261.8034%	423.6068%	685.4102%	1109.0170%	1794.4272%
832,040	161.8034%	261.8034%	423.6068%	685.4102%	1109.0170%	1794.4272%

FIGURE 4.3 Fibonacci Ratios above 100%

For ratios above 100%, the results are as shown in Figure 4.3.

These generate ratios of 161.8%, 261.8%, 423.6%, 685.4%, 1,109%, and 1,794.4%.

Figure 4.4 shows Fibonacci Ratios below 100%.

Projection and Retracement Ratios

	1	2	3	4	5	6
0						
1						
1	100.0000%					
2	50.0000%	50.0000%				
3	66.6667%	33.3333%	33.3333%			
5	60.0000%	40.0000%	20.0000%	20.0000%		
8	62.5000%	37.5000%	25.0000%	12.5000%	12.5000%	
13	61.5385%	38.4615%	23.0769%	15.3846%	7.6923%	7.6923%
21	61.9048%	38.0952%	23.8095%	14.2857%	9.5238%	4.7619%
34	61.7647%	38.2353%	23.5294%	14.7059%	8.8235%	5.8824%
55	61.8182%	38.1818%	23.6364%	14.5455%	9.0909%	5.4545%
89	61.7978%	38.2022%	23.5955%	14.6067%	8.9888%	5.6180%
144	61.8056%	38.1944%	23.6111%	14.5833%	9.0278%	5.5556%
233	61.8026%	38.1974%	23.6052%	14.5923%	9.0129%	5.5794%
377	61.8037%	38.1963%	23.6074%	14.5889%	9.0186%	5.5703%
610	61.8033%	38.1967%	23.6066%	14.5902%	9.0164%	5.5738%
987	61.8034%	38.1966%	23.6069%	14.5897%	9.0172%	5.5724%
1,597	61.8034%	38.1966%	23.6068%	14.5899%	9.0169%	5.5729%
2,584	61.8034%	38.1966%	23.6068%	14.5898%	9.0170%	5.5728%
4,181	61.8034%	38.1966%	23.6068%	14.5898%	9.0170%	5.5728%
6,765	61.8034%	38.1966%	23.6068%	14.5898%	9.0170%	5.5728%
10,946	61.8034%	38.1966%	23.6068%	14.5898%	9.0170%	5.5728%
17,711	61.8034%	38.1966%	23.6068%	14.5898%	9.0170%	5.5728%
28,657	61.8034%	38.1966%	23.6068%	14.5898%	9.0170%	5.5728%
46,368	61.8034%	38.1966%	23.6068%	14.5898%	9.0170%	5.5728%
75,025	61.8034%	38.1966%	23.6068%	14.5898%	9.0170%	5.5728%
121,393	61.8034%	38.1966%	23.6068%	14.5898%	9.0170%	5.5728%
196,418	61.8034%	38.1966%	23.6068%	14.5898%	9.0170%	5.5728%
317,811	61.8034%	38.1966%	23.6068%	14.5898%	9.0170%	5.5728%
514,229	61.8034%	38.1966%	23.6068%	14.5898%	9.0170%	5.5728%
832,040	61.8034%	38.1966%	23.6068%	14.5898%	9.0170%	5.5728%
100.00%	38.1966%	61.8034%	76.3932%	85.4102%	90.9830%	94.4272%

FIGURE 4.4 Fibonacci Ratios below 100%

For ratios less than 100% the following are generated:
5.6%, 9%, 14.6%, 23.6%, 33.3%, 38.2%, 50%, 61.8%, 66.6%, 76.4%, 85.4%, 91%, and 94.4%

	23.60%	38.20%	61.80%	161.80%	261.80%	423.60%	685.40%
23.60%	5.6%	9.0%	14.6%	38.2%	61.8%	100.0%	161.8%
38.20%	61.8%	100.0%	161.8%	423.6%	685.3%	1108.9%	1794.2%
61.80%	38.2%	61.8%	100.0%	261.8%	423.6%	685.4%	1109.1%
	23.60%	38.20%	61.80%	161.80%	261.80%	423.60%	685.40%
23.60%	100.0%	161.9%	261.9%	685.6%	1109.3%	1794.9%	2904.2%
38.20%	61.8%	100.0%	161.8%	423.6%	685.3%	1108.9%	1794.2%
61.80%	38.2%	61.8%	100.0%	261.8%	423.6%	685.4%	1109.1%

FIGURE 4.5 Multiplying and Dividing Ratios

A further interesting feature of Fibonacci ratios is that when dividing or multiplying one ratio by another, the result will be another Fibonacci ratio (as shown in Figure 4.5).

The higher grid provides the results when ratios are multiplied by each other while the lower grid provides the results from dividing one ratio by another.

Before moving on to how these can be applied to the Wave Principle, I would like to just cover the ratios provided by harmonic ratios.

The Square Root of Two

The square root of two, also known as Pythagoras's constant, is the positive real number that, when multiplied by itself, gives the number 2. Geometrically the square root of two is the length of a diagonal across a square with sides of one unit of length; this follows from the Pythagorean theorem. It was probably the first number known to be irrational. Its numerical value truncated to five decimal places is: 1.41421.

In mathematics, an irrational number is any real number that is not a rational number; that is, it is a number which cannot be expressed as a fraction x/y, where x and y are integers, with y being non-zero. Basically, this means numbers that cannot be represented as simple fractions. It can be proven that irrational numbers are precisely those real numbers that cannot be

Projection and Retracement Ratios

represented as terminating or repeating decimals, although mathematicians do not take that to be the definition.

I do not profess to be a skilled mathematician and will go no further than this brief explanation. I was introduced to the use of the square root of two by an acquaintance in the market, who described the ratio as commonly occurring within musical notes. At first I wasn't quite sure how to use this, until I began to sit down and study wave relationships and noted that two derivations of the number frequently occurred: 41.4% and its "opposite" 58.6%, being 100 – 41.4.

Alternative Wave Relationships

From many hours of research into the common relationships between waves I noted those that are generated directly from both Fibonacci and the square root of two. However, I found more commonly in the trending wave sequence other ratios that can be derived from Fibonacci ratios.

What I noted was that specifically with Wave (iii) it is possible to take the ratios less than 100% and add them to 100%, 200% and occasionally 300% and 400%. Earlier I listed these ratios as:

5.6%, 9%, 14.6%, 23.6%, 33.3%, 38.2%, 50%, 61.8%, 66.6%, 76.4%, 85.4%, 91%, and 94.4%

To this list we can add 41.4% and 58.6%.

Mostly commonly, extensions I find on a very frequent basis are: 138.2%, 176.4%, 223.6%, 261.8%, 276.4%, and 285.4%

In addition, on a less frequent basis I find 158.6%, 166.7%, 238.2% and have even noted 361.8%, occasionally 423.6% and also 461.8%.

Common Wave Relationships

Here I shall provide the wave relationships most often noted in each wave position.

Wave (i) There is no relationship to any prior wave given that it is the start of a five-wave sequence. If we are to consider any stalling point then it may be the span of the prior Wave (b) of Wave (v) or possibly close to the most recent swing high or low.

Where we can begin to identify where Wave (i) will complete is by observing the most frequent projections in Wave -c- of the anticipated Wave (i).

Wave (ii) Wave (ii) is a retracement of Wave (i).

This is probably the most difficult to assess before it starts. If looking at a straight retracement ratio then I have seen these to be as shallow as 14.6% and as much as 100%. We can also consider the span of the Wave -b- of Wave (i).

When observing a Wave (ii) in a five-minute chart, for example, it is often difficult to really observe the individual waves that construct the correction, whether this be a simple abc move, a Triple Three, or an even more complex correction. However, in a daily chart we can see the development of Wave (ii) within the shorter time-frame charts and observe the sequence of individual abc moves.

Wave (iii) Wave (iii) is an extension of Wave (i) and projected from the end of Wave (ii). It is in Wave (iii) that we can begin to consider more reliable and consistent projection ratios.

The most common ratios are: 176.4%, 185.4%, 190.02%, 223.6%, 276.4%, and 285.4%.

Less frequent ratios are: 138.2%, 166.7%%, and 261.8%.

Occasional ratios are: 123.6%, 238.2%, 361.8%, 423.6%, and 476.4%.

Needless to say, when reviewing a chart all potential ratios should be kept in mind as long as they are both accurate and the projections in Wave (c) also match that target.

Wave (iv) Wave (iv) is a retracement of Wave (iii).

Wave (iv) is one of my favorite corrections since, as long as the Wave (ii) and Wave (iii) of the sequence have been identified accurately and we have noted the implications of alternation with Wave (ii) or Wave (b), we have a much stronger basis to identify the completion of this pullback.

Projection and Retracement Ratios

For shallow retracements: 14.6%, 23.6%, 33.3%, and 38.2%.
For fuller retracements: 41.4% and 50%.
For deep retracements: 58.6% and infrequently 61.8% or 66.7%.

It is also important to understand the underlying characteristics of the particular market that is being analyzed. For example, I find that Dollar–Swiss Franc and British Pound–Dollar have a greater tendency to stall at 41.4% and 58.6%.

Wave (v) Wave (v) is an extension of the entire move from the start of Wave (i) to the end of Wave (iii) and projected from Wave (iv).

Again, having identified Wave (iv) it is much easier to develop projections for Wave (v). In particular the projections in Wave (v), given they will be coming at the end of a Wave (C) of one higher degree, should also match the target of this higher degree.

The majority of projection ratios are: 61.8%, 66.7%, or 76.4%.

In a truncated Wave (v), common ratios are: 58.6% and less frequently 50%.

In an extended Wave (v), common ratios are: 85.6%, 100%, 114.4%, and occasionally 123.6% and 138.2%.

Wave (A) As with Wave (i), there is no uniform way of identifying where this will stall as it is not related to any prior wave. It is possible to consider the prior Wave b of Wave (v) and occasionally the prior Wave (iv), especially when this is a key swing high or swing low in a trend. Markets tend to shun testing a swing low/high on the first test. Other areas to consider are pivot levels, which I find of particular benefit.

If this is a Wave (A) in a daily chart then again we should be watching the development of the five waves that construct Wave (A) and matching the projections in the internal Wave v with any of the prior Wave b of Wave (v), the prior Wave (iv), or pivot level.

Wave (B) Wave (B) is a retracement of Wave (A).

Being the correction within a correction, Wave (B) can prove to be the most complicated and erratic of all waves. It is probably one where the most errors can be made. We could be talking about a simple Wave (B) within a Zigzag or a complex correction such as a

Flat, Expanded Flat, or Triangle correction. Depending on which area of the entire wave sequence in which the Wave (B) is developing, we may also have to consider the impact of alternation.

If looking at a straight retracement ratio then I have seen these to be as shallow as 14.6% and as much as 100%. We can also consider pivot levels and key swing highs or swing lows.

When observing a Wave (B) in a five-minute chart, for example, it is often difficult to really observe the individual waves that construct the correction, whether this be a simple abc move, a Triple Three, or an even more complex correction. However, in a daily chart we can see the development of Wave (B) within the shorter time-frame charts and observe the sequence of individual five-wave moves.

Wave (B) of Wave (III) tends to be 50% on average, but unlike any other Wave (B) position it is subject to the guideline of alternation and may be very brief if Wave (II) has been exceptionally deep, or alternatively very deep—as much as 66.7%—if Wave (II) has been exceptionally shallow.

Wave (C) Wave (C) is an extension of Wave (A) projected from the end of Wave (B).

The most common ratios are: 100%, 105.6%, 109.2%, 114.4%, 138.2%, and 161.8%.

Less frequent ratios are: 76.4%, 85.6%, 123.6%, and 176.4%.

Occasional ratios are: 123.6%, 223.6%, and 261.8% or as short as 61.8%.

Needless to say, when reviewing the targets for Wave (C) it is important to relate this to the targets in both the next higher degree and also lower degree. Therefore, take note that the internal Wave v of the Wave (C) should match the extension of Wave (A) and also, if this is part of a Wave (iii) or Wave (v), the potential projection targets for this higher degree.

Wave (x) Generally this intermediate corrective wave between Zigzag patterns tends to retrace in the same way as a Wave (b). However, one common guideline is that if the previous Wave (b) was

Projection and Retracement Ratios

very deep, perhaps as much as 76.4%, then Wave (x) will likewise have a greater tendency to be also deep.

Triangles Wave ^a will normally retrace quite deeply. In a Wave (iv) position this will often be quite sharp and to at least 50% of Wave (iii), and possibly more as long as this does not imply a move too close to the prior Wave (b) of Wave (iii).

Wave ^b: Will commonly be a 76.4% retracement of Wave ^a, or occasionally 85.6%.

Wave ^c: 66.7%, 76.4% of Wave ^a projected from the end of Wave ^b.

Wave ^d: 66.7% to 76.4% of Wave ^b from the end of Wave ^c.

Wave ^e: In my experience I have found this to normally be a simple Zigzag, but it rarely moves beyond 61.8% to 66.7% and may, on occasion, be less than 61.8%.

Expanded Flat Corrections Wave efa: Generally 50% or less of the preceding wave.

Wave efb: Most commonly 14.6% to 38.2%%. On occasions as shallow as 9% and, rarely, 41.4%.

Wave efc: Back to the area around Wave efa can fall short or move beyond Wave efa to a retracement suitable to the wave.

General Observations on Using Ratios

I have listed the ratios I tend to commonly find. However, each market tends to display its own characteristics as an "individual" price. In addition, it can have different tendencies in a range of time frames. It may be that in a five-minute or hourly chart you may commonly see a 23.6% expansion in Wave efb of an Expanded Flat, while a daily Wave efb may expand a fuller 38.2%.

As an example, in short time-frames I find the Euro–Dollar most often expands 38.2% while the Dollar–Swiss Franc expands mostly only 23.6%. It is always important to get to know the markets you are analyzing and their characteristics and foibles in all time frames.

EXAMPLES OF HOW THE MODIFIED WAVE STRUCTURE PROVIDES SUPERIOR RESULTS

Having covered the modifications in Chapter 3 together with the common wave relationships in this chapter, the key now is to prove that these modifications produce superior results. Having applied this approach for some years I have found it to produce astounding success, and many of my subscribers comment on the accuracy of my support and resistance levels. These are a direct reflection of both the structure and ratios I employ.

First let us take a look at the first example of a five-wave move (Figure 4.6). This was shown in Figure 3.3 that identified a rally in the five-minute market of EURUSD.

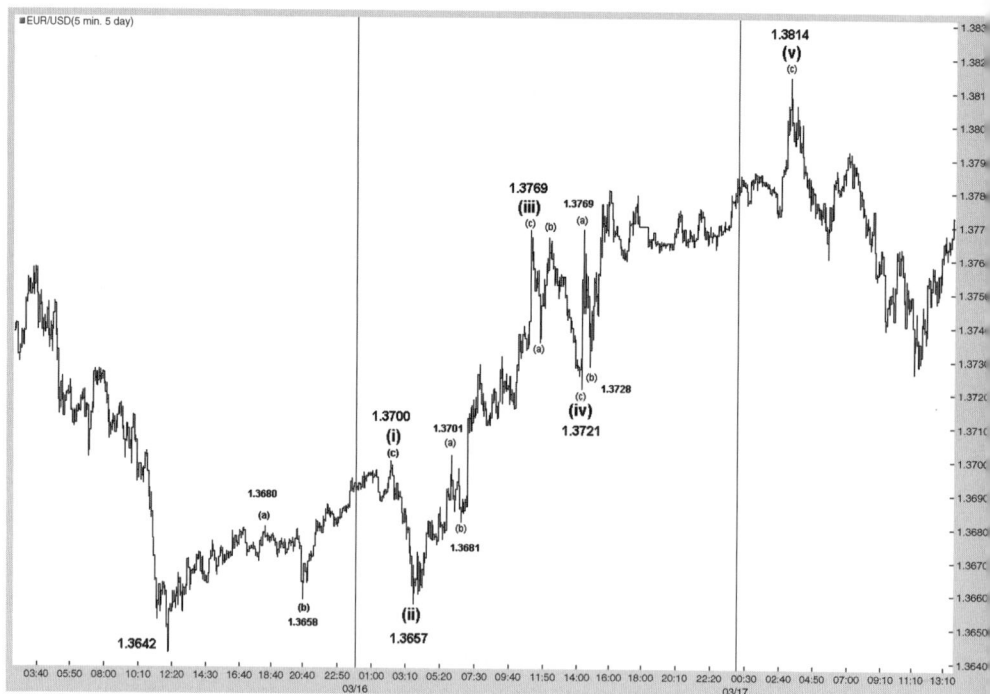

FIGURE 4.6 A Five-Wave Rally in the Five-Minute EURUSD market
Source: FXtrek IntelliChart™ in collaboration with FX-Strategy.com Pro Charts™

Projection and Retracement Ratios **83**

TABLE 4.1 Wave Relationships for the Five-Wave Rally in Figure 4.6

Five-wave rally		Ratio	Projection	Actual
Wave (a)	1.368			1.3680
Wave (b)	1.3680 −	Wave (a) * 58.6% =	1.3658	1.3658
Wave (c)	1.3658 +	Wave (a) * 114.6% =	1.3702	1.3700
Wave (i)	**1.37**			**1.3700**
Wave (ii)	**1.3700 −**	Wave (i) * 76.4% =	**1.3656**	**1.3657**
Wave (a)	1.3701			1.3701
Wave (b)	1.3701 −	Wave (a) * 50.0% =	1.3680	1.3681
Wave (c)	1.3681 +	Wave (a) * 185.6% =	1.3763	1.3769
Wave (iii)	**1.3757 +**	Wave (i) * 185.6% =	**1.3765**	**1.3769**
Wave (a)	1.3735			1.3735
Wave (b)	1.3735 +	Wave (a) * 90.02% =	1.3766	1.3766
Wave (c)	1.3766 −	Wave (a) * 138.2% =	1.3719	1.3721
Wave (iv)	**1.3769 −**	Wave (iii) * 41.4% =	**1.3723**	**1.3721**
Wave (a)	1.3769			1.3769
Wave (b)	1.3769 −	Wave (a) * 90.02% =	1.3726	1.3728
Wave (c)	1.3728 +	Wave (a) * 176.4% =	1.3813	1.3814
Wave (v)	**1.3721 +**	Wave (i) > (iii) * 76.4% =	**1.3818**	**1.3814**

The levels of the major turning points have been labeled in this chart. Table 4.1 displays the wave relationships for each section of the rally.

Very clearly the wave relationships of the major five waves have a maximum variance of four points, and the (a)(b)(c) waves which form the five waves have a maximum variance of just two points, with just one exception being the Wave (c) of Wave (iii) which had a variance of six points.

This type of corroboration between the impulsive waves and the individual (a)(b)(c) waves of which they are formed together with the relationship of the entire five-wave sequence is crucial and confirms the entire move. A traditional five-wave development (or extended five-wave) in Elliott's original structure would not hold relationships between the waves.

Extended Wave Examples

In Chapter 3, I covered examples of how Elliott's extended wave appears to be a misjudgment of the real underlying harmonic structure. In Figure 3.8 I provided the example of a rally in GBPUSD and provided the harmonic wave count (shown in Figure 4.7).

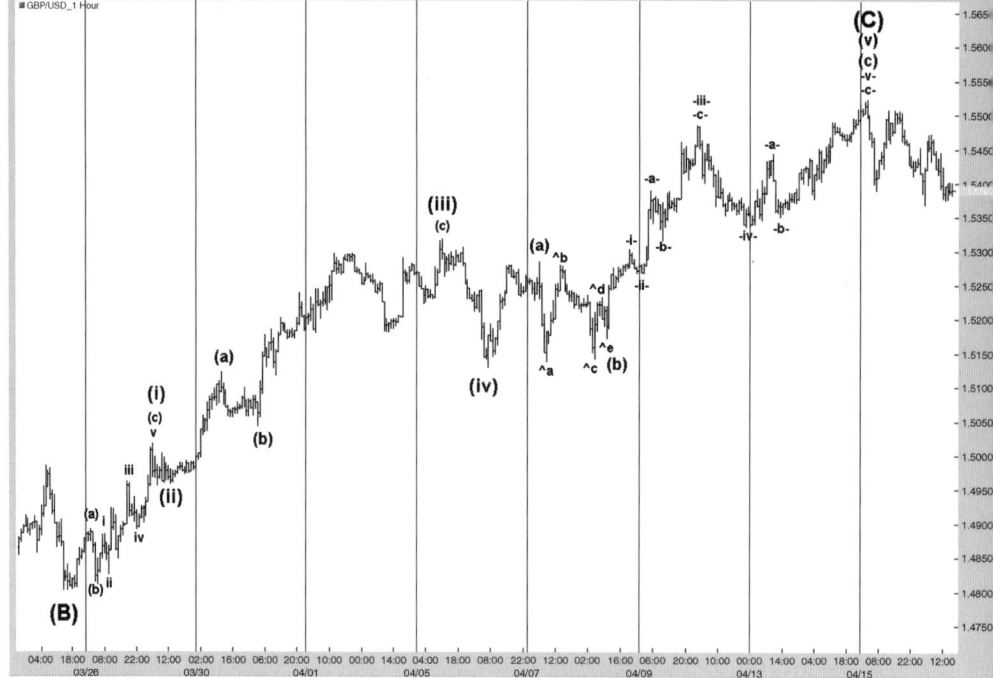

FIGURE 4.7 A Five-Wave Rally in the Hourly GBPUSD Market
Source: FXtrek IntelliChart™ in collaboration with FX-Strategy.com Pro Charts™

Projection and Retracement Ratios

TABLE 4.2 Wave Relationships for the Five-Wave Rally in Figure 4.7

Wave (C)				
Wave (a)	1.4891			1.4891
Wave (b)	1.4891 −	Wave (a) * 90.02% =	1.4811	1.4810
Wave i	1.4884			1.4884
Wave ii	1.4884 −	Wave i * 76.4% =	1.4827	1.4825
Wave iii	1.4825 +	Wave i * 185.4% =	1.4962	1.4961
Wave iv	1.4961 −	Wave iii * 50.0% =	1.4893	1.4891
Wave v	1.4891 +	Wave i > iii * 85.4% =	1.5020	1.5017
Wave (c)	1.4810 +	Wave (a) * 238.2% =	1.5022	1.5017
Wave (i)	**1.5017**			**1.5017**
Wave (ii)	**1.5017 −**	Wave (i) * 23.6% =	1.4966	1.4956
Wave (a)	1.5122			1.5122
Wave (b)	1.5122 −	Wave (a) * 50.0% =	1.5040	1.5043
Wave (c)	1.5043 +	Wave (a) * 166.7% =	1.5316	1.5317
Wave (iii)	**1.4956 +**	Wave (i) * 166.7% =	1.5316	1.5317
Wave (iv)	**1.5317 −**	Wave (iii) * 50.0% =	1.5137	1.5129
Wave (a)	1.5284			1.5284
Wave ^a	1.5284 −	Wave (a) * 95.43% =	1.5136	1.5138

Table 4.2 provides the ratios in all waves.

The extremely close correlations of the key waves are highlighted, with all projections and retracements being linked to Fibonacci ratios. Such ratios can provide extremely precise targets, or if the structure has been complex then identification of exactly what has occurred once that part of the structure has been completed. Above all, it generates more confidence in understanding each section of the structure and leaves fewer instances where subjective judgment needs to be applied.

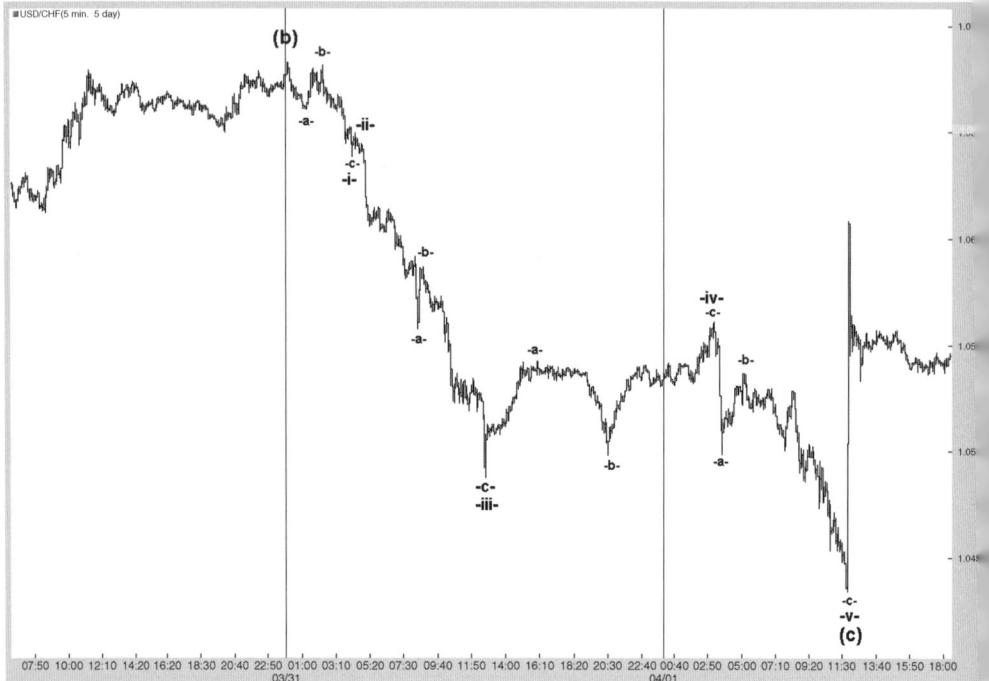

FIGURE 4.8 A Five-Wave Decline with a Strong Extended Wave -iii- in Five-Minute USDCHF Market
Source: FXtrek IntelliChart™ in collaboration with FX-Strategy.com Pro Charts™

Also in Chapter 3 I provided an example of a harmonic version of a stronger extended wave (shown in Figure 4.8).

In this example the wave relationships are exceptionally accurate (as shown in Table 4.3). It is very important to note how the internal ABC relationships confirm the projections of Waves -i- through Wave -v-. In addition, while not shown, the end of Wave (c) at 1.0434 should also be a close relationship with that of Wave (a).

These fractal relationships across the entire wave structure of all degrees is very noticeable and, in my mind, is conclusive proof that R. N. Elliott (probably quite understandably) made an error of judgment when defining the five-wave impulsive structure.

Projection and Retracement Ratios

TABLE 4.3 Wave Relationships for the Five-Wave in Figure 4.8

Wave (c)		Ratio	Projection	Actual
Wave -a-	1.0661			1.0661
Wave -b-	1.0661 +	Wave -a- * 100% =	1.0683	1.0682
Wave -c-	1.0682 −	Wave -a- * 194.43% =	1.0639	1.0638
Wave -i-	**1.0638**			1.0638
Wave -ii-	**1.0638 +**	Wave -i- * 23.6% =	1.0649	1.065
Wave -a-	1.0557			1.0557
Wave -b-	1.0557 +	Wave -a- * 33.3% =	1.0588	1.0587
Wave -c-	1.0587 −	Wave -a- * 109.02% =	1.0486	1.0488
Wave -iii-	**1.0650 −**	Wave -i- * 361.8% =	1.0487	1.0488
Wave -a-	1.0543			1.0543
Wave -b-	1.0543 −	Wave -a- * 85.4% =	1.0496	1.0498
Wave -c-	1.0498 +	Wave -a- * 114.6% =	1.0561	1.0561
Wave -iv-	**1.0488 +**	Wave -iii- * 41.4% =	1.0555	1.0561
Wave -a-	1.0498			1.0498
Wave -b-	1.0498 +	Wave -a- * 61.8% =	1.0537	1.0537
Wave -c-	1.0537 −	Wave -a- * 161.8% =	1.0435	1.0434
Wave -v-	**1.0561 −**	Wave -i- > -iii- * 66.7% =	1.0431	1.0434

As a second example of a clearly extending Wave (iii), in Chapter 3, I offered the hourly chart of a decline in Wave (c) in what I considered then to be Wave (iii).

Figure 4.9 displays the same chart as provided in Chapter 3 as an example of an extended wave and also one with a deep Wave (b). The key to identifying the harmonic structure is in synthesizing the different fractal elements of the entire wave. Each impulsive wave must have a projection in Wave (c) that is a normal ratio of

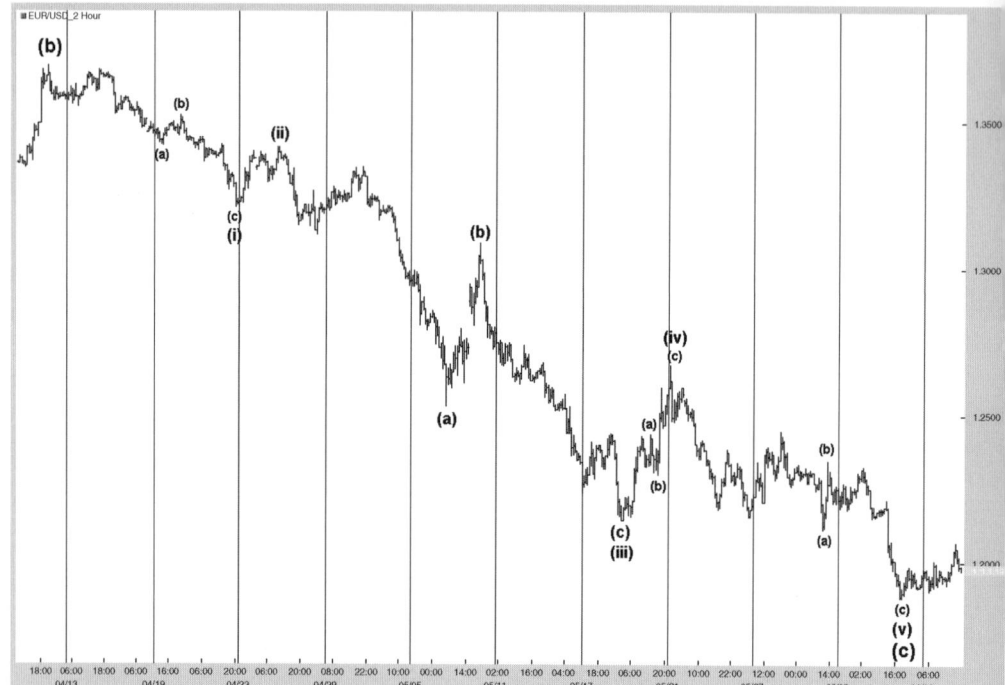

FIGURE 4.9 A Five-Wave Decline in Hourly EURUSD with an Effective Extended Wave (iii)
Source: FXtrek IntelliChart™ in collaboration with FX-Strategy.com Pro Charts™

Wave (a). Waves (iii) and (v) must in addition have targets from extensions of Wave (i) and Wave (i) to (iii) respectively.

Table 4.4 shows the harmonic fractal nature of the modified structure and in general holds quite accurate targets throughout. Note the deep Wave (b) of 61.8% but which slots in nicely with the projection in Wave (iii). Both Wave (ii) and Wave (iv) were modestly shallow at 41.4%. While the final 50% projection in Wave (v) is not uncommon, it is not one that I usually look for but should be considered if there is a discrepancy with the targets of one higher degree. In this case the larger Wave (c) lower displayed was a normal extension ratio of Wave (a) and also of Wave (i).

Projection and Retracement Ratios

TABLE 4.4 Wave Relationships for the Five-Wave Decline in Figure 4.9

Wave (c)		Ratio	Projection	Actual
Wave (a)	1.3417			1.3417
Wave (b)	1.3417 +	Wave (a) * 38.2% =	1.3522	1.3520
Wave (c)	1.3520 −	Wave (a) * 114.6% =	1.3206	1.3206
Wave (i)	1.3208			1.3206
Wave (ii)	1.3208 +	Wave (i) * 41.4% =	1.3408	1.3412
Wave (a)	1.253			1.2530
Wave (b)	1.2530 +	Wave (a) * 61.8% =	1.3075	1.3086
Wave (c)	1.3086 −	Wave (a) * 109.2% =	1.2124	1.2143
Wave (iii)	1.3412 −	Wave (i) * 261.8% =	1.2142	1.2143
Wave (a)	1.2436			1.2436
Wave (b)	1.2436 −	Wave (a) * 50.0% =	1.2290	1.2297
Wave (c)	1.2297 +	Wave (a) * 123.6% =	1.2660	1.2670
Wave (iv)	1.2143 +	Wave (iii) * 41.4% =	1.2668	1.2670
Wave (a)	1.2113			1.2113
Wave (b)	1.2113 +	Wave (a) * 41.4% =	1.2344	1.2353
Wave (c)	1.2353 −	Wave (a) * 85.4% =	1.1877	1.1877
Wave (v)	1.2670 −	Wave (i) -> (iii) * 50.0% =	1.1896	1.1877

Extended Fifth Wave These are always very tough but there are normally some pointers to guide or suggest that an extension may occur. The following example was provided in Chapter 3 and was of an extended Wave -v- of Wave (c) of Wave (v).

In Chapter 3 I provided Figure 3.13 as an example of an extended fifth wave (shown in Figure 4.10). The wave relationships are shown in Table 4.5. Note that the common Wave (c) projection at 105.43% offered a potential target at 1.1353, while the wave

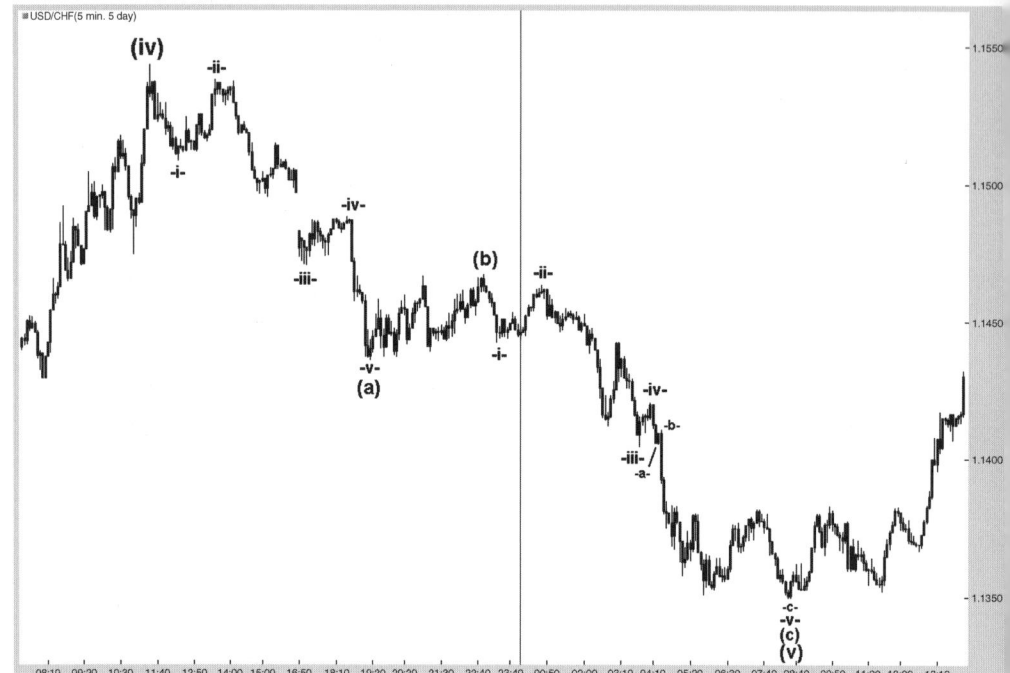

FIGURE 4.10 A Three-Wave Decline in Five-Minute USDCHF with an Extended Wave -v- of Wave (c)
Source: FXtrek IntelliChart™ in collaboration with FX-Strategy.com Pro Charts™

TABLE 4.5 Wave Relationships for the Three-Wave Decline in Figure 4.10

Wave (v)		Ratio	Projection	Actual
Wave -i-	1.1509			**1.1509**
Wave -ii-	1.1509 +	Wave -i- * 85.4% =	1.1539	**1.1538**
Wave -iii-	1.1538 −	Wave -i- * 195.4% =	1.1470	**1.1471**
Wave -iv-	1.1471 +	**Wave -iii- * 23.6% =**	1.1487	**1.1488**
Wave -v-	1.1488 −	Wave -i- −> -iii- * 66.7% =	1.1439	**1.1436**
Wave (a)	1.1436			**1.1436**
Wave (b)	1.1436 +	Wave (a) * 33.33% =	1.1472	**1.1467**

Projection and Retracement Ratios **91**

Wave -i-	1.1443			1.1443
Wave -ii-	1.1443 +	Wave -i- * 85.4% =	1.1463	1.1463
Wave -iii-	1.1463 −	Wave -i- * 238.2% =	1.1406	1.1405
Wave -iv-	1.1405 +	Wave -iii- * 23.6% =	1.1419	1.1421
Wave -a-	1.1405			1.1405
Wave -b-	1.1405 +	Wave -a- * 38.2% =	1.1411	1.1411
Wave -c-	1.1411 −	Wave -a- * 384.5% =	1.1349	1.1350
Wave -v-	1.1421 −	Wave -i- -> Wave -iii- * 100% =	1.1349	1.1350
Wave (c)	1.1467 −	Wave (a) * 105.43% =	1.1353	1.1350
Wave (v)	1.1544 −	Wave (i) -> Wave (iii) * 66.7% =	1.1361	1.1350

equality target in a Wave -v- extension was implied at 1.1349. Overall, the 66.7% target in Wave (v) was at 1.1361. Therefore, the general 1.1350–60 area was implied by several different measurements. Even the 385.4% projection in Wave -c- of Wave -v- pointed to 1.1349 also but would be observed as being able to fit that target. Attempting to predict such excessive moves is always accompanied by some uncertainties.

ELLIOTT STRUCTURE RELATIONSHIPS VERSUS THE MODIFIED HARMONIC RELATIONSHIPS

As another example of how the extended waves in Elliott's original structure fail to stand up to rigorous wave relationships, I will provide an example of an apparent impulsive decline in hourly GBPUSD and compare wave relationships between Elliott's structure and the harmonic structure.

Figure 4.11 displays the decline in the hourly GBPUSD market. This appears to decline in a complex five-wave move in which Wave (3) has a double extension. Apart from the correction in Wave (2), all

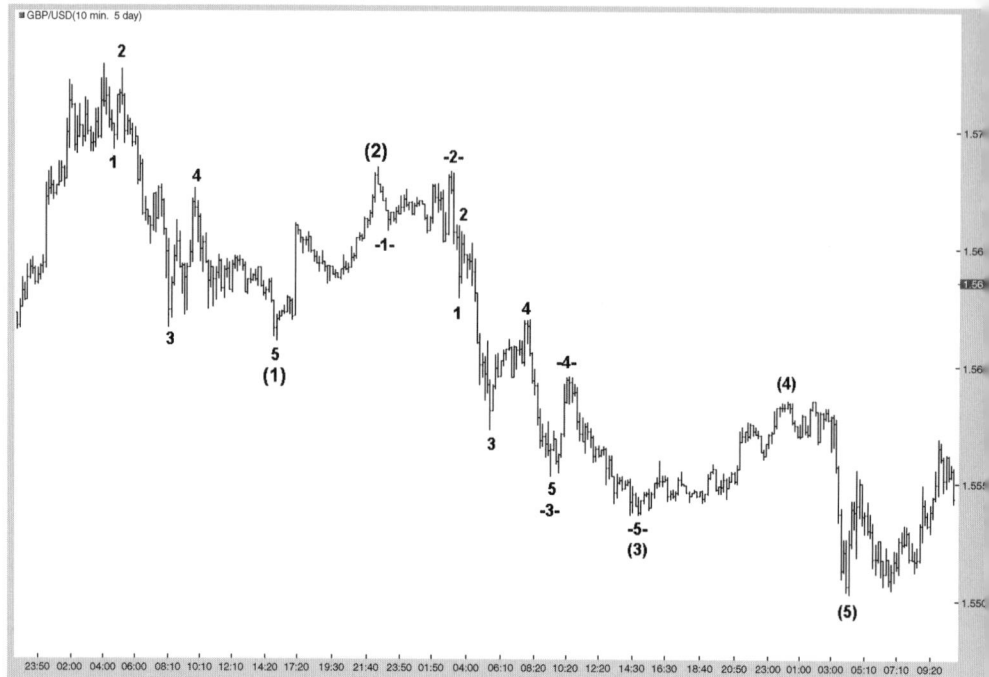

FIGURE 4.11 A Complex Five-Wave Decline in GBPUSD
Source: FXtrek IntelliChart™ in collaboration with FX-Strategy.com Pro Charts™

the swing highs and swing lows are declining, confirming a bearish move. This decline followed a previous move lower and therefore the implication is for another five-wave decline.

The decline in Wave (1) does follow Elliott's structure of five waves with Wave 3 being the longest and providing the main thrust of the decline. The correction in Wave (2) appears normal, and this is followed by a Wave (3) which has extended twice. Wave -2- is an Expanded Flat with the rest of the decline developing normally.

The problems I habitually encountered with Elliott's structural development were twofold. Firstly, these extended waves frequently lacked any consistent wave relationships, and this generated the second problem of being able to forecast where price should stall. To demonstrate the frustration I commonly encountered, the wave relationships are displayed in Table 4.6.

Projection and Retracement Ratios

TABLE 4.6 Wave Relationships

Elliott complex wave		Ratio
Wave 1	1.5692	
Wave 2	1.5726	Wave 1 * 94.4%
Wave 3	1.5616	**Wave 1 * 305.6%**
Wave 4	1.5675	Wave 3 * 53.6%
Wave 5	1.5611	**Wave 1 > 3 * 57.14%**
Wave (1)	1.5611	
Wave (2)	1.5685	Wave (1) * 63.25%
Wave -1-	1.5658	
Wave -2-	1.5683	Wave -1- * 92.6%
Wave 1	1.5629	
Wave 2	1.5657	Wave 1 * 51.2%
Wave 3	1.5572	**Wave 1 * 157.4%**
Wave 4	1.562	Wave 3 * 56.5%
Wave 5	1.5553	Wave 1 > 3 * 60.4%
Wave -3-	1.5553	Wave -1- * 481.5%
Wave -4-	1.5595	Wave -3- * 32.3%
Wave -5-	1.5536	**Wave -1- > -3- * 44.7%**
Wave (3)	1.5536	**Wave (1) * 127.3%**
Wave (4)	1.5585	Wave (3) * 32.9%
Wave (5)	1.5503	**Wave (1) > (3) * 42.7%**

As can be seen, there is a mixture of wave relationships. While there are some that have the normal wave relationships I look for, within a reasonable deviation, I have highlighted those which really would have posed serious issues in forecasting.

It was this type of imprecision that I found difficult to accept. On many occasions the failure to be able to identify turns within a

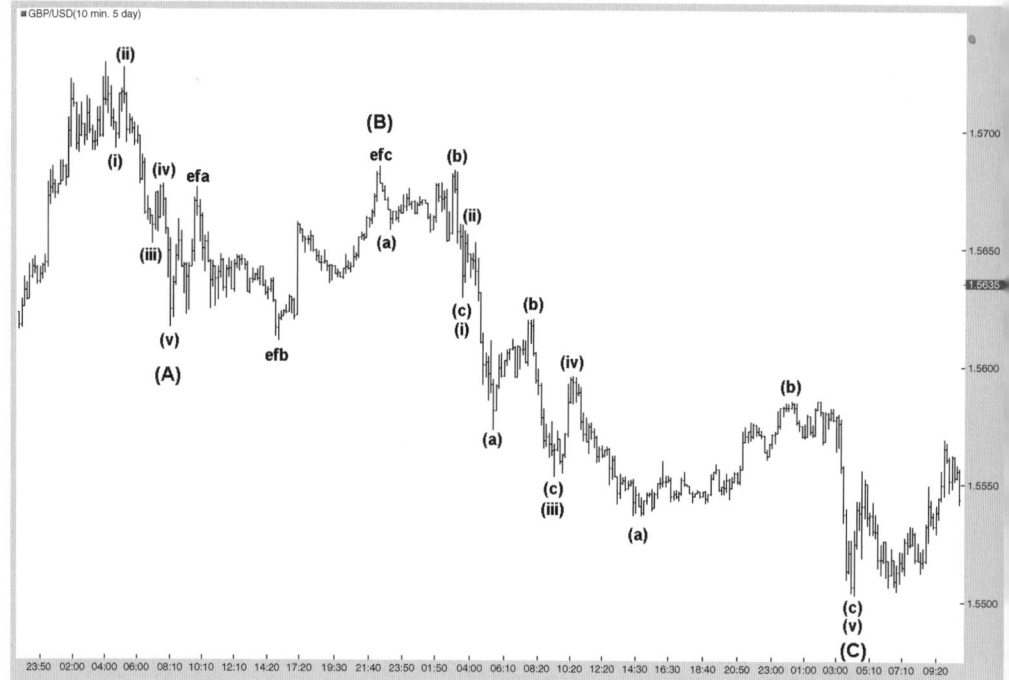

FIGURE 4.12 A Harmonic Three-Wave Decline in GBPUSD
Source: FXtrek IntelliChart™ in collaboration with FX-Strategy.com Pro Charts™

reasonable margin saw reversals much earlier and left me in no-man's land wondering whether a correction was being seen and not a reversal. Anticipating extended waves and where each Wave 1 would stall was a hit-or-miss affair, and then everything became much more problematic.

Now let's look at the same decline employing the harmonic wave structure.

Figure 4.12 labels this completely differently as a three-wave decline. There will be many Elliott Wave practitioners who will question this, but the evidence for the count comes through the wave relationships which in this case provide exceptionally accurate ratios that provided me with a much easier call for a reversal higher.

The clarity of the wave relationships stands out from the first five-wave decline in Wave (A) (as shown in Table 4.7). All relationships are common for their position; the 198.4% projection in Wave

Projection and Retracement Ratios

TABLE 4.7 Wave Relationships for Three-Wave Decline in Figure 4.12

Harmonic wave		Ratio	Projection	Actual
Wave (i)	1.5692			
Wave (ii)	**1.5692 +**	Wave (i) * 95.4% =	**1.5726**	**1.5726**
Wave (iii)	**1.5726 −**	Wave (i) * 198.4% =	**1.5655**	**1.5652**
Wave (iv)	**1.5652 +**	Wave (iii) * 33.3% =	**1.5677**	**1.5677**
Wave (v)	**1.5677 −**	Wave (i) > (iii) * 76.4% =	**1.5619**	**1.5616**
Wave (A)	1.5616			
Wave (B)	**1.5616 +**	Wave (A) * 61.8% =	**1.5685**	**1.5685**
Wave (a)	1.5658			
Wave (b)	**1.5658 +**	Wave (a) * 90.2% =	**1.5682**	**1.5683**
Wave (c)	**1.5683 −**	Wave (a) * 198.4% =	**1.5629**	**1.5629**
Wave (i)	1.5629			
Wave (ii)	**1.5659 +**	Wave (i) * 50.0% =	**1.5657**	**1.5657**
Wave (a)	1.5572			1.5572
Wave (b)	**1.5572 +**	Wave (a) * 58.6% =	**1.5622**	**1.562**
Wave (c)	**1.5620 −**	Wave (a) * 76.4% =	**1.5555**	**1.5553**
Wave (iii)	**1.5657 −**	Wave (i) * 185.4% =	**1.5553**	**1.5553**
Wave (iv)	**1.5553 +**	Wave (iii) * 41.4% =	**1.5596**	**1.5595**
Wave (a)	1.5536			1.5536
Wave (b)	**1.5536 +**	Wave (a) * 85.4% =	**1.5586**	**1.5585**
Wave (c)	**1.5585 −**	Wave (a) * 138.2% =	**1.5503**	**1.5503**
Wave (v)	**1.5595 −**	Wave (i) > (iii) * 66.7% =	**1.5507**	**1.5503**
Wave (C)	**1.5685 −**	Wave (A) * 161.8% =	**1.5504**	**1.5503**

(iii), the 33.3% retracement in Wave (iv), and the 76.4% projection in Wave (v). The maximum variance was just three points.

The correction in Wave (B) developed as an Expanded Flat with the pullback being exactly 61.8%. These common relationships

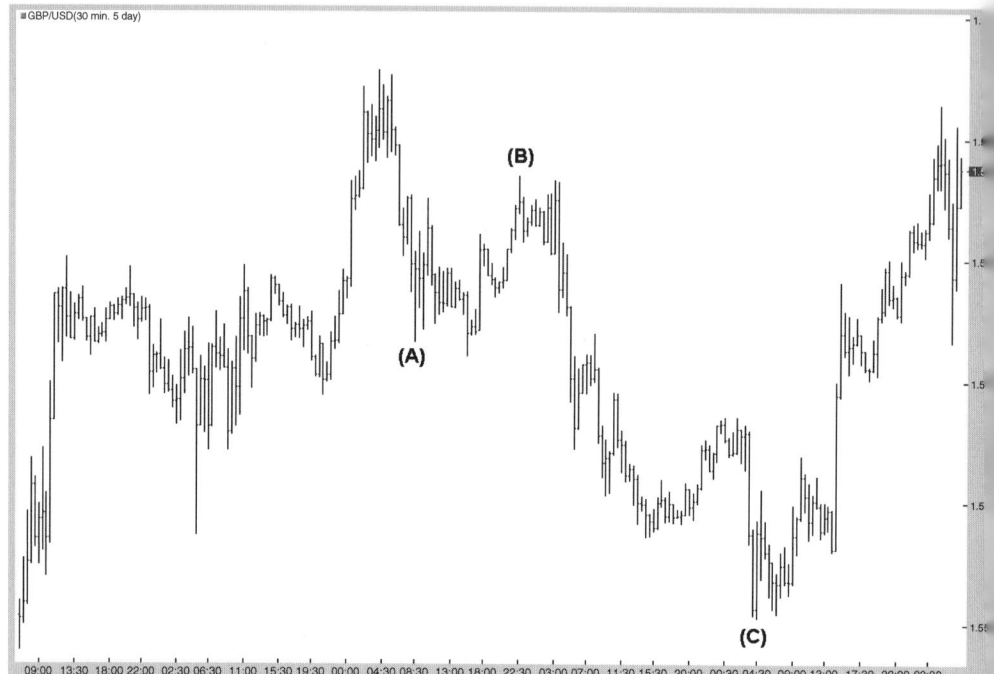

FIGURE 4.13 Rally Following the (A)(B)(C) Decline in GBPUSD
Source: FXtrek IntelliChart™ in collaboration with FX-Strategy.com Pro Charts™

continued throughout the entire decline, even to the end where the extension in Wave (v) of Wave (C) was only four points while the projection in Wave (C) was one point away from the exact 161.8% projection of Wave (A).

Figure 4.13 displays the resulting reversal higher to confirm the accuracy of the harmonic structure.

OTHER EXAMPLES OF THE STRENGTH AND ACCURACY OF THE MODIFIED HARMONIC STRUCTURE

Next in Chapter 3, I provided the example of Figure 3.17 which displayed a Zigzag higher in 30-minute EURUSD with overlap in

Projection and Retracement Ratios

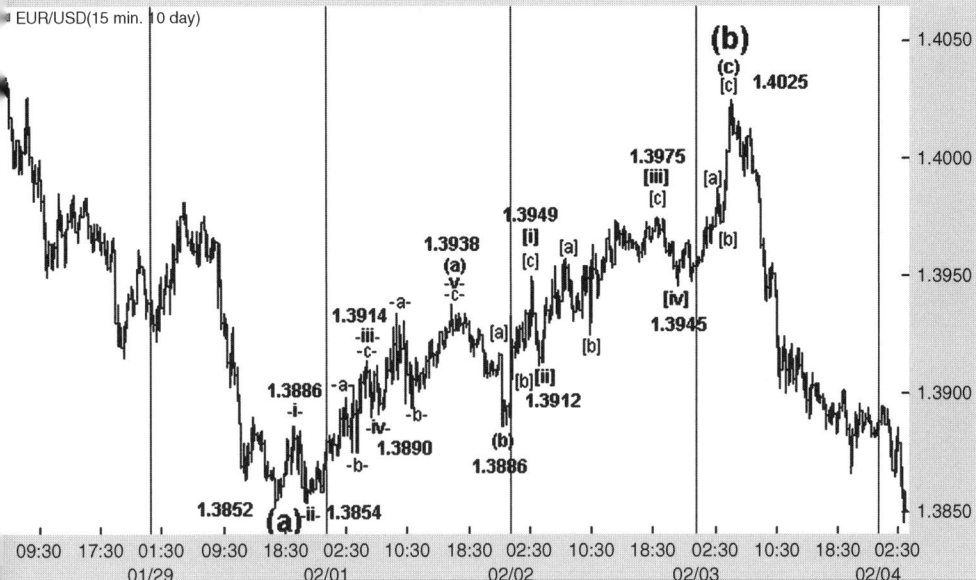

FIGURE 4.14 Zigzag Higher in 30-Minute EURUSD with Overlap in Wave [i] and Wave [iv]
Source: FXtrek IntelliChart™ in collaboration with FX-Strategy.com Pro Charts™

Wave [i] and Wave [iv]. I have reproduced the image with key price levels listed (Figure 4.14).

Table 4.8 displays the wave relationships for each section of the corrective rally.

TABLE 4.8 Wave Relationships for the Zigzag higher in Figure 4.14

Entire Wave (b)		Ratio	Projection	Actual
Wave (a)	1.3938			1.3938
Wave (b)	1.3939 −	Wave (a) * 61.8% =	1.3885	1.3886
Wave (c)	1.3886 +	Wave (a) * 161.8% =	1.4025	1.4025
Wave (a)		Ratio	Projection	Actual
Wave -i-	1.3886			1.3886
Wave -ii-	1.3886 −	Wave -i- * 100% =	1.3852	1.3854

(*continued*)

TABLE 4.8 (Continued)

Entire Wave (b)		Ratio	Projection	Actual
Wave -a-	1.3898			1.3898
Wave -b-	1.3898 −	Wave -a- * 50.0% =	1.3876	1.3875
Wave -c-	1.3875 +	Wave -a- * 85.6% =	1.3913	1.3914
Wave -iii-	1.3886 +	Wave -i- * 176.4% =	1.3914	1.3914
Wave -iv-	1.3914 −	Wave -iii- * 38.2% =	1.3891	1.3890
Wave -a-	1.3934			1.3934
Wave -b-	1.3934 −	Wave -a- * 85.6% =	1.3896	1.3894
Wave -c-	1.3894 +	Wave -a- * 100% =	1.3938	1.3938
Wave -v-	1.3890 +	Wave -i- > -iii- * 76.4% =	1.3937	1.3938
Wave (c)		**Ratio**	**Projection**	**Actual**
Wave [a]	1.3932			1.3932
Wave [b]	1.3932 −	Wave [a] * 58.6% =	1.3905	1.3906
Wave [c]	1.3906 +	Wave [a] * 100% =	1.3952	1.3949
Wave [i]	1.3949			1.3949
Wave [ii]	1.3949 −	Wave [i] * 58.6%	1.3912	1.3912
Wave [a]	1.3957			1.3957
Wave [b]	1.3957 −	Wave [a] * 50.0% =	1.3922	1.3925
Wave [c]	1.3925 +	Wave [a] * 114.4% =	1.3976	1.3975
Wave [iii]	1.3912 +	Wave [i] * 100% =	1.3975	1.3975
Wave [iv]	1.3975 −	Wave [iii] * 50.0% =	1.3944	1.3945
Wave [a]	1.3987			1.3987
Wave [b]	1.3987 −	Wave [a] * 38.2% =	1.3972	1.3972
Wave [c]	1.3972 +	Wave [a] * 138.2% =	1.4027	1.4025
Wave [v]	1.3975 +	Wave [i] > [iii] * 85.6%	1.4021	1.4025

Projection and Retracement Ratios

I have separated each specific wave and listed the results. The first section is nothing new as it merely relates to the Zigzag development in the overall Wave (b), developing in an (a)(b)(c) move. Wave (b) was a 61.8% retracement of Wave (a) and Wave (c) a 161.8% projection of Wave (a).

The modified structure is highlighted in the construction of Wave (a) and Wave (c), each comprising five waves but all of them in three-wave structures.

In Wave -iii- of Wave (a), note that Wave -c- had a projection at 1.3914 while the extension in Wave -iii- was the common 176.4% projection of Wave -i-. Given Wave -ii- was just about a 100% retracement of Wave -i- we can see that Wave -iv- was a shallow 38.2%. This gave rise to a 76.4% projection in Wave -v- to the same target as a wave equality projection of Wave -a- in Wave -c-.

In Wave (c) it can be seen that a similar process provided remarkably accurate targets in Wave [c] of Wave [iii] and the extension of Wave [i], which turned out to be a wave equality target with Wave [i]. Similarly the targets for Wave [c] of Wave [v] and Wave [v] itself were within six points.

This larger Wave (b) was actually a deep Wave (b) of a declining Wave (iii) which retraced an exact 66.7% of Wave (a).

In another example in Chapter 3 I offered the five-wave decline in Wave efc in USDCAD (as shown in Figure 4.15).

Table 4.9 shows the table of the individual waves that constructed the decline.

Here I have separated each of the impulsive waves and also the breakdown of Wave -a- and Wave -c- of Wave -v-.

The modified structure in this example is remarkably accurate, with the majority of individual wave targets matching the internal abc waves to within one point. Only in the final Wave -c- of Wave -v- was there a difference of six points, but then the Wave v of Wave -c- did have a 66.7% projection that matched the 66.7% Wave -v- projection at 1.0545. All waves adhered to the normal ratios seen in the modified wave structure.

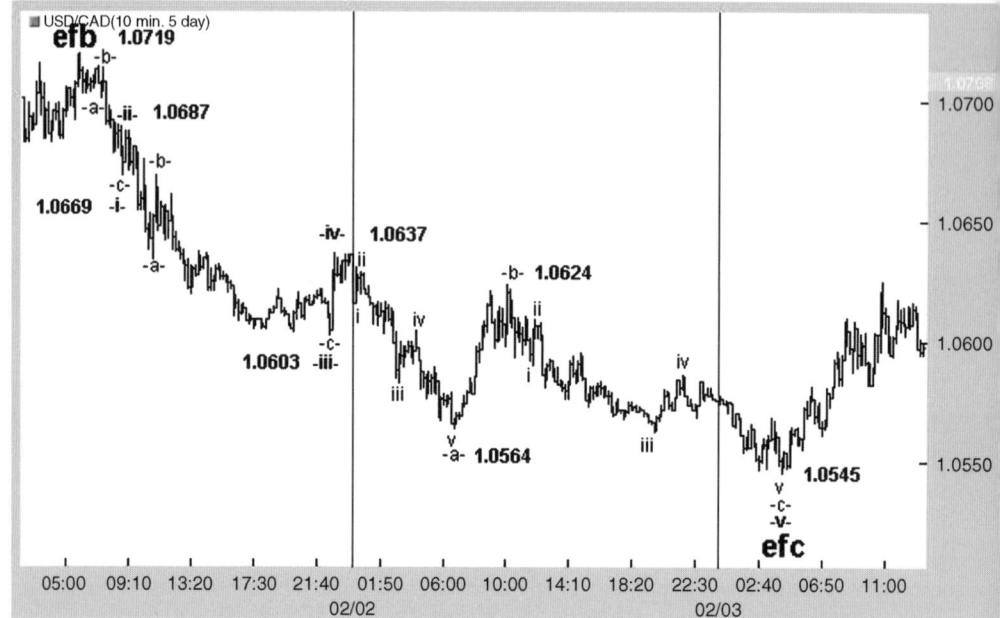

FIGURE 4.15 A Decline in Wave efc in 10-minute USDCAD to Complete what was a Wave (iv)
Source: FXtrek IntelliChart™ in collaboration with FX-Strategy.com Pro Charts™

TABLE 4.9 Wave Relationships for the Decline in Wave efc in Figure 4.15

Wave -i-		Ratio	Projection	Actual
Wave -a- =	1.0702			1.0702
Wave -b- =	1.0702 *	Wave -a- * 38.2% =	1.0708	1.0708
Wave -c- =	1.0708 −	Wave -a- * 223.6% =	1.0670	1.0669
Wave -ii- & Wave -iii-		Ratio	Projection	Actual
Wave -ii- =	1.0669 +	Wave -i- * 38.2% =	1.0688	1.0687
Wave -a- =	1.0634			1.0634
Wave -b- =	1.0634 +	Wave -a- * 66.7% =	1.0669	1.0669
Wave -c- =	1.0669 −	Wave -a- * 123.6% =	1.0603	1.0603
Wave -iii- =	1.0687 −	Wave -i- * 166.7% =	1.0604	1.0603

Projection and Retracement Ratios

Wave -iv- & Wave -v-		Ratio	Projection	Actual
Wave -iv- =	1.0603 +	Wave -iii- * 50.0% =	**1.0636**	1.0637
Wave -v- =	1.0637 −	Wave -i- > -iii- * 66.7% =	**1.0547**	1.0545
Wave -v-		Ratio	Projection	1.0545
Wave -a-	1.0564			1.0564
Wave -b- =	1.0564 +	Wave -a- * 85.6% =	**1.0626**	1.0624
Wave -c-	1.0624 −	Wave -a- * 100% =	**1.0551**	1.0545
Wave -a- of -v-		Ratio	Projection	Actual
Wave i =	1.0616			1.0616
Wave ii =	1.0616 −	Wave i * 66.7%	**1.0630**	1.0631
Wave iii =	1.0631 −	Wave i * 223.6%	**1.0584**	1.0583
Wave iv =	1.0583 +	Wave iii * 41.4%	**1.0603**	1.0604
Wave v =	1.0604 −	Wave i > Wave iii * 76.4%	**1.0563**	1.0564
Wave -c- of -v-		Ratio	Projection	Actual
Wave i =	1.0590			1.0590
Wave ii =	1.0590 +	Wave i * 58.6%	**1.0610**	1.0609
Wave iii =	1.0609 −	Wave i * 138.2%	**1.0562**	1.0562
Wave iv =	1.0562 +	Wave iii * 50.0%	**1.0586**	1.0586
Wave v =	1.0586 −	Wave i > Wave iii * 66.7%	**1.0545**	1.0545

As a third example, in Figure 4.16, I have taken the deep Wave -b- of Wave -iii- that was shown in Figure 3.21 in the hourly USDCHF market.

Table 4.10 shows the individual waves that constructed the rally.

In Wave (A) we had a standard five-wave move in which Wave (v) ended midway between the 76.4% and 85.4% projections. The retracement in Wave (B) was just over 33.3%.

After seeing the pullback in Wave (B), we would be looking for a rally in Wave (C) and thus we should be concentrating on normal

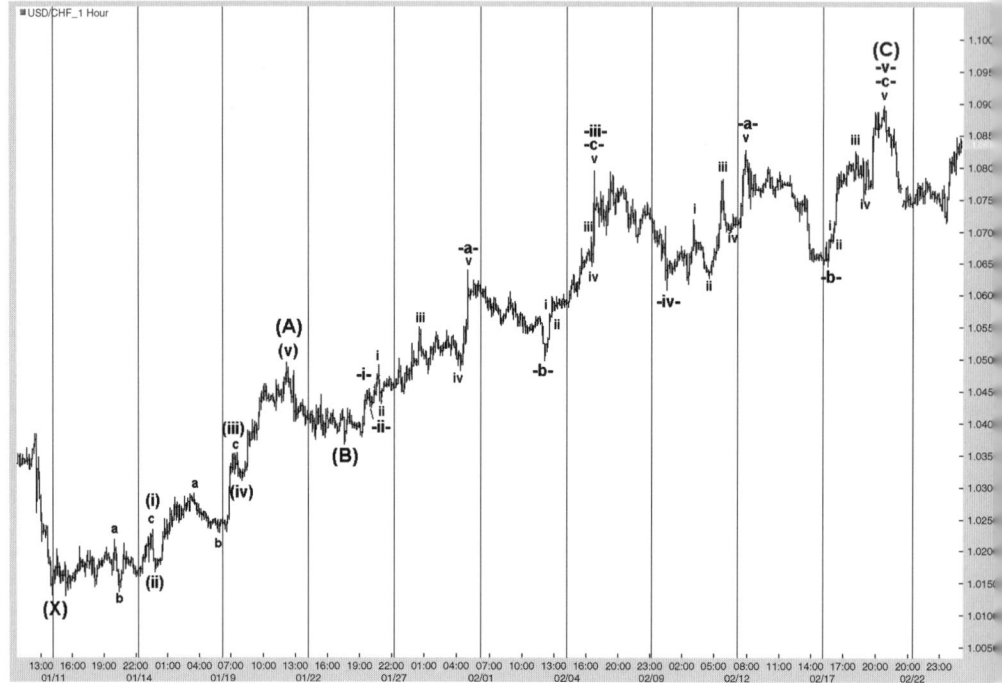

FIGURE 4.16 An (A)(B)(C) with a Deep Wave -b- in Wave -iii- in Hourly USDCHF
Source: FXtrek IntelliChart™ in collaboration with FX-Strategy.com Pro Charts™

TABLE 4.10 Wave Relationships for the (A)(B)(C) in Figure 4.16

Wave (C)		Ratio	Projection	Actual
Wave i	1.0218			1.0218
Wave ii	1.0218 −	Wave i * 90.98% =	**1.0137**	1.0136
Wave a	1.0212			1.0212
Wave b	1.0212 −	Wave a * 66.7% =	**1.0161**	1.0159
Wave c	1.0159 +	Wave a * 261.8% =	**1.0358**	1.0354
Wave iii	1.0218 +	Wave i * 238.2% =	**1.0348**	1.0354
Wave iv	1.0354 −	Wave iii * 23.6% =	**1.0303**	1.0310
Wave a	1.0388			1.0388
Wave b	1.0388 −	Wave a * 33.3% =	**1.0362**	1.0362

Projection and Retracement Ratios

Wave c	1.0362 +	Wave a * 166.7% =	**1.0492**	**1.0495**
Wave v	1.0354 +	Wave i > iii * 85.6% =	**1.0503**	**1.0495**
Wave (C)		Ratio	Projection	Actual
Wave (A)	1.0495			1.0495
Wave (B)	1.0495 −	Wave (A) * 33.3% =	1.0373	1.0366
Wave (C)	1.0366	Wave (A) * 141.4% =	**1.0884**	**1.0897**

projections generated from Wave (A). These produced potential targets at:

$$100.0\% = 1.0732$$
$$114.6\% = 1.0785$$
$$138.2\% = 1.0872$$
$$161.8\% = 1.0958$$

Table 4.11 displays the relationship in Wave (C).

TABLE 4.11 Wave Relationships for the Wave (C) Rally in Figure 4.16

Wave (C)		Ratio	Projection	Actual
Wave -i-	1.0454			1.0454
Wave -ii-	1.0454 −	Wave -i- * 33.3% =	1.0425	1.0425
Wave -a-	1.0639			1.0639
Wave -b-	1.0639 −	Wave -a- * 66.7% =	1.0496	1.0497
Wave -c-	1.0497 +	Wave -a- * 138.2% =	**1.0793**	**1.0794**
Wave -iii-	1.0425 +	Wave -i- * 423.6% =	**1.0798**	**1.0794**
Wave -iv-	1.0794 −	Wave -iii- * 50.0% =	1.0611	1.0608
Wave -a-	1.0827			1.0827
Wave -b-	1.0827 −	Wave -a- * 85.6% =	1.0640	1.0646
Wave -c-	1.0646 +	Wave -a- * 114.4%	**1.0897**	**1.0897**
Wave -v-	1.0608 +	Wave -i- > -iii- * 66.7% =	**1.0893**	**1.0897**

Here I am concentrating on the rally from the 1.0366 Wave (B) low until the completion of Wave (C) at 1.0897. In terms of projections of Wave (A) the final 1.0897 high was not particularly accurate, which disappoints. However, the Wave -v- projection of 66.7% came within three points and the 114.6% projection in Wave -c- of Wave -v- was actually perfect.

Once again, the rally in Wave (C) was fueled by common wave ratios. Note the relatively shallow 33.3% retracement in Wave -ii- that spurred a deeper Wave -b- of Wave -iii- that was the very common 66.7% retracement. In addition the 138.2% projection in Wave -c- and the 423.6% projection of Wave -i-, both arrived at the same area with only four points variance.

In this case, the Wave -iv- was probably deeper than would normally be expected at 50% and this would have had to have been managed by observing the nature and structure of the decline in the five-minute chart.

The 66.7% projection in Wave -v- and the 114.4% projection in Wave -c- also matched with a variance of four points.

I should add at this point that the 85.6% and 114.4% projections in Wave -c- are surprisingly common. I can only imagine that there is a common observation that wave equality relationships occur quite frequently and the slightly shorter and slightly longer are reflections of early profit taking and stop losses being triggered from reversal positions at the wave equality target respectively. However, from the analyst's perspective, what we are looking for are matching targets drawn from both the larger projection of Wave -a- and the internal Wave v of Wave -c-.

In Figure 3.22, I also covered the rather unusual structure in Wave -a- of Wave -v-. Therefore, we should also take a closer look at the internal structure and wave relationships (as shown in Figure 4.17).

The related table of wave relationships is shown in Table 4.12.

This type of price development is not the easiest to forecast due to the number of less common wave relationships. An 85.6% retracement in Wave b (of Wave i) must always be one of the areas to watch out for, but it can begin to cause some doubts when approached. The 141.4% projection in Wave c is not one I'd usually look for, but since

Projection and Retracement Ratios

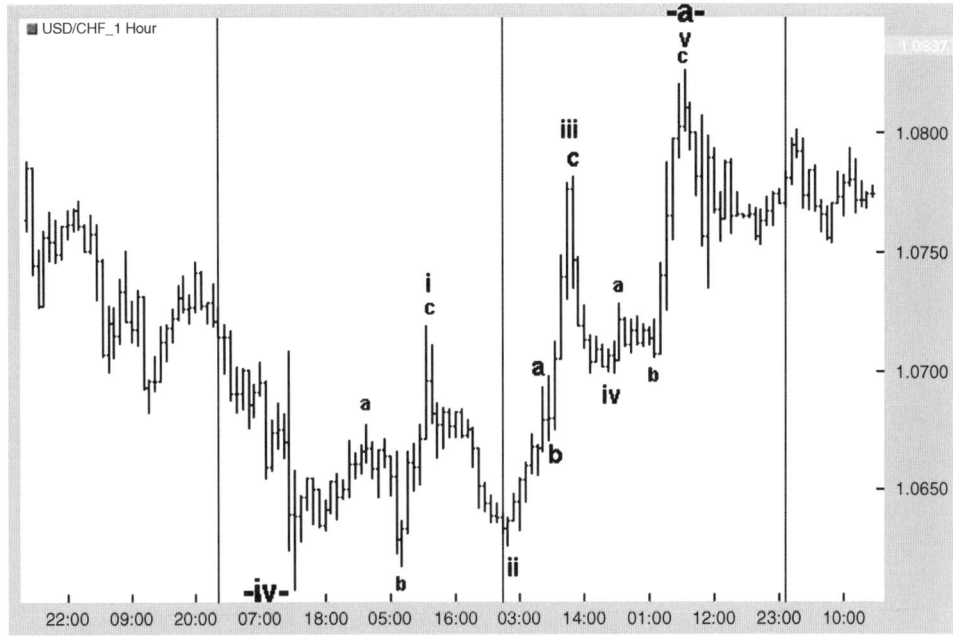

FIGURE 4.17 Internal Structure of Wave -a- of Wave -v- Higher in USDCHF
Source: FXtrek IntelliChart™ in collaboration with FX-Strategy.com Pro Charts™

TABLE 4.12 Wave Relationships of the Wave -a- of Wave -v- Higher in Figure 4.17

Wave -a- of -v-		Ratio	Projection	Actual
Wave a	1.0677			1.0677
Wave b	1.0677 −	Wave a * 85.6% =	1.0618	1.0618
Wave c	1.0618 +	Wave a * 141.4% =	1.0716	1.0719
Wave i	1.0719			1.0719
Wave ii	1.0719 −	Wave i * 85.6% =	**1.0624**	**1.0626**
Wave a	1.0693			1.0693
Wave b	1.0693 −	Wave a * 33.3% =	1.0671	1.0671
Wave c	1.0671 +	Wave a * 166.7% =	**1.0783**	**1.0782**
Wave iii	1.0626 +	Wave i * 141.4% =	**1.0783**	**1.0782**

(continued)

TABLE 4.12 (Continued)

Wave -a- of -v-		Ratio	Projection	Actual
Wave iv	1.0782 −	Wave iii * 50.0% =	1.0704	1.0699
Wave a	1.0728			1.0728
Wave b	1.0728 −	Wave a * 76.4% =	1.0706	1.0705
Wave c	1.0705 +	Wave a * 423.6%	1.0828	1.0827
Wave v	1.0699 +	Wave i > iii * 76.4% =	1.0832	1.0828

this is an hourly chart the wave development in the five-minute chart should have provided some indication. The 85.6% retracement in Wave ii would have again raised some doubts but the key was the fact the Wave b low was not breached.

Given that both Wave b and Wave ii were exceptionally deep, the guideline of alternation would warn that Wave b may well be short and shallow. Indeed it was, and then Wave c of Wave iii extended by 166.7% which again is less frequently seen. To have it match again with a 141.4% extension of Wave i is not high on the list of common projections.

Even after a 50% retracement in Wave iv the 76.4% projection in Wave v is very common, but the 423.6% projection in Wave c is not.

Wave (iv) Retracements with Reference to Wave (b) of Wave (iii)

Again in Chapter 3, I provided an example of a decline in Wave (c) which demonstrated how Wave -iv- never retraces beyond the prior Wave -b- of Wave -iii-. (This was also shown in Figure 4.8 detailing the ratios in an extended Wave (iii).) There is nothing more to gather from this chart but I present it again to demonstrate the remarkable harmonious relationships between all parts of the wave structure (Figure 4.18).

The ratios are displayed in Table 4.13. It should be noted that the reaction following the completion of this Wave (c) was not too surprising as this completed a Triple Three correction in Wave (X) from the 1.0897 high.

Projection and Retracement Ratios

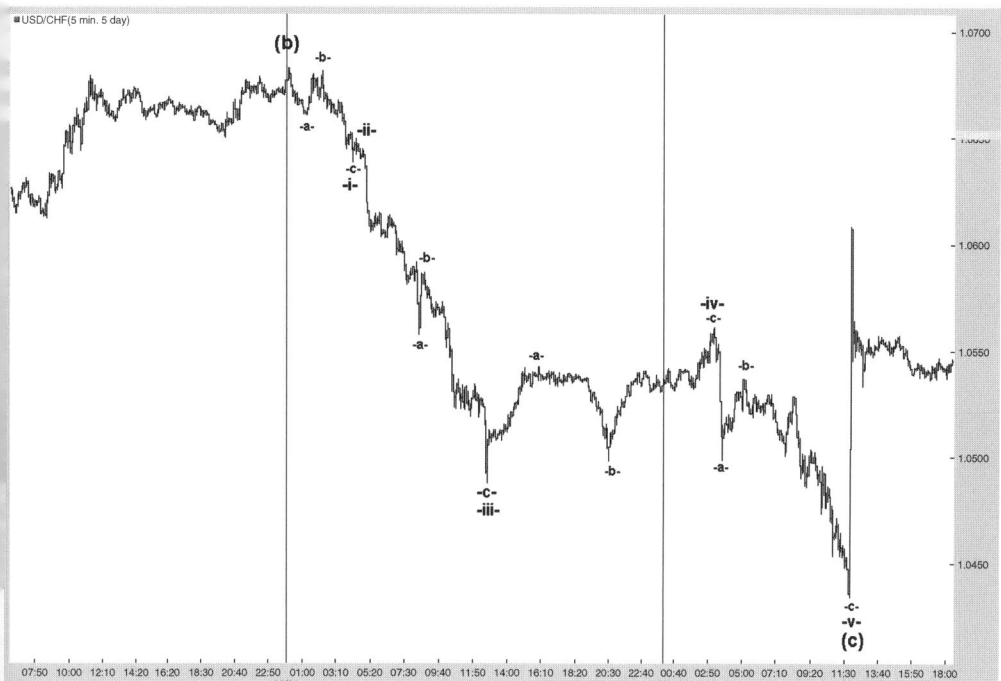

FIGURE 4.18 Wave (c) Decline in Five-Minute USDCHF Displaying the Limited Pullback in Wave -iv-
Source: FXtrek IntelliChart™ in collaboration with FX-Strategy.com Pro Charts™

TABLE 4.13 Wave Relationships for the Shallow Wave -iv- in Figure 4.18

Wave (c)		Ratio	Projection	Actual
Wave -a-	1.0661			1.0661
Wave -b-	1.0661 +	Wave -a- * 100% =	1.0683	1.0682
Wave -c-	1.0682 −	Wave -a- * 194.43% =	1.0639	1.0638
Wave -i-	**1.0638**			1.0638
Wave -ii-	**1.0638 +**	Wave -i- * 23.6% =	1.0649	1.0650
Wave -a-	1.0557			1.0557
Wave -b-	1.0557 +	Wave -a- * 33.3% =	1.0588	1.0587

(continued)

TABLE 4.13 *(Continued)*

Wave (c)		Ratio	Projection	Actual
Wave -c-	1.0587 −	Wave -a- * 109.02% =	**1.0486**	**1.0488**
Wave -iii-	**1.0650** −	Wave -i- * 361.8% =	**1.0487**	**1.0488**
Wave -a-	1.0543			1.0543
Wave -b-	1.0543 −	Wave -a- * 85.4% =	1.0496	1.0498
Wave -c-	1.0498 +	Wave -a- * 114.6% =	**1.0561**	**1.0561**
Wave -iv-	**1.0488** +	Wave -iii- * 41.4% =	1.0555	1.0561
Wave -a-	1.0498			1.0498
Wave -b-	1.0498 +	Wave -a- * 61.8% =	**1.0537**	**1.0537**
Wave -c-	1.0537 −	Wave -a- * 161.8% =	**1.0435**	**1.0434**
Wave -v-	**1.0561** −	Wave -i- > -iii- * 66.7% =	1.0431	1.0434

Deep Wave (x) in Wave (B) in USDCAD 15-Minute Chart

In Figure 2.8 in Chapter 2, I described the situation where a deep Wave (b) in a Triple Three can often cause a similarly deep Wave (x). I have reproduced the Wave (B) pullback in Figure 4.19 to show more clearly how this develops.

I have placed in the table displaying the wave relationships the entire Triple Three decline (Table 4.14). The first Wave (b) retraced by 66.7% and this was followed by a 76.4% retracement in Wave (x) to the same level (plus one point) at 1.0267.

The decline continued in two further (a)(b)(c) structures to reach a very deep Wave (B) of 85.4% which was just 19 points above the prior Wave (x) at 1.0150.

Deep Wave -b- of Wave -iii- in Wave (c) Higher in USDCAD

As another example of a deep Wave (b) Figure 4.20 was shown in Chapter 3 in which a Wave (IV) higher was developing in

Projection and Retracement Ratios

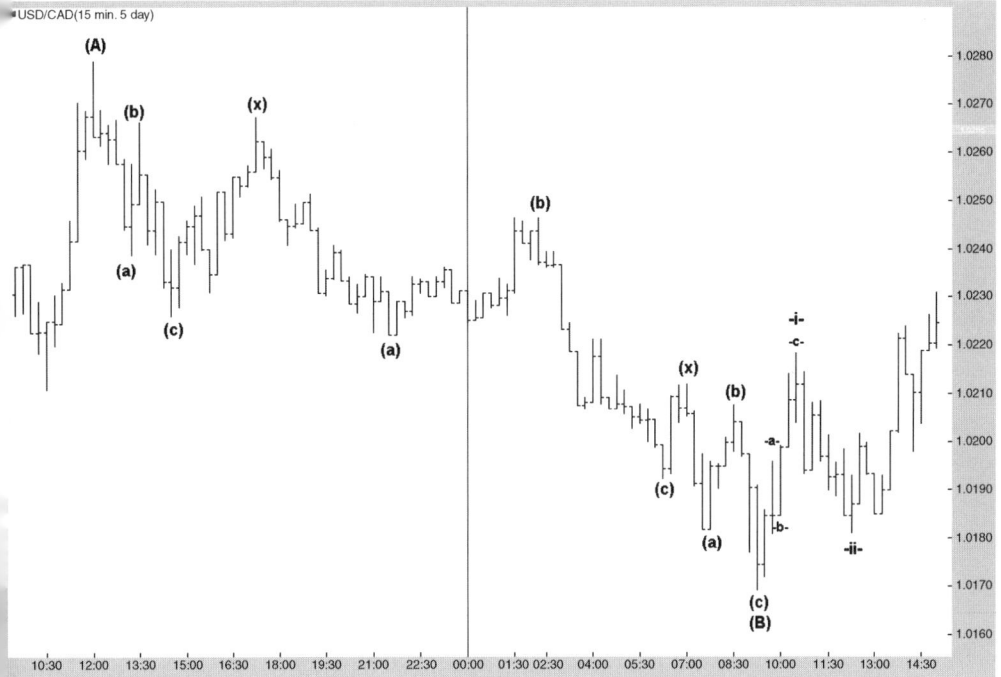

FIGURE 4.19 A deep Wave (x) in a declining Wave (B) in 15-minute USDCAD
Source: FXtrek IntelliChart™ in collaboration with FX-Strategy.com Pro Charts™

TABLE 4.14 A Deep Wave (x) in a Declining Wave (B) in 15-Minute USDCAD

Wave (B)		Ratio	Projection	Actual
Wave (a)	1.0239			1.0239
Wave (b)	1.0239 +	Wave (a) * 66.7% =	1.0266	1.0266
Wave (c)	1.0266 −	Wave (a) * 100.0% =	1.0226	1.0226
Wave (x)	1.0226 +	Wave (a) > (c) * 76.4% =	1.0266	1.0267
Wave (a)	1.0222			1.0222
Wave (b)	1.0222 +	Wave (a) * 50.0% =	1.0245	1.0246
Wave (c)	1.0246 −	Wave (a) * 114.6% =	1.0194	1.0192

(continued)

TABLE 4.14 (Continued)

Wave (B)		Ratio	Projection	Actual
Wave (x)	1.0192 +	Wave (a) > (c) * 23.6% =	1.0210	1.0212
Wave (a)	1.0182			1.0182
Wave (b)	1.0182 +	Wave (a) * 85.4% =	1.0208	1.0208
Wave (c)	1.0208 –	Wave (a) * 138.2% =	1.0167	1.0169
Wave (B)	1.0279 –	Wave (A) * 85.4% =	**1.0169**	**1.0169**

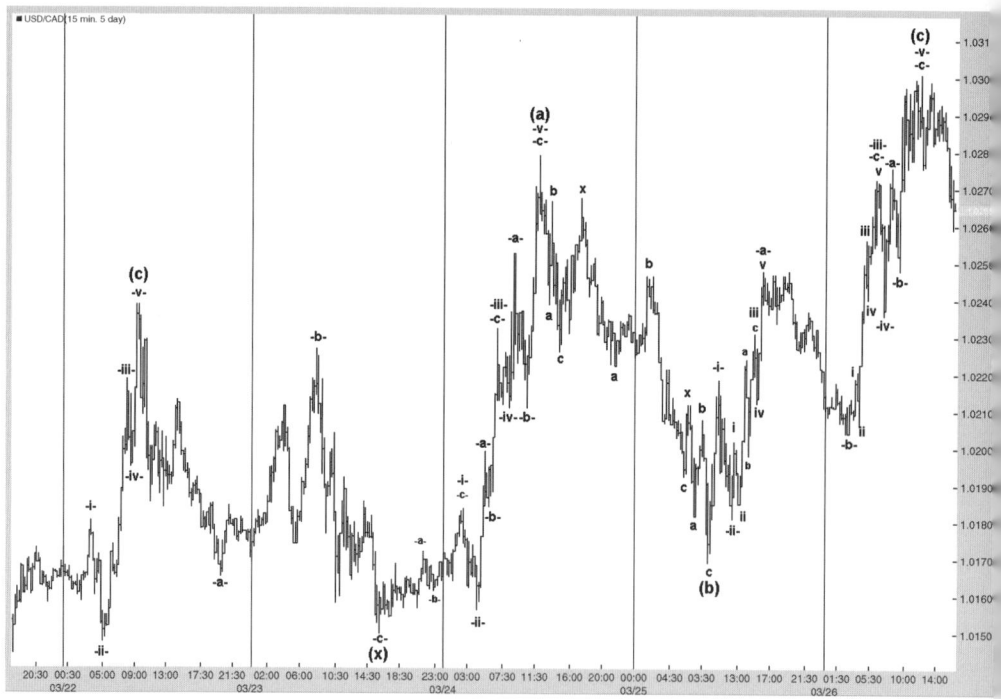

FIGURE 4.20 A Deep Wave -b- in Wave -iii- Higher in Wave (c) of Wave (IV) in Hourly USDCAD
Source: FXtrek IntelliChart™ in collaboration with FX-Strategy.com Pro Charts™

Projection and Retracement Ratios

TABLE 4.15 Wave Relationships for the Wave (a) Shown in Figure 4.20

Wave (a)		Ratio	Projection	Actual
Wave -a-	1.0172			1.0172
Wave -b-	1.0172 −	Wave -a- * 50.0% =	1.0161	1.0161
Wave -c-	1.0161 +	Wave -a- * 100.0% =	1.0183	1.0184
Wave -i-	1.0184			1.0184
Wave -ii-	1.0184 −	Wave -i- * 85.4% =	**1.0155**	**1.0156**
Wave -a-	1.0199			1.0199
Wave -b-	1.0199 −	Wave -a- * 38.2% =	1.0183	1.0184
Wave -c-	1.0184 +	Wave -a- * 114.6% =	1.0233	1.0232
Wave -iii-	1.0156 +	Wave -i- * 223.6% =	**1.0232**	**1.0232**
Wave -iv-	1.0232 −	Wave -iii- * 23.6% =	**1.0214**	**1.0211**
Wave -a-	1.0252			1.0252
Wave -b-	1.0252 −	Wave -a- * 100.0% =	1.0211	1.0211
Wave -c-	1.0211 +	Wave -a- * 166.7% =	1.0279	1.0279
Wave -v-	1.0211 +	Wave -i- > -iii- * 85.6% =	**1.0281**	**1.0279**

USDCAD. The ratios are quite startling (see Tables 4.15, 4.16, and 4.17).

To highlight the accuracy I shall provide the ratios for Wave (a), Wave (b), and Wave (c).

This completed Wave (a) from where a pullback in Wave (b) was anticipated. It would not be possible to know how deep this correction would be. The ratios were shown in Table 4.14 as an example of a deep Wave (x) following a deep correction in Wave (b).

Having identified the Wave (b) low there would therefore be projections for Wave (c), and being within a Wave (IV) there would also be ratios for this pullback. Figure 4.21 displays Wave (c) in more detail.

TABLE 4.16 Wave Relationships for the Wave (b) Shown in Figure 4.20

Wave (b)		Ratio	Projection	Actual
Wave -a-	1.0239			1.0239
Wave -b-	1.0239 +	1.0239 * 66.7% =	**1.0266**	1.0267
Wave -c-	1.0267 −	Wave -a- * 100.0% =	**1.0226**	**1.0226**
Wave -x-	1.0226 +	Wave -a- > Wave -c- * 76.4% =	**1.0266**	1.0267
Wave -a-	1.0222			1.0222
Wave -b-	1.0222 +	Wave -a- * 50.0% =	**1.0245**	1.0246
Wave -c-	1.0246 −	Wave -a- * 114.6% =	**1.0194**	**1.0192**
Wave -x-	1.0192 +	Wave -a- > Wave -c- * 23.6% =	**1.0210**	1.0212
Wave -a-	1.0182			1.0182
Wave -b-	1.0182 +	Wave -a- * 85.4% =	**1.0208**	1.0208
Wave -c-	1.0208 −	Wave -a- * 138.2% =	**1.0167**	**1.0169**
Wave (b)	1.0279 −	Wave (a) * 85.4% =	**1.0169**	**1.0169**

TABLE 4.17 Wave Relationships for Wave (c) in Figure 4.21

Wave (c)		Ratio	Projection	Actual
Wave -a-	1.0196			1.0196
Wave -b-	1.0196 −	Wave -a- * 41.4% =	**1.0185**	1.0185
Wave -c-	1.0185 +	Wave -a- * 123.6% =	**1.0218**	1.0218
Wave -i-	1.0218			1.0218
Wave -ii-	1.0218 −	Wave -i- * 76.4% =	**1.0181**	1.0181
Wave -a-	1.0248			1.0248
Wave -b-	1.0248 −	Wave -a- * 66.7% =	**1.0203**	1.0204
Wave -c-	1.0204 +	Wave -a- * 100.0% =	**1.0271**	1.0273
Wave -iii-	1.0181 +	Wave -i- * 185.4% =	**1.0272**	1.0273

Projection and Retracement Ratios

Wave -iv-	1.0273 −	Wave -iii- * 41.4% =	1.0235	1.0236
Wave -a-	1.0276			1.0276
Wave -b-	1.0236 −	Wave -a- * 66.7% =	1.0249	1.0248
Wave -c-	1.0248 +	Wave -a- * 138.2% =	1.0303	1.0301
Wave -v-	1.0236 +	Wave -i- > -iii- * 61.8% =	1.0300	1.0301
Wave (c)	1.0169 +	Wave (a) * 100.0% =	1.0298	1.0301

In Elliott's structure this would not even be considered, as Wave 3 is generally considered to be the strongest and most powerful wave of the entire sequence. However, the ratios provide compelling evidence that this is not the case.

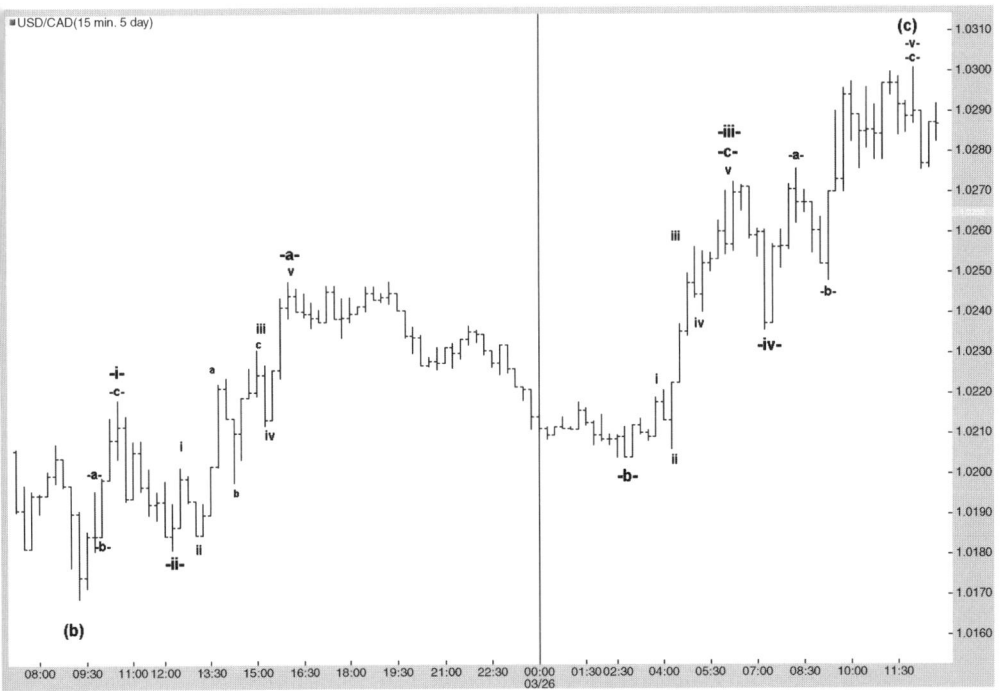

FIGURE 4.21 A Deep Wave -b- in Wave -iii- Higher in Wave (c) in Hourly USDCAD
Source: FXtrek IntelliChart™ in collaboration with FX-Strategy.com Pro Charts™

The key points to note here are:

- The 185.4% projection in Wave -iii- provided a projection target at 1.0272.
- The wave equality target in Wave -c- provided a projection target at 1.0271.
- Given Wave -ii- had a deep retracement of 76.4% the retracement in Wave -iv- of 41.4% was in line with normal ratios.
- The 61.8% projection in Wave -v- arrived at the same area as the wave equality target in Wave (c).

This is the typical development of a directional move that includes a deep Wave (b), and demonstrates very clearly the degree of synchronicity that develops within the Harmonic Elliott Wave structure.

Deep Wave (b) in Wave (iii) in EURUSD Daily Chart

I have provided several examples of how accurate the modified structure can be within the short time frames. Moving up the scale to daily charts (Figure 4.22), the degree of variance in projections certainly becomes larger in point terms (Table 4.18).

Very clearly some of the ratios implied are rather unusual but closely related to Fibonacci or harmonic ratios as an extension to prior waves. What it does highlight is that while the ratios are all valid, forecasting can end up being very trying.

Such events can end up being a 20/20 hindsight forecast, and certainly I found the sequence in Wave (C) one of the most difficult. Strangely enough, I did forecast the 1.5143 high, my target being 1.5146, but by using a different structure in the move higher. Thus, once the decline developed I had been looking for a much shallower correction, specifically at 1.4207 and 1.4048. Indeed, there were reactions from 1.4217 and 1.4028 respectively, but by this time the momentum conditions were still quite bearish and did not indicate any

Projection and Retracement Ratios

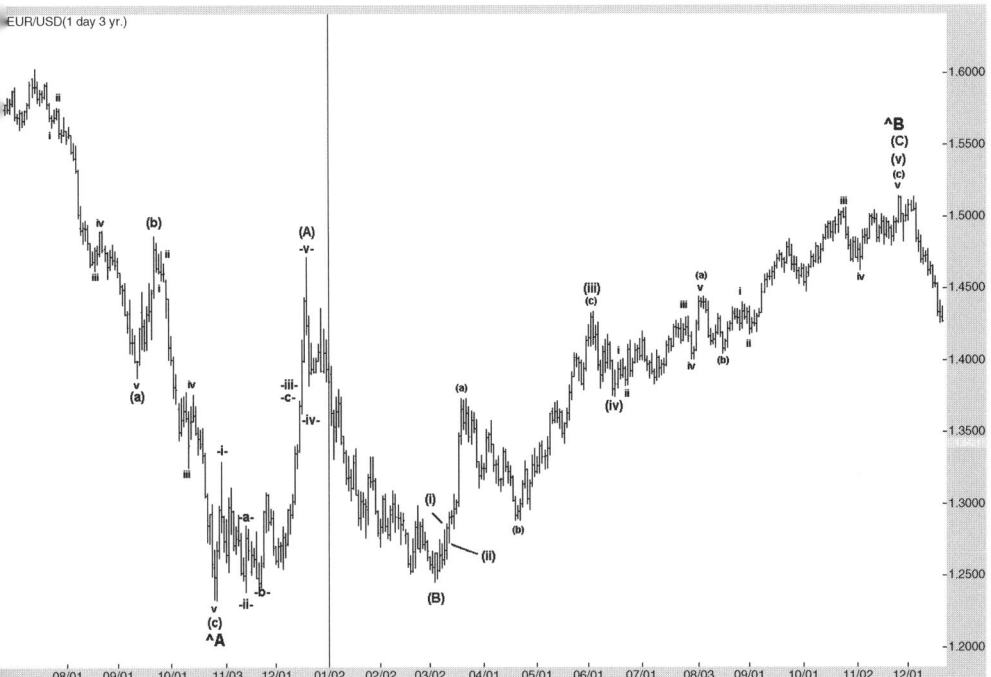

FIGURE 4.22 Potential Development of a Daily Triangle in EURUSD Including a Deep Wave (b) of Wave (iii)
Source: FXtrek IntelliChart™ in collaboration with FX-Strategy.com Pro Charts™

TABLE 4.18 Wave Relationships for the Potential Development of a Daily Triangle Shown in Figure 4.22

Wave (A)		Ratio	Projection	Actual
Wave -i-	1.3297			1.3297
Wave -ii-	1.3297 −	Wave -i- * 94.43% =	**1.2382**	**1.2387**
Wave -a-	1.2855			1.2855
Wave -b-	1.2855 −	Wave -a- * 94.43% =	1.2413	1.2422
Wave -c-	1.2422 +	Wave -a- * 276.4% =	1.3716	1.3721
Wave -iii-	1.2387 +	Wave -i- * 138.2% =	**1.3726**	**1.3721**

(continued)

TABLE 4.18 (Continued)

Wave (A)		Ratio	Projection	Actual
Wave -iv-	1.3721 −	Wave -iii- * 5.57% =	1.3643	1.3628
Wave -v-	1.3628 +	Wave -i- > -iii- * 76.4% =	1.4692	1.4717
Wave (B) & (C)				
Wave (A)	1.4717			1.4717
Wave (B)	1.4717 −	Wave (A) * 94.43% =	1.2461	1.2455
Wave (C)	1.2455 +	Wave (A) * 114.6% =	1.5193	1.5143
Wave (C)		Ratio	Projection	Actual
Wave (i)	1.2862			1.2862
Wave (ii)	1.2862 −	Wave (i) * 33.3% =	1.2726	1.2731
Wave (a)	1.3737			1.3737
Wave (b)	1.3737 −	Wave (a) * 85.4% =	1.2878	1.2885
Wave (c)	1.2885 +	Wave (a) * 141.4% =	1.4307	1.4338
Wave (iii)	1.2731 +	Wave (i) * 394.43% =	1.4336	1.4338
Wave (iv)	1.4338 −	Wave (iii)* 38.2% =	1.3724	1.3747
Wave (a)	1.4445			1.4445
Wave (b)	1.4445 −	Wave (a) * 58.6% =	1.4036	1.4048
Wave (c)	1.4048 +	Wave (a) * 158.4% =	1.5154	1.5143
Wave (v)	1.3747 +	Wave (i) > (iii) * 76.4% =	1.5186	1.5143

potential for a reversal, and price actually penetrated the anticipated support levels forcing a change in outlook.

There are always multiple potential projections in most areas of the wave structure, and while tying together projections from different wave degrees, both higher and lower, can generate high confidence areas of wave terminations, use of other complementary techniques can help to fine-tune or even identify when a target is not going to hold.

Projection and Retracement Ratios

I should stress that even if there are times when price conditions are clouded and uncertain, the eventual end of a move that is finally realized after the event does constitute valuable information since it actually provides clarification of the wave structure of one higher degree. From that point it provides guidance for the expectations of the subsequent wave development.

In Chapter 5, I will cover this subject and provide some tips on how to approach forecasting and recognizing when anticipated structures begin to break down, and general signals that can forewarn you of confirmation or denial of structures.

CHAPTER 5

Working with the Modified Wave Structure in Forecasting

INTRODUCTION

Until this point in the book, I have concentrated on describing Elliott's basically brilliant findings, his observations on the structure in which market prices develop, and then laying down the foundations for my claim that the impulsive wave structure was misjudged. I repeat the view that Elliott did not have the benefit of having modern spreadsheets which calculate a wide range of projection ratios that can be used for any time frame, from one minute to monthly. Elliott had to do all this in long hand, which limited his ability to fully analyze wave relationships in detail.

The majority of examples I gave in Chapter 4 were live as I have been writing, and clearly I have picked them as, in my opinion, they demonstrate the validity of the modifications I am proposing and which I use every day in my analysis. The ratios match not only in one wave degree but harmoniously across all wave degrees. Above all, this attracts me as I feel this is the way the natural order of the world works.

Did I forecast all of the examples? No I didn't, but I did get quite a few correct, and with pinpoint accuracy.

Is this the Holy Grail? Not at all. It is a very intensive method of analysis and requires constant attention. When it all comes together, the accuracy astonishes not only my subscribers but even takes my breath away at times. Some subscribers appear to think I am psychic. Unfortunately the new ones then forget money management and raise the risk levels, so that when the structure adapts or morphs into another pattern they lose too much.

So as in just about all books the examples look like great, shining examples of the power of the technique; however, this chapter is intended to provide guidance on how to approach the Harmonic Elliott Wave method, clues to spot when the structure is breaking down, how to integrate the different wave degrees to ensure a higher level of accuracy, and how to identify whether a projection or retracement is going to hold a particular forecast level.

I have chosen examples that replicate some of the issues I have faced after first recognizing that Elliott's original impulsive structure was incorrect and offering practical guidance in how to approach forecasting, the difficulties that can be faced, and general hints and tips to assist your progress in mastering the technique.

To provide a reminder of the relationships between waves I shall repeat those provided in Chapter 3.

The Modified Impulse Wave

Wave c in Wave (i) should be related to Wave a.

Wave (ii) should be related to Wave (i).

Wave (iii) should be related to Wave (i).

Within Wave (iii) Wave c should be related to Wave a and match the target in Wave (iii).

Wave (iv) should be related to Wave (iii).

Wave (v) should be related to a ratio of the beginning of Wave (i) to the end of Wave (iii).

Within Wave (v) Wave c should be related to Wave a and match the target in Wave (v).

Working with the Modified Wave Structure in Forecasting **121**

To introduce the topic of forecasting it would first be useful to go through each of the impulsive waves in turn, noting common patterns and stalling areas.

Wave (i) Targets

The simplest target to watch for is a projection in Wave (c) that is a ratio of Wave (a). In Chapter 4 covering retracement and projection targets I highlighted the following:

There is no uniform way of identifying where this will stall as it is not related to any prior wave. It is possible to consider the prior Wave b of Wave (v) and occasionally the prior Wave (iv), especially when this is a key swing high or swing low in a trend. Markets tend to shun testing a swing low/high on the first test. Other areas to consider are pivot levels, which I find of particular benefit.

If this is a Wave (a) of Wave (i) in a daily chart then again we should be watching the development of the five waves that construct Wave (a) and matching the projections in the internal Wave v with any of the prior Wave b of Wave (v), the prior Wave (iv) or pivot level.

Following this we shall need to observe the pullback in Wave (b) and then calculate projections in Wave (c).

Take the example of a pullback in Wave (B) in the AUDJPY market and the subsequent development of Wave (I) of Wave (C) (shown in Figure 5.1).

In Figure 5.1, I have shown the decline in Wave (c) of Wave (B) within a rally in AUDJPY. Naturally for a Wave (C) the expectation will be for a rally in five waves that should reach a projection of a ratio of Wave (A) commencing from the Wave (B) low.

Within Wave (I) of Wave (C) there first needs to be a Wave ((a)) constructed of five waves followed by a Wave ((b)) and then projection in Wave ((c)).

Normally the easiest guideline is to look for the prior Wave b of Wave -v-. In this case this is not discernable and therefore the next stronger resistance will be the span of the prior Wave -iv-. Above there we can see the broad sideways congestion area from the top of

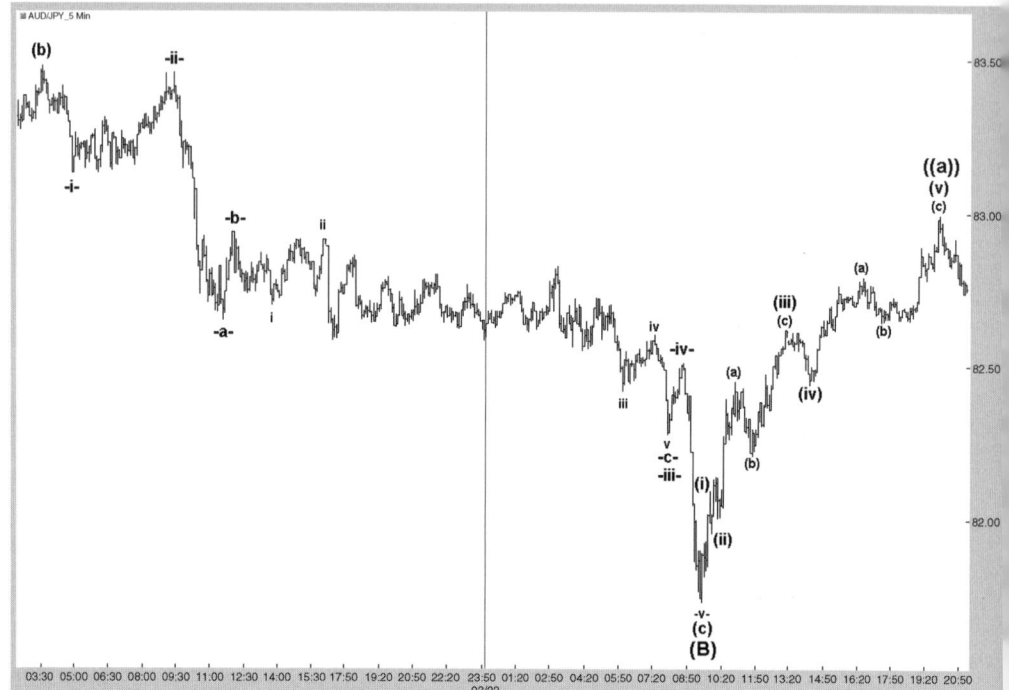

FIGURE 5.1 The Early Stages of a Reversal Higher in Wave (C) from a Wave (B) Retracement Low
Source: FXtrek IntelliChart™ in collaboration with FX-Strategy.com Pro Charts™

the prior Wave -b- to the lows just below Wave -a-. These areas can be expected to provide resistance and normally cause corrections.

In the early stages of this wave development, consideration needs to be given to the potential of Wave a, Wave b, and Wave c to form the first Wave (i) of Wave ((a)). A possible initial target would be the prior Wave (b). This is often the stalling point of the Wave a of Wave (i). This will be followed by a Wave b and then a projection of Wave a to complete Wave c. This will be Wave (i). In trying to determine whether Wave (i) is in approximately the right area we should consider a minimum target of a 176.4% projection of Wave (i) that would imply a Wave (iii) that would stall in around the right area that would allow a pullback in Wave (iv), then follow through in Wave (v) to reach close to a realistic target for Wave ((a)).

Thus, approximate estimations should be made to qualify the first abc rally in Wave (i) and ensure that Wave b is a ratio of Wave a and then Wave c a projection of Wave a. In this example, while it is too small to label, Wave b was a 41.4% retracement of Wave a while Wave c was a 176.4% projection of Wave a. This formed Wave (i) at 82.10. Wave (ii) was a 38.2% retracement of Wave (i).

At this point projections in Wave (iii) can be generated. I shall cover these later in this chapter.

Wave (i)'s can develop in different ways, at times with a very tight abc move and sometimes with a long Wave c followed by steep or shallow wave (ii)'s. There has been an interesting rally in the GBPUSD market which includes the development of several Wave (i)'s that can be used as solid examples (shown in Figure 5.2)

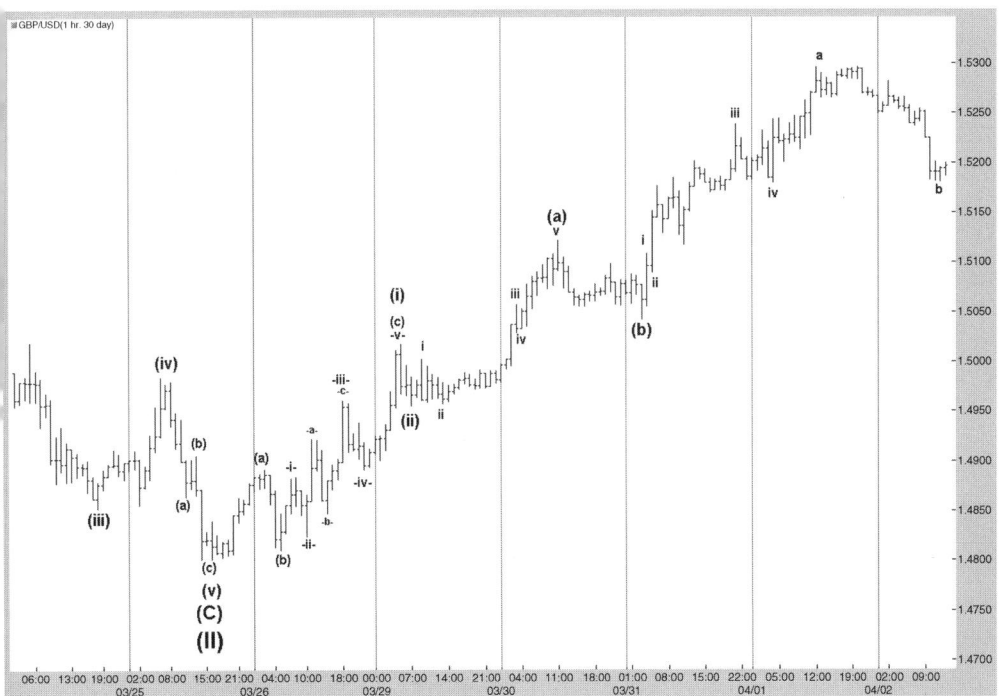

FIGURE 5.2 The Initial Stages of a Rally in Wave (A) of Wave (III) in Hourly GBPUSD
Source: FXtrek IntelliChart™ in collaboration with FX-Strategy.com Pro Charts™

Figure 5.2 displays the initial stages of development in Wave (A) of Wave (III) in the hourly GBPUSD market. Within this are four instances of Wave (i)'s, and all are different in structural development in terms of pullbacks and extensions. Also included are various examples of alternation between Wave (ii) and Wave (iv) and, indeed, while the final Wave v of Wave (c) could not fit into the image there is also an example of how Wave b of Wave v can also be deep when Wave ii and Wave iv are both shallow.

To highlight the different structures I shall zoom in on the key areas with the use of lower time-frame charts (Figure 5.3).

Figure 5.3 displays the first Wave (i) within which there are instances of Wave i in both Wave (a) and Wave (c).

The initial Wave i higher from the Wave (II) low is more often than not impossible to predict. As long as the end of Wave (II) was expected

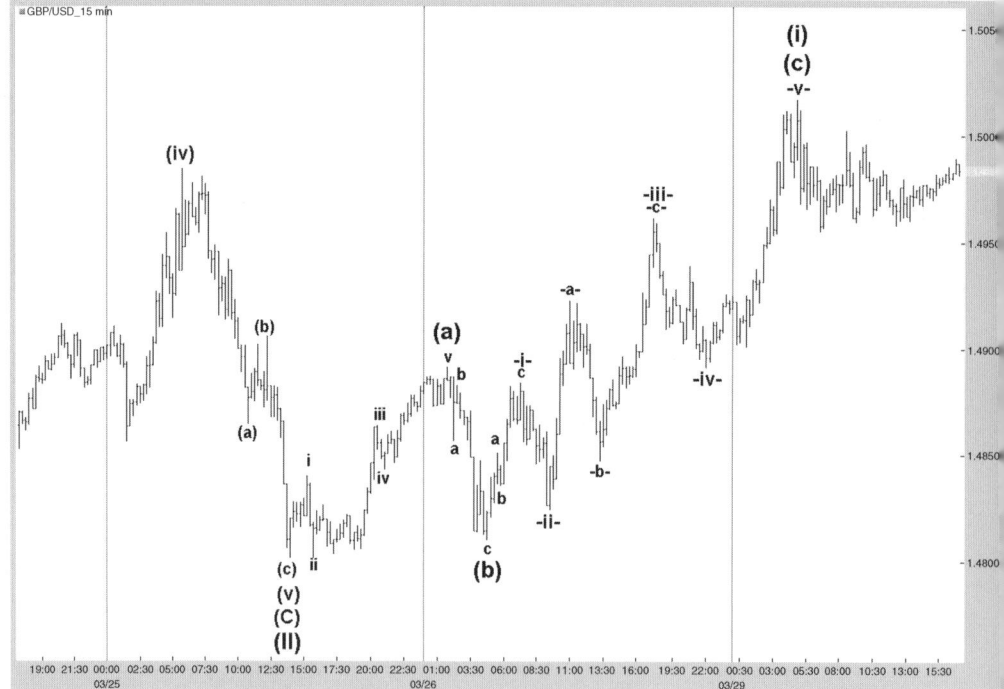

FIGURE 5.3 Development of Wave (i) Including the Wave i of Wave (a) and Wave (c)
Source: FXtrek IntelliChart™ in collaboration with FX-Strategy.com Pro Charts™

it really sets a marker down for subsequent wave development. However, the prior Wave (b) of Wave (v) lower is a common target on initial reversals. In this case, although not labeled, there was a brief Wave a followed by a sideways consolidation in what appears to be a Triangle before the rally in Wave c to reach Wave iii. The extension in Wave iii was 166.7%. Given the deep Wave ii, the expectation is for a shallow Wave iv (33.3%) followed by a final Wave v (76.4%) into the span of the prior Wave (b) of Wave (v) lower. This five-wave rally can then be labeled as Wave (a) of Wave (i).

How deep Wave (b) will retrace would be unknown, and in the end it turned out to be a deep 90.02% retracement to 1.4810 which was exactly in the middle of the Wave b Triangle in Wave iii. The next step will be to consider where a probable target for Wave (i), and therefore Wave (c), could end. To judge this, a strong idea of the larger wave structure must be known. This Wave (i) will be part of Wave (A) of Wave (III). The Wave (iv) high is a possibility if it represents a key swing high that would confirm a swing reversal of the previous downtrend, which is more often than not the case. Wave (iv) was at 1.4984. Projections of Wave (a) should also be made.

$$100.0\% = 1.4886$$
$$114.6\% = 1.4912$$
$$138.2\% = 1.4933$$
$$161.8\% = 1.4954$$

Therefore the broad 1.4886–1.4933 area is where the Wave (c) is most likely to end, with a lower risk of the 161.8% projection at 1.4954.

Wave -i- rallied in three waves to the high of the prior Wave b of Wave (b). The correction was quite deep, to two points below the 76.4% retracement. From here a target in Wave -iii- can be estimated:

$$138.2\% = 1.4927$$
$$176.4\% = 1.4956$$
$$185.4\% = 1.4962$$

Wave -a- rallied and reached 1.4922 with Wave -b- being also very deep to the 76.4% retracement. It is possible that some doubts could arise over the depth of retracements as there doesn't appear to be much evidence of alternation. However, a target for Wave -c- can be generated and matched with targets for Wave -iii-.

$$85.4\% = 1.4931$$
$$100.0\% = 1.4949$$
$$114.6\% = 1.4959$$

With Wave -a- having completed at 1.4922 the 85.4% projection can be eliminated. That leaves a target area of around 1.4956–59 and possibly 1.4962. In fact, Wave -iii- ended at 1.4961.

Now, with Wave -iii- having ended at 1.4961 it has already exceeded the 161.8% projection in Wave (c) at 1.4954. Therefore deep projections should be considered. At the same time, a retracement in Wave -iv- and then extension in Wave -v- should also be considered.

In Wave (c):

$$185.4\% = 1.4975$$
$$223.6\% = 1.5009$$
$$238.2\% = 1.5022$$
$$261.8\% = 1.5043$$

With the depth of retracement in all corrections until this point it would seem probable that a shallower correction would be most likely. In the event even Wave -iv- was a full 50% to 1.4891, and this provided projections of:

$$61.8\% = 1.4984$$
$$66.7\% = 1.4992$$
$$76.4\% = 1.5006$$
$$85.4\% = 1.5020$$
$$100.0\% = 1.5042$$

There are several matching projections here; the 223.6% Wave (c) with 76.4% Wave -v-, the 238.2% Wave (c) with the 85.4% Wave -v-, and the 261.8% Wave (c) with the wave equality target in Wave -v-.

Working with the Modified Wave Structure in Forecasting

Identifying just where this final wave will end requires supporting analysis, a projection in Wave c of Wave -v-, and the use of momentum.

In Figure 5.4 I have added my own RSI, a more sensitive version that tends to swing more frequently between high and low extremes and identify divergences more effectively. The high finally came at 1.5017.

From this point, focus can be made on identifying the Wave (ii) and resumption of the uptrend in Wave (a), Wave (b), and Wave (c) of Wave (iii).

Figure 5.5 displays the development of Wave (a) and most of Wave (c) of Wave (iii). I shall not go into as much detail for these as the intention is more to provide examples of the different ways a

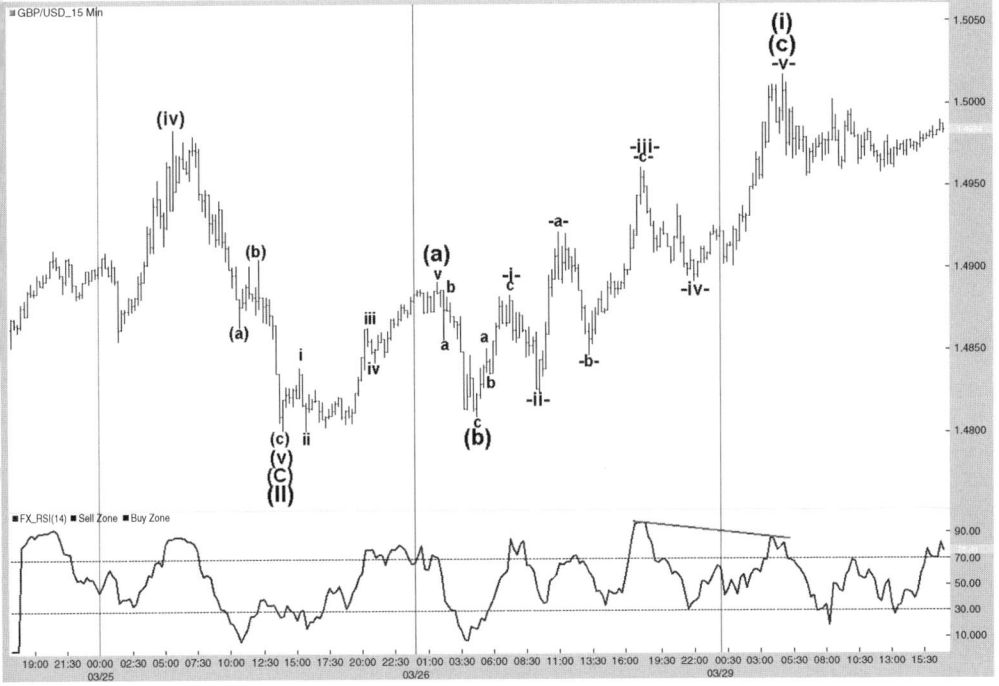

FIGURE 5.4 Identifying the Completion of Wave -v- and Wave (c) Using Momentum
Source: FXtrek IntelliChart™ in collaboration with FX-Strategy.com Pro Charts™

FIGURE 5.5 Extension in Wave (a), Wave (b), and Wave (c) of Wave (iii) Higher in GBPUSD
Source: FXtrek IntelliChart™ in collaboration with FX-Strategy.com Pro Charts™

Wave (i) can develop. Here, Wave (ii) was exceptionally brief and therefore highlights the risk of a long and deep Wave (iv) (which eventually did happen). In Wave (a) the Wave i stalled a little short of the Wave (i) high and saw a deep Wave ii, while in Wave (c) there was a similar strong extension in Wave c to complete Wave i and a shallow Wave ii as was seen in Wave (i) and Wave (ii).

Ambiguous Projections in Wave (c) of Wave (i)

The start of a new five-wave sequence can cause some confusion on occasion. The issue is to identify the Wave (a), (b), and (c) that make up the first Wave (i). Occasionally what appears to be a straightforward first structure isn't quite so obvious.

Working with the Modified Wave Structure in Forecasting 129

Figure 5.6 displays the end of what was considered a possible Wave (b) of Wave (iii) and the subsequent rally. The call for a rally was correct, but there was a problem in identifying the Wave -iii-. It can be seen that an initial rally was counted as Wave -a- with an Expanded Flat Wave -b-, followed by a Wave -c- that ended at a wave equality target. This was followed by another Expanded Flat Correction, this time in Wave -ii-.

Taking the normal type of projections of 176.4%–185.4% and 261.8%–285.4% I have marked on the chart the 176.4% and 285.4% projection areas. Price stalled close to the 176.4% but nowhere close to the 285.4%. Could it be assumed that the peak where I have labeled Wave -iii- is correct? Well, a 76.4% projection from the Wave -iv- does end just about at the final peak. However, there is a problem with this

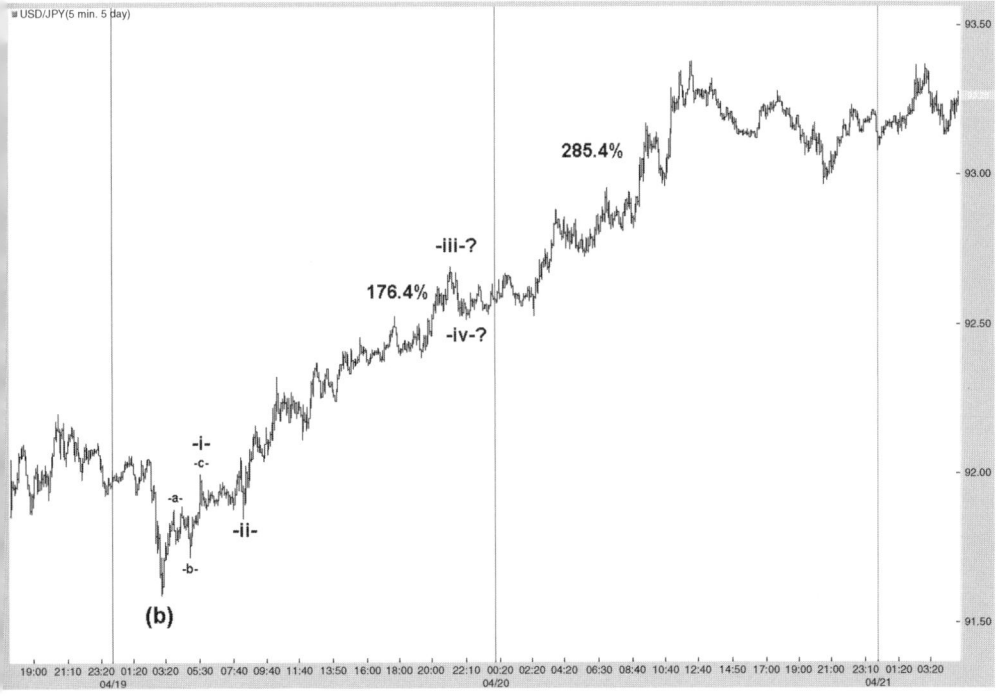

FIGURE 5.6 The Start of a New Five-Wave Sequence Higher in the Five-Minute USDJPY Market
Source: FXtrek IntelliChart™ in collaboration with FX-Strategy.com Pro Charts™

structure. Wave -ii- was around a 38.2% retracement of Wave -i- and the labeled Wave -iv- is just under a 23.6% retracement. Although alternation is only a guideline it does raise the question whether this is a valid wave count.

Let us take a look at the start of the rally again (Figure 5.7).

Figure 5.7 displays the same chart but with a change to the positions of Wave -i- and Wave -ii-. Taking further measurements and on the assumption that the Wave v of Wave -a- was an extended (wave equality) move, a 114.6% projection in Wave -c- came exactly to the new Wave -i- peak. Then taking a 176.4% projection in Wave -iii- it came precisely to the final peak at 93.38.

The expectations must be for a deeper Wave -iv- and probably a full 58.6% retracement before the Wave -v- can develop.

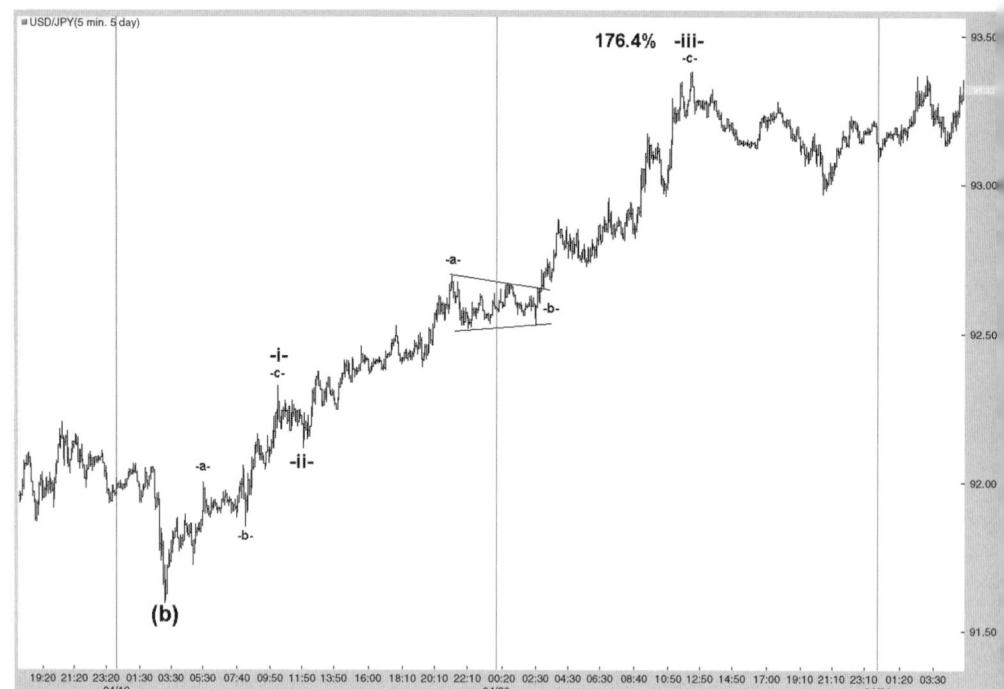

FIGURE 5.7 The Start of a New Five-Wave Sequence Higher in the Five-Minute USDJPY Market
Source: FXtrek IntelliChart™ in collaboration with FX-Strategy.com Pro Charts™

Wave (iii) targets

Once Wave (i) and Wave (ii) have been established the immediate task is to identify where Wave (iii) will probably end. After all, there are multiple projections that could occur. Most common are 176.4%, 185.4%, 223.6% and in stronger moves 276.4% and 285.4%.

There are several elements to this, and I shall cover each in turn.

The Wave Structure of One Higher Degree   A Wave (iii) only occurs in two waves: Wave (A) or Wave (C).

The positions of Waves (A) and Wave (C) generate different implications and may occur within:

- Wave (i), Wave (iii), Wave (v);
- a Zigzag, Double Zigzag, or Triple Three;
- a Triangle.

Wave (A) will always follow Wave (C). Wave (C) will always end in a Wave (v).

Wave iii of Wave (a) in Larger Wave (i)   A common initial target following the completion of a Wave (v) will be the Wave (b) of Wave (v). This may be the new Wave i, Wave iii, or indeed the full Wave (a). The target for Wave iii should therefore be considered within this structure.

Wave (iii) of Wave (a) of Wave (III)   There is no universal guideline for this and it will depend on exactly what is happening in the larger wave degree. The more important guide will be the expectation of where Wave (A) is to end, which in turn will provide an idea of where the Wave (a) of Wave (III) will need to complete to be within striking distance for Wave (v) to reach the target.

In Figure 5.8, I will show an example of how this may be achieved.

In Chapter 3 I provided an example of a deep Wave -b- of Wave -iii- within a Wave (c) higher in USDCAD. This was within

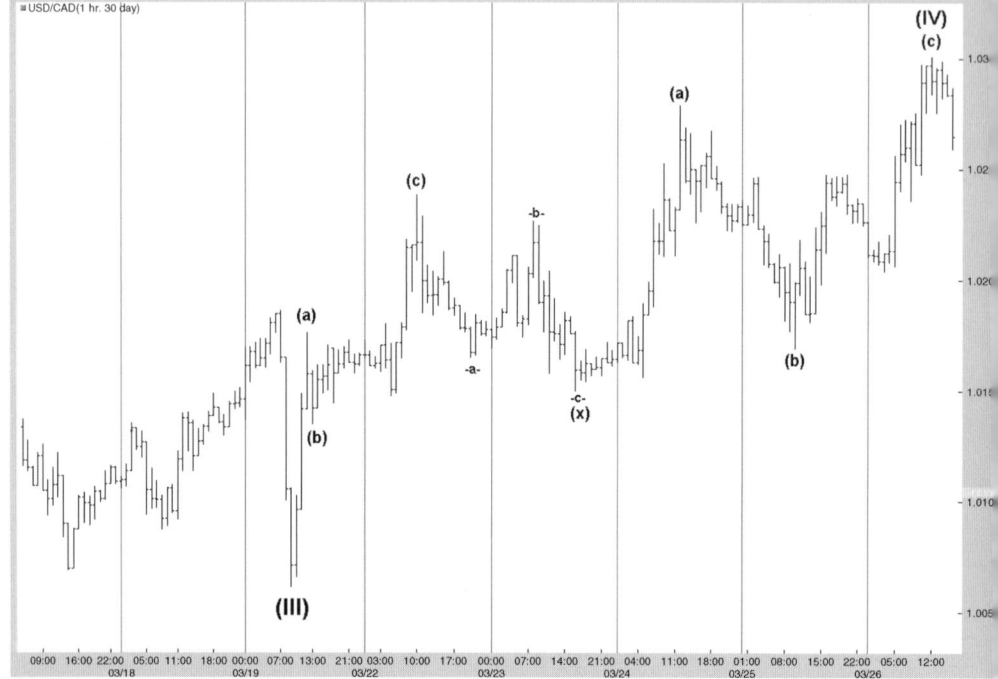

FIGURE 5.8 Wave (IV) Correction in Hourly USDCAD
Source: FXtrek IntelliChart™ in collaboration with FX-Strategy.com Pro Charts™

a Wave (IV) of one higher degree. In Chapter 4 I demonstrated the amazing accuracy and synchronicity of the final (a)(b)(c) waves.

The first problem to be considered is whether this actually completed Wave (IV). The recovery from 1.0062 developed in a Double Zigzag. If this represented a full 50% or perhaps 58.6% retracement in Wave (IV) then it would be a clearer implication that the 1.0301 high was indeed Wave (IV). In this instance the 50% retracement was at 1.0317. This was also around where two prior corrective highs were situated in the Wave (c) of Wave (III) decline. The Wave (II) retracement was 41.4%.

Therefore, this case was not a clear-cut certainty that a third ABC structure would not occur. A move below the prior Wave (b) at 1.0169 would assist that view, and also below the prior Wave (x) at 1.0150 being another key swing low. The market tends to avoid

Working with the Modified Wave Structure in Forecasting 133

breaking key swing highs/lows on the first test and therefore some reactions should be expected. The guideline of a reaction from the prior Wave (b) would also be a factor. Therefore the approach to this general area will need to be observed in order to assess whether the decline was developing in line with what should be a Wave (A) of Wave (V) if this was to confirm whether the Wave (V) would develop rather than a Wave (x) and followed by a third ABC rally.

If this is the start of a Wave (V) then normally Wave (A) will stall somewhere in the region of the Wave (III) low. This would provide a general idea where Wave (iii) of Wave (A) needs to fall to allow Wave (v) to reach the area around the Wave (III) low.

Figure 5.9 displays how the first decline develops. The chart displays the final Wave -c- of Wave -iii- from the deep Wave -b-, followed by the three-wave rally in Wave -v-. In either a Wave (x)

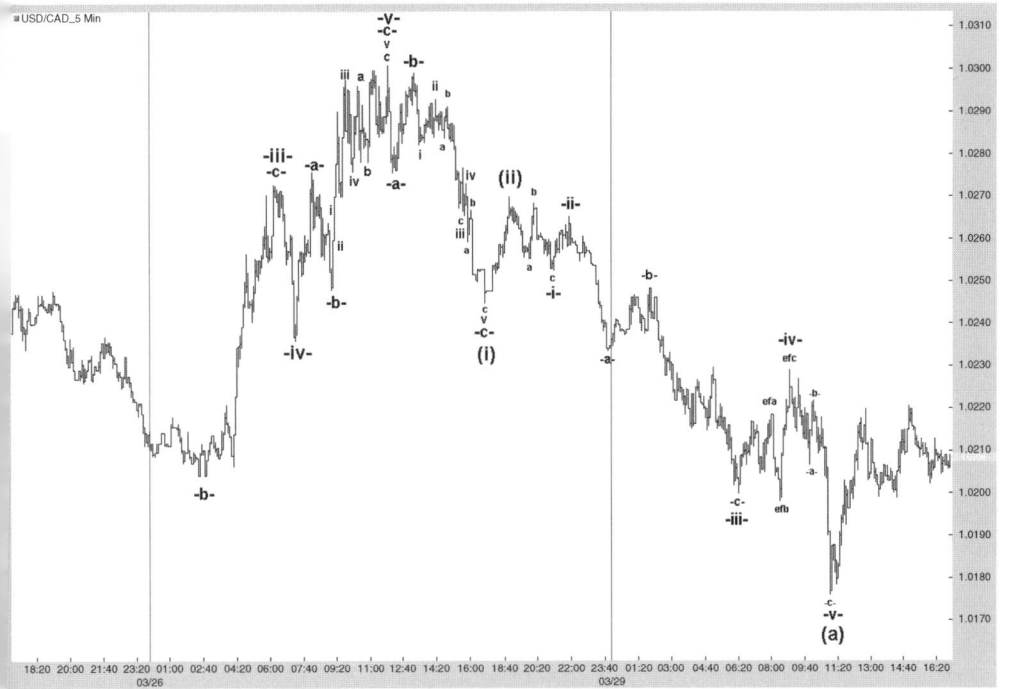

FIGURE 5.9 Initial Decline from the 1.0301 Peak in Five-Minute USDCAD
Source: FXtrek IntelliChart™ in collaboration with FX-Strategy.com Pro Charts™

correction that would lead to a new ABC structure higher in Wave (IV) or a five-wave decline in Wave (A), the first development must be an ABC move.

As should be expected, the initial decline in Wave -a- reached the area of the prior Wave iv and Wave b of Wave v. Identifying the five waves in Wave -a- (and therefore the Wave iii) in a five-minute chart is normally impossible. Wave -b- then followed, and then five waves in Wave -c- to reach the prior Wave -b- of Wave -v- higher and just below but holding above the prior Wave -iv-. Wave -c- was just over 223.6% of Wave -a-. This was at 1.0245.

At this point there is no way of knowing precisely whether this decline formed Wave (I) of Wave (A) or whether it was a pullback in Wave (x), or perhaps just one ABC decline within a Wave (x). The recovery from the 1.0245 Wave -c- low ended between the 41.4% and 50% retracement at 1.0270 and between the prior Wave b of Wave v and the peak of Wave iv.

The next move should define the structure of the decline. For this to be a Wave (x) the next three-wave decline must see the Wave C below the 1.0245 low unless it was to turn into a complex correction in Wave (x).

If this was to be Wave (a) of Wave (III) then the next move should be five waves lower in Wave (a). It should also test the prior Wave (b) at 1.0169 and possibly the 1.0150 prior Wave (x). This would enable a retracement in Wave (b) and extension in Wave (c) of Wave (III) to reach closer to the prior higher degree Wave (III) low at 1.0062. To identify where Wave -iii- should stall the projections for Wave -iii- should be observed in conjunction with those of Wave -c- (once Wave -b- had been completed).

Wave -c- projections:

$$85.4\% = 1.0222$$
$$100.0\% = 1.0217$$
$$114.6\% = 1.0212$$
$$123.6\% = 1.0210$$
$$138.2\% = 1.0205$$
$$161.8\% = 1.0198$$

Wave -iii- projections:

$$176.4\% = 1.0235$$
$$185.4\% = 1.0233$$
$$223.6\% = 1.0227$$
$$261.8\% = 1.0220$$
$$285.4\% = 1.0216$$
$$423.6\% = 1.0193$$

From these we could consider a potential target around 1.0216–20.

In fact, what transpired was Wave -iii- measuring a rather unusual 376.4% projection of Wave -i- and Wave -c- of Wave -iii- being 161.8% of Wave -a- reaching 1.0200. This begins to highlight the issue of also identifying the individual wave structure of Wave -c-.

Wave -iv- was then two points above a 41.4% retracement of Wave -iii- and Wave -v- was precisely 76.4% at 1.0176. This was perfect in terms of the retest of the prior Wave (b) in Wave (IV) higher. Thus this could now be confirmed as a developing Wave (A) lower, and the next step was to identify a correction in Wave (b) and then extension in Wave (c) to complete Wave (III).

The next step would be to identify an approximate target for Wave (III) from where a Wave (IV) retracement would develop and provide somewhere between a 61.8% and 76.4% (or possibly an extended wave of 85.4%) to reach close to the 1.0062 low.

Wave (III) projections:

$$176.4\% = 1.0171$$
$$185.4\% = 1.0166$$
$$223.6\% = 1.0145$$
$$261.8\% = 1.0123$$
$$285.4\% = 1.0110$$

Since Wave (a) had reached 1.0176, the first two projections can be ruled out. The 223.6% projection at 1.0145 may well be possible, as well as the 261.8% projection at 1.0123. The 285.4% is rather deep but shouldn't really be ruled out.

Next the retracements in Wave (b) can be derived:

$$38.2\% = 1.0212$$
$$41.4\% = 1.0215$$
$$50.0\% = 1.0223$$
$$58.6\% = 1.0231$$

Note should be taken of the prior Wave -b- of Wave -v- and also the Wave -iv-. These were at 1.0229 and 1.0222. This would lead to the favored retracement being between 1.0212 and 1.0223.

The recovery from 1.0176 reached 1.0221 and thus two points below the 50.0% retracement (see Figure 5.10). Compared to the decline in Wave (a) it was quite brief, but the likelihood is that it would be considered as Wave (b).

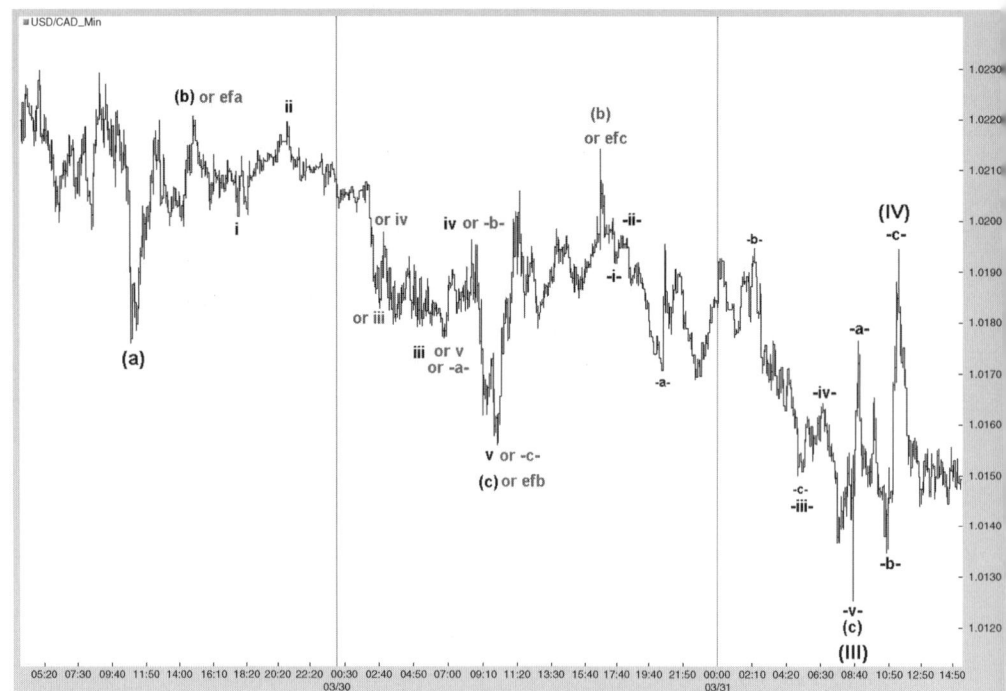

FIGURE 5.10 Wave (c) Decline in Wave (III) in Five-Minute USDCAD
Source: FXtrek IntelliChart™ in collaboration with FX-Strategy.com Pro Charts™

Working with the Modified Wave Structure in Forecasting **137**

From that peak the wave development became more uncertain. I have marked a five-wave decline which did hold quite good relationship ratios. However, the low was at 1.0156 and above the prior swing low at the 1.0150 Wave (x). This does not satisfy a Wave (III) target.

The possibility of these being a mistake in the bearish wave count should be considered, although the breach of the prior Wave (b) is normally (but not always) a sign that there has been a reversal.

On a closer look there was a secondary wave count that implied a three-wave decline with the alternative Wave -c- being 85.4% of Wave -a-. It is also therefore possible that this is an Expanded Flat. If so, the 1.0156 low should represent an expansion of the alternative Wave efa. Indeed, this was a 41.4% expansion which would imply a five-wave rally in Wave efc to around the Wave efa high. This occurred with the Wave efc stalling at 1.0214, and this would then be counted as Wave (b).

A target in Wave (c) could then be calculated:

$$85.4\% = 1.0134$$
$$100.0\% = 1.0120$$
$$114.6\% = 1.0106$$

Matching with the projections anticipated in Wave (III) between 1.0212–1.0223, it would appear that Wave (c) would also likely stall in the same area. The five waves lower developed with normal ratios to reach 1.0125.

Wave (IV) developed with an almost 50% retracement to 1.0195. Finally, this allowed targets for Wave (V):

$$61.8\% = 1.0086$$
$$66.7\% = 1.0078$$
$$76.4\% = 1.0061$$

The Wave (III) low of one higher degree was at 1.0062 and the Wave (V) to complete Wave (A) completed at 1.0065 (see Figure 5.11).

This walk-through demonstrates the technique of estimating the Wave (iii) targets, both internally from the Wave (c) target within

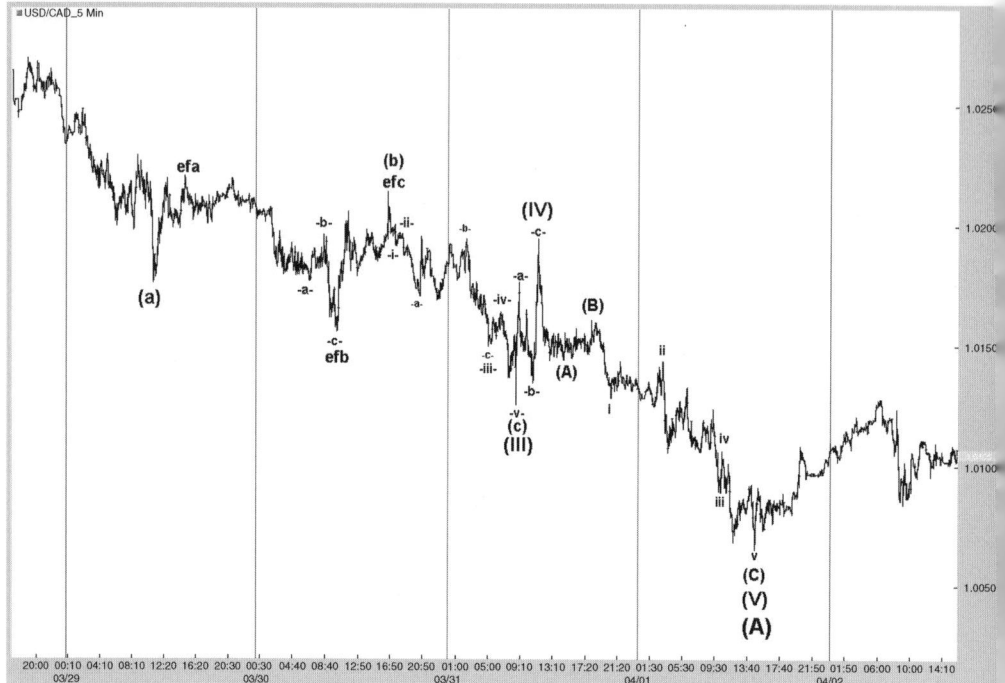

FIGURE 5.11 Wave (V) Decline in Wave (A) in Five-Minute USDCAD
Source: FXtrek IntelliChart™ in collaboration with FX-Strategy.com Pro Charts™

Wave (iii), and also as a projection of Wave (i) and a general expectation of where a Wave (iii) should fall if the target in the Wave (A) or Wave (C) is to be achieved.

This process provides several factors in bringing confidence to the expected wave count or whether it begins to break down:

- A move will always be expected in either five waves or three waves, dependent on the location within the larger wave count.
- The early stages can be linked to the prior Wave (b) and/or Wave -b- of Wave -iv- of the preceding move.
- Estimates can be made for the general area where Wave (iii) should be expected to end.

- If a five-wave move is anticipated then there should be valid relationships between them. If not, then an alternative structure may be developing.
- Relationships between Wave (i), Wave (iii), and Wave (v) need be confirmed by projections of the internal Wave abc.
- The general adherence to ratios normally provides excellent break levels to the anticipated wave count. For example, if a Wave iii reaches a common expansion ratio in a possible complex correction then this can be highlighted by a break through the anticipated Wave iv retracement.

Wave (v) targets   Before considering the possible targets that can be considered for a Wave (v), we have to overcome the problem of knowing which projection ratio to use for the extension of the prior wave development.

As already explained in Chapter 4, a Wave (v) most commonly extends by a ratio of the distance traveled from the start of Wave (i) to the end of Wave (iii) and from the completion of Wave (iv). In Figure 5.12 this would imply:

Wave (iv) + (X − Y) * ratio

In my experience I have found 66.7% probably to be the most frequent extension. However, there is no way of truly knowing in advance whether it will stall at the shorter 61.8% or even the extended wave ratio 85.4%. Indeed, it is not impossible for an extended Wave (v) to meet a wave equality target.

Perhaps the simple answer is that since internally a Wave (v) is constructed of an (a)(b)(c) move, we should look for a normal extension ratio of Wave (a). The problem here is that Wave (c) can extend by possibly just 85.4% of Wave (a) or as much as 261.8%. I have also found to my frustration at times that, for example, a wave equality target in Wave (c) matches with a 61.8% projection in Wave (v) while a 138.2% projection in Wave (c) matches with a 66.7% projection in Wave (v), and possibly even a 161.8% projection in Wave (c) matches with a 76.4% projection in Wave (v).

Therefore we have to look at other possible methods of identifying the eventual wave (v) completion. What we do know is that a

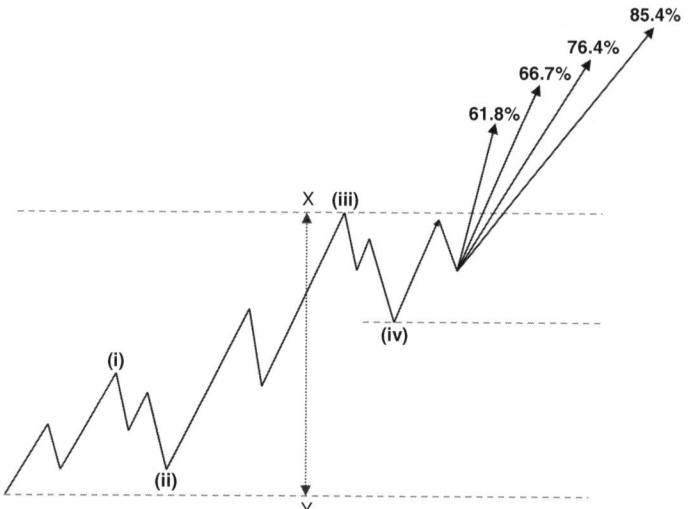

FIGURE 5.12 Potential Projection Ratios in Wave (v)

Wave (v) will also always occur either at the conclusion of a Wave (A) or a Wave (C) of a larger degree. Of the two, identifying the completion of a Wave (A) is probably one of the most difficult when considering forecasting. A Wave (v) of Wave (C) should have the same targets as the projection of Wave (A).

Since the first instance of a Wave (v) after a reversal comes in the first Wave (a), the guidelines I provided earlier in this chapter concerning targets for Wave (i) (and inherently the Wave (a) of Wave (i)) are relevant. The sort of areas that were discussed were the Wave (b) of Wave (v), then the Wave (iv) extreme if it represented a key swing level in the prior trend. It is also not too unusual for a prior low in a downtrend (or high in an uptrend) to provide a pivotal barrier on the reversal.

Other areas to observe are periods of congestion which generally provoke a reaction when retested, and in a non-aggressive Wave (iii) the Wave v of Wave (a) can often stall around the extreme of the Wave (i). Another fairly common occurrence I have noted on many occasions is that in an extended Wave (iii) in which the Wave (a) of Wave (iii) stalls some distance past the extreme of Wave (i), the

Working with the Modified Wave Structure in Forecasting **141**

stalling point can be a projection of Wave (i). For example, it may be a wave equality target of Wave (i) or even a 138.2% projection of Wave (i). If the structure of the Wave (a) is rather messy it can cause confusion as to whether the end of Wave (a) is actually Wave (a) or the end of Wave (iii). It is therefore important to be attentive to the structure of the move from the Wave (ii). Even then, if there is a wave equality target in Wave V of Wave (a) that ends at a 138.2% projection of Wave (i), it can be mistaken as being a short Wave (iii).

Instead of repeating several examples I would suggest that the reader should scan over previous examples and note the various types of targets in Wave (v).

Extended Wave (v) The topic of extended fifth waves was covered in both Chapters 3 and 4 to demonstrate how they develop. However, these can be some of the most difficult to anticipate, and due to the common sharp and aggressive development the final stalling point can be difficult to predict.

The same situations described for identification of common chart barriers such as prior Wave (iv)'s, swing peaks or troughs, or even congestion areas applies also to extended fifth waves. However, it is good practice to observe prior wave projections, especially in Wave (c) developments as a stalling point for intermediate waves can occur at these levels. This occurred in the hourly USDCHF market as I was writing this chapter.

Figure 5.13 displays a rally in Wave (i) and Wave (ii) followed by a Wave (a) with extended Wave -v- in the hourly USDCHF market. In some ways it was an unusual and somewhat complicated structure to follow, as the Wave -b- of Wave -iii- was unusually deep for the prior Wave -ii- but then translated into a shallow Wave -iv- in a Triangle in which Wave ^b was expanded. The final Wave -v- extended by 114.6% of the distance from Wave (ii) to the end of Wave -iii-.

While being an extension ratio I have seen on several occasions, it is not that common and to anticipate this without any other factor would be difficult. However, it will be noticed that the entire rally originated from the 1.0501 low which is labeled Wave (B). The Wave -v- came to an end just two points below the wave equality

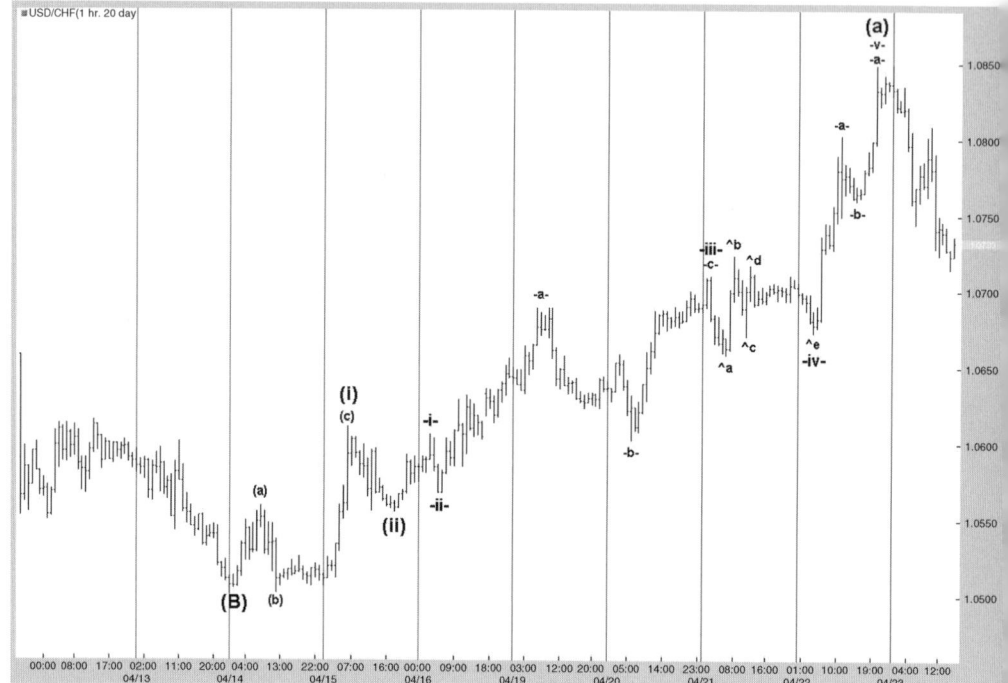

FIGURE 5.13 Wave (a) Rally in Wave (iii) in Hourly USDCHF Ending in an Extended Fifth Wave
Source: FXtrek IntelliChart™ in collaboration with FX-Strategy.com Pro Charts™

target in Wave (C). While this move is still in progress at the time of writing and I cannot be totally certain that the final high has not been seen at 1.0849, the structure of the rally to that point does not appear to be in five waves. Indeed, I suspect that the entire rally began from the Wave (X) low at 1.0434 which I provided in an earlier example of an extended Wave (iii). If that count proves correct then we must see an eventual move to a new high above the 1.0897 high that was seen on February 19, 2010. From this point I am therefore anticipating a Wave (b) of Wave (iii) and will then match the projections in Wave (c) with those of Wave (iii).

While in this example the Wave (a) of Wave (iii) ended at the wave equality target in Wave (C), I have also noticed that they can stall at short Wave (iii) projections such as the 176.4% extension.

Working with the Modified Wave Structure in Forecasting

After the Wave (b) retracement and follow-through in Wave (c) the final Wave (iii) extension could be around 261.8% or 276.4% or more.

Using Momentum to Assist in Identifying Breakdown or Targets

I fully believe that Harmonic Elliott Wave provides a solid base for forecasting, but as I wrote in my first book, *Integrated Technical Analysis*, the need for complementary analysis is vital to bring strength to the forecasting and also a sense of practicality when trading. The production of anticipated projections and targets can be generated easily but it does rely on the identification of the correct beginning of the wave structure. If Waves (i) and (ii) are not identified accurately then any projection in Wave (iii) and retracement in Wave (iv) may be wrong. Thus, blind placing of orders at these levels can cause losses.

I find momentum can provide excellent support at these events. I tend to use my own form of RSI, which is more sensitive, swings between overbought and oversold more frequently even in trending markets, and provides excellent divergence indications.

Earlier in this chapter when discussing the identification of Wave (i) and (ii) I offered an example of a rally in USDJPY. This described the potential confusion in recognizing both Wave (a) and Wave (c), which impacts on the identification of Wave (iii). The following charts offer a method of checks and controls.

Figure 5.14 displays the same chart as in Figure 5.6 earlier in this chapter but this time with my version of RSI. I have placed labels of Wave (i) and Wave (ii) where there may have been an error of judgment, along with what became the correct wave count. I have also labeled where the 176.4% and 285.4% projections in Wave (iii) would be implied.

It can be seen that at the Wave -i- and Wave -a- peaks the five-minute RSI displayed bearish divergences. This was not true for the peak in Wave (i) nor at the series of peaks at the 176.4% projection in Wave (iii). In fact, at this projection area the RSI peaks were rising, which is a sign of strong momentum. At the 285.4% projection of Wave (iii) there was a mild bearish divergence, again at the final Wave -iii- peak.

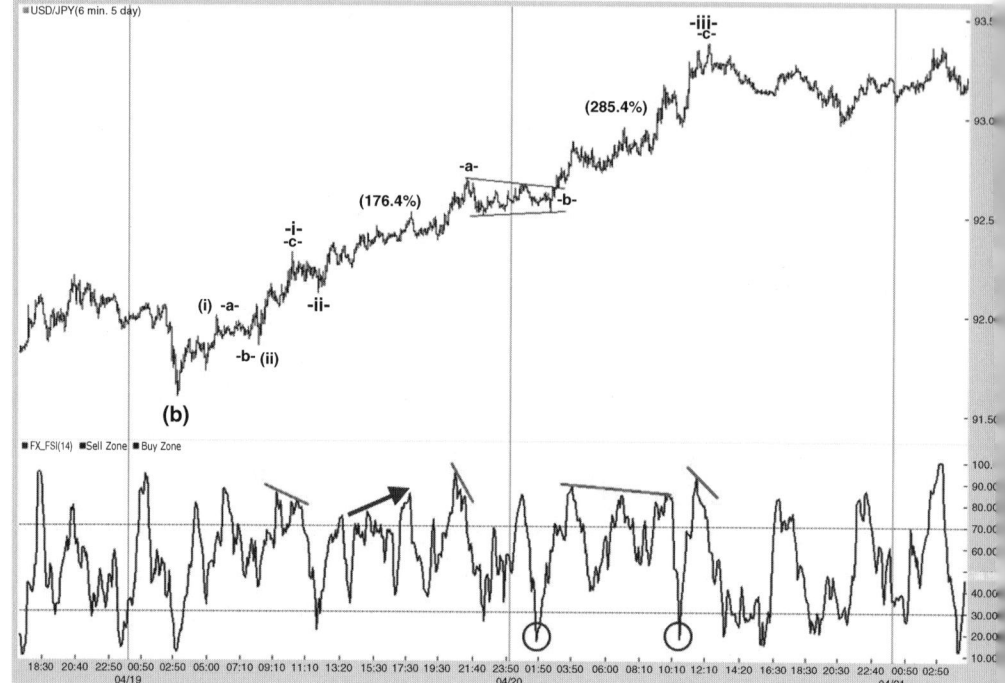

FIGURE 5.14 Potential Confusion in Identifying Targets in a Rally in Five-Minute USDJPY
Source: FXtrek IntelliChart™ in collaboration with FX-Strategy.com Pro Charts™

It can be seen that this version of RSI also allows moves to oversold levels even in an uptrend. This occurred at Wave -ii-, again at the final low in the Wave -b- Triangle, and then at the final pullback before the Wave -iii- high.

However, this is just five-minute momentum, and this can turn within several bars. It is never wise to base analysis and trades on a single time frame. Therefore it is preferable to also consider the momentum in a higher time frame.

In Figure 5.15 I have applied the same version of RSI to the 30-minute chart. It can be seen that momentum rose right through the Wave (i) that could have been considered, and all the way to the Wave -i- high before beginning to drift lower. Thus there was a bearish

Working with the Modified Wave Structure in Forecasting

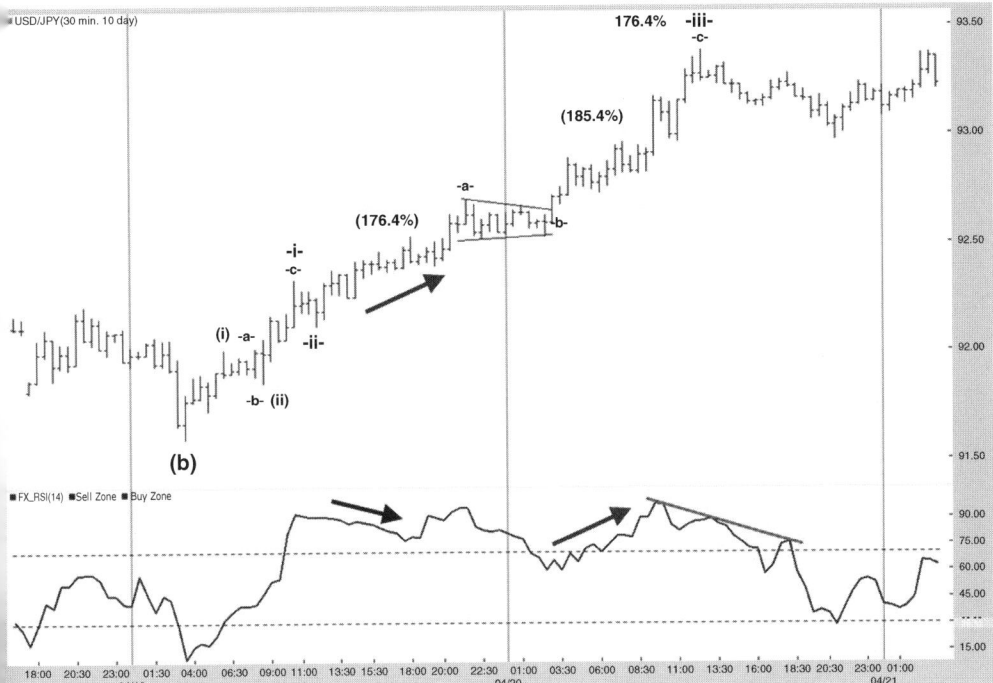

FIGURE 5.15 Confirming Momentum Conditions in 30-Minute USDJPY
Source: FXtrek IntelliChart™ in collaboration with FX-Strategy.com Pro Charts™

divergence in the five-minute chart but none in the 30-minute. It would imply a correction, although we would have no idea at that point how deep the correction may be. It should also force us to reconsider the Wave (i) label and at least seek alternatives. This could have provided us with an earlier opportunity to identify the correct wave count.

As the 30-minute RSI began to drift lower, price rose to a new high and stalled for a few bars. The potential for this to be an Expanded Flat could be considered. However, in the five-minute chart there was a small abc pullback before again rising, and at this point the Wave -ii- was confirmed and projections for Wave -iii- generated.

Note that at the time price approached the 176.4% projection in the original Wave (iii) while 30-minute RSI was declining, the five-minute RSI was recording new highs—a bullish factor. Therefore emphasis is on identifying Wave -a- of Wave -iii-. As noted earlier the five-minute chart recorded a bearish divergence at the Wave -a- peak. However, the 30-minute chart saw RSI rising again by this time to a new high—a bullish factor. Thus the risk that we would just see a correction was high.

The Triangle price rallied again, forcing five-minute RSI to successive high levels while 30-minute RSI rose back to new highs for a third time. This was occurring around the 185.4% projection in Wave (iii), so once again there was no indication from momentum that the rally was due to end. However, by the time price reached the 176.4% projection in Wave -iii- both time frames recorded bearish divergences. This provides a much stronger basis for a trade.

Thus, the use of a good momentum tool to confirm projection levels and avoid trades at inappropriate targets is a vital addition to the armory. It need not just end with momentum; the addition of a favored indicator that provides support or resistance can also be useful. Figure 5.16 displays the same 30-minute chart with an Equilibrium Cloud that I designed to identify market equilibrium.

The Equilibrium Cloud provides a reliable area of support or resistance in directional moves. Note how this supported almost the entire rally once price had reversed above the Cloud.

Most traders and analysts have favored tools. As long as these are complementary and not providing the same information (such as applying RSI, Stochastics, and MACD), the quality of the analysis is enhanced and provides more confidence in the wave structure. In addition to confirming a wave count, indicators can forewarn of a breakdown in the anticipated structure.

Figure 5.17 provides an example of how a wave count may break down an anticipated bullish rally in Wave (C). It is impossible to identify the correct wave structure 100% of the time. We all make errors of judgment and sometimes wave structures can morph into more complex corrections.

In this example, it is assumed that the first high marks the completion of a Wave (A) where momentum displayed a bearish divergence. In the pullback the analyst feels that it developed in

Working with the Modified Wave Structure in Forecasting

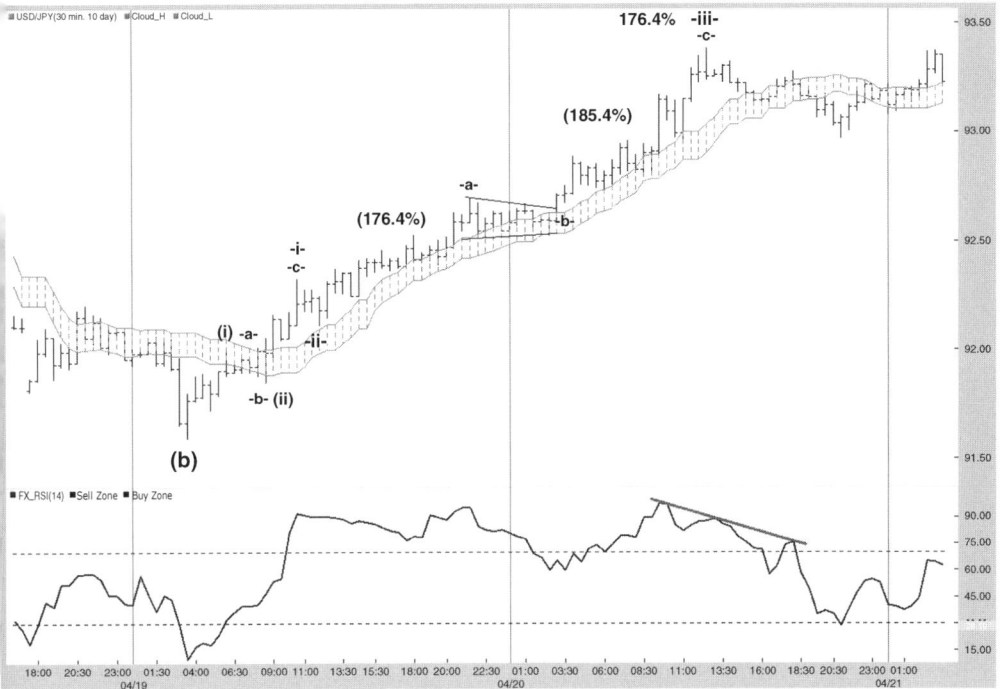

FIGURE 5.16 Confirming Momentum Conditions in 30-minute USDJPY
Source: FXtrek IntelliChart™ in collaboration with FX-Strategy.com Pro Charts™

three waves and, due to other factors, feels there is more risk of Wave (C) developing to new highs directly.

Price rallies to stall just below the Wave (A) high, and being bullish the analyst labels this as Wave (i) and the correction as Wave (ii). However, the subsequent follow-through fails, with a second bearish divergence having developed. This could be due to a possible Expanded Flat in Wave (ii), but the clean break lower through the anticipated Wave (ii) low with price also reversing below the Equilibrium Cloud extends the decline to a wave equality target.

Thus the alternative is for the first correction to be labeled Wave (a), the corrective peak as Wave (b), and the new corrective low as Wave (c) to complete Wave (B).

Use of momentum can assist in providing warning signals. It is possible to remain bullish believing that price will rally to break the

FIGURE 5.17 Using Indicators to Forewarn of a Breakdown in a Bullish Wave Count
Source: FXtrek IntelliChart™ in collaboration with FX-Strategy.com Pro Charts™

bearish divergence. However, the signal is there to keep as a warning that if price doesn't rally a second decline can be expected in a possible Flat correction.

Similar movements can occur with Expanded Flat corrections as price pushes to a new high but then fails amid a bearish divergence. While these occurrences are frustrating, the important point to remember is that once the preferred count is proven incorrect there is often an immediate alternative. In this case the breakdown automatically signals a Flat correction and a new target identified.

Using Cycles to Identify Larger Directional Forces Harmonic Elliott Wave is an amazing tool that provides structure, expectation, and a great deal of accuracy that can be even pin point in the shorter time frames. However, as with any technique

Working with the Modified Wave Structure in Forecasting **149**

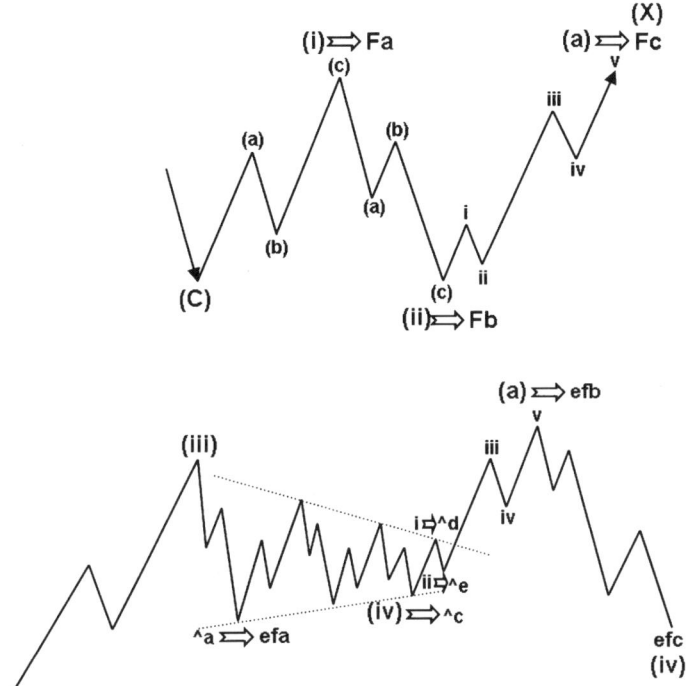

FIGURE 5.18 Two Examples of how Assumed Wave Structures can Change

it is not foolproof as patterns and structures can change as markets evolve.

For example, Figure 5.18 displays two examples of how assumed wave structures can change and yet retain the same internal wave development. The top structure shows an assumed Wave (i), almost 100% retracement in Wave (ii), followed by a Wave (a) to just above the Wave (i) high that is actually the same wave count as a Flat correction. The bottom example shows a rally in a Wave (iii) followed by what looks to be a break out from a Triangle Wave (iv) that could extend above Wave (iii) and then stall to reverse in an Expanded Flat. This would imply the rally in what had been assumed to be Wave ^b was actually an abc move and then the Triangle extends so that what had been Wave i was Wave ^d followed by Wave ^e where a Wave ii is labeled. This in turn would be counted as Wave (x) followed by a second abc move (instead of the assumed Wave iii, iv, and v) to complete a Double Zigzag in Wave efb.

When these types of situations occur in the shorter time frames such as five minutes, it can be frustrating; in the hourly charts recipients of the analysis may shrug their shoulders but when this occurs in the daily or weekly charts they will wonder how the analysis was so wrong. Of course, full attention should be given to momentum, but the larger picture application of cyclic tools is one option to consider.

Over the 21 years I have been a technical analyst I have met several analysts who employ cycles. One Japanese trader showed me his Mercury cycles, which forecast the timing and approximate pattern of how USDJPY would move during the following three to four months after the 79.70 historic low in April 1995. I have a subscriber who uses lunar cycles with astonishing accuracy to identify turning dates. Others use astrology, though most seem to be applying Fibonacci-calculated turning points.

In forex, I have found the use of simple fixed cycles provides quite solid indications on weekly and monthly charts, though daily cycles tend to be a little less reliable. I do like the cycles to generally correlate across the major currencies, with only relatively minor variances in the timing of major reversals. The following three charts provide the cycles I have been following for several years and which all appear to suggest a multi-decade dollar low around the first half of 2012 approximately. I have not included the Euro since it is such a new currency pair, and even synthetically generated history is just not long enough.

Figure 5.19 displays the monthly chart of USDJPY with cycles applied. Note that the correction from the late 1970s lasted only around one-quarter of the period of the largest cycle. The same occurred after the 1995 low. This represents quite significant right translation (that the decline lasts much longer than the earlier recovery), indicating a bearish market and most probably a new historic price low. The approximate timing is in the first half of 2012,

Working with the Modified Wave Structure in Forecasting

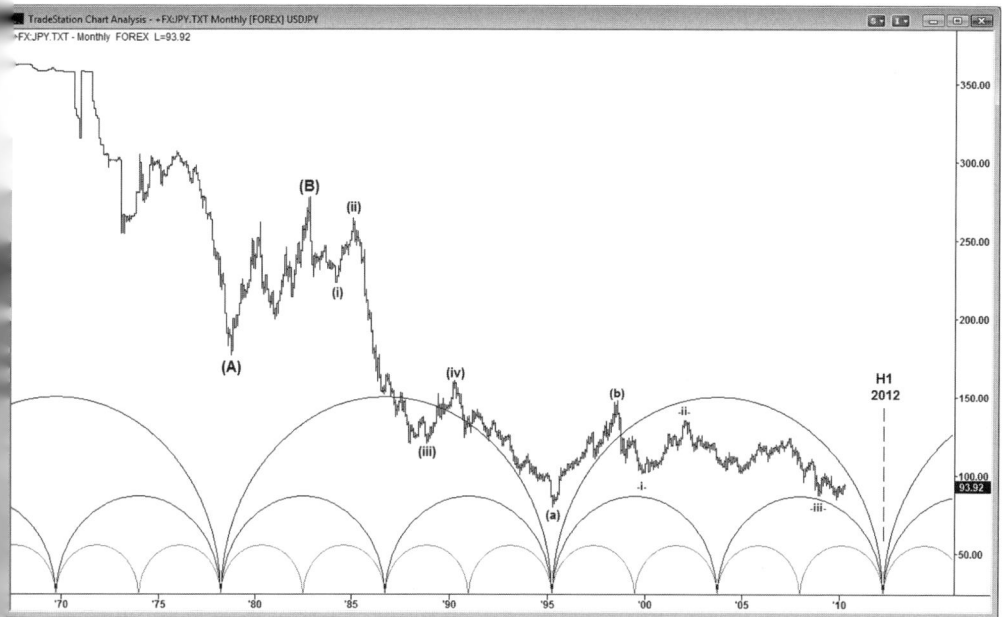

FIGURE 5.19 Cycles in the Monthly Chart of USDJPY
Source: Created with TradeStation. ©TradeStation Technologies, Inc. All rights reserved.

and this has caused me to look more for a bearish structure. I suspect the 147.66 high in August 1988 was a Wave (b) retracement high of a Wave (v) lower. Common targets for the projection in Wave (v) and in Wave (c) are around 60.00–64.00. This also matches a target generated from the descending Triangle starting from the Wave -i- low.

Figure 5.20 displays the monthly chart of USDCHF with cycles applied. In this chart too the strong right translation in the cycles is evident in the corrections from the Wave (A) low and Wave efb low being less than half of the largest cycle. This major cycle is also due to find a low around the end of the second quarter of 2012, to match the same approximate time target of USDJPY. I have labeled the 1.8300 high in October 2000 as the end of a long Expanded Flat correction in Wave (iv), and thus the current decline would logically be Wave (v). Common targets for the Wave (v) and Wave (c) of Wave (v) appear to around the 0.5000 area.

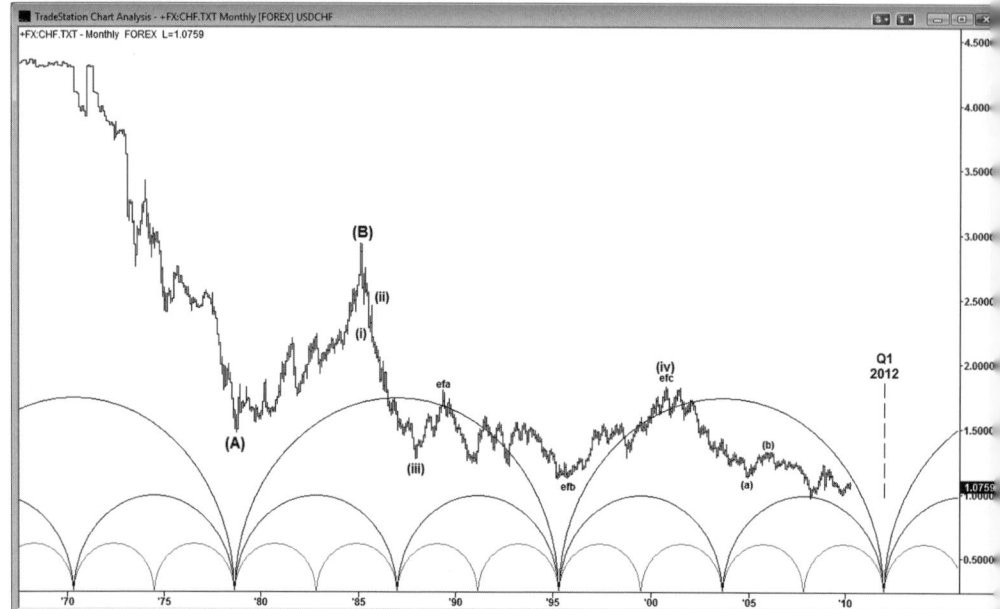

FIGURE 5.20 Cycles in the Monthly Chart of USDCHF
Source: Created with TradeStation. ©TradeStation Technologies, Inc. All rights reserved

Finally, Figure 5.21 displays the monthly chart of GBPUSD with cycles attached. Since GBPUSD is quoted as dollars per pound, the chart is necessarily "reversed" compared to the other two cycle charts. The wave count is less certain here, but due to the cyclic implications I feel we may be seeing a large multi-decade Flat Wave (x) or even an Expanded Flat Wave (x).

The sharp decline from the 2.1160 high in November 2007 appeared to develop in five waves and thus suggest this may have been a Wave (a). Therefore we are in the middle of a Wave (b) correction. Where the current bullish cycle will finally stall is not yet clear, but from a timing perspective the earliest would appear to be soon after the smallest cycle begins to turn lower around October 2011 and the latest by the time the middle cycle begins to turn down around July 2013. This does, of course, tend to match the expectations of a major US dollar low somewhere around the first half of

Working with the Modified Wave Structure in Forecasting

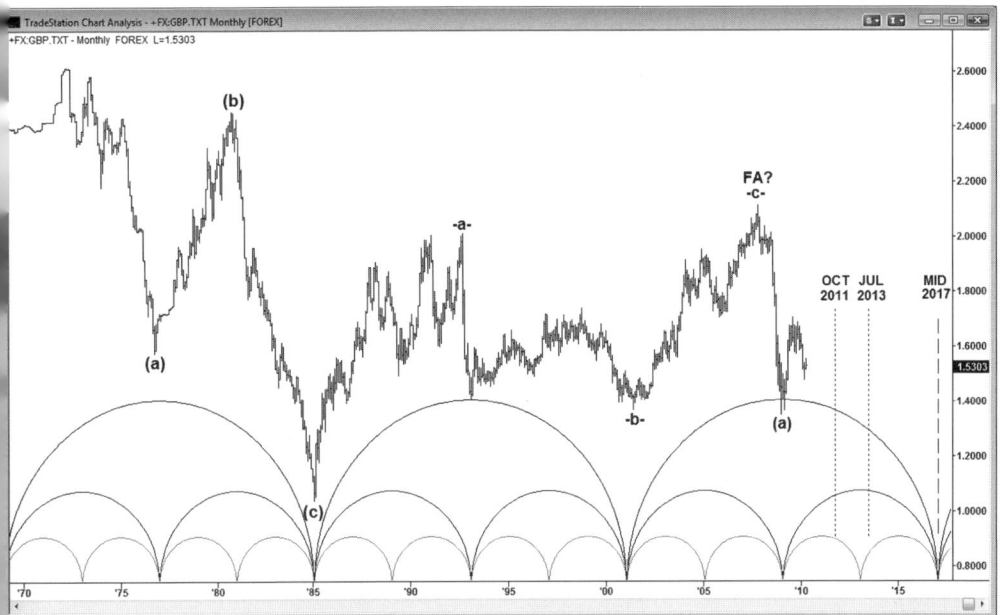

FIGURE 5.21 Cycles in the Monthly Chart of GBPUSD
Source: Created with TradeStation. ©TradeStation Technologies, Inc. All rights reserved.

2012. Note the larger cycle low is not due until around the middle of 2017.

The application of fixed time cycles is certainly an approximate guide only, but can provide the general outlook which can often differentiate between two conflicting wave counts and, in conjunction with observance of momentum, warn of a breakdown of a possible wave count being followed in favor of a larger complex correction. They also help to retain a certain perspective of whether a general move higher or lower should be anticipated. Additional complementary tools are always beneficial for comprehensive analysis.

Ambiguous Wave Counts It is easy to sit and write about forecasting, providing examples that hold perfect wave relationships that give the impression that all your problems are solved. I have always taken the view that if a forecasting technique is easy then everyone will learn the process with the idea that it will be a self-fulfilling prophesy. Very clearly this is not the case, since if everyone knows what the market is going to do there'll be the contrarian with large funds to push around to hammer stop losses. As much as Harmonic Elliott Wave is a fabulous tool, there are still numerous barriers to overcome, confusing wave development that seems to lack any relationships, and difficulties in identifying Wave (i) and Wave (ii) in particularly erratic beginnings to a new wave.

Not all wave counts are obvious, and on occasion, because of the natural order of Fibonacci ratios in particular, the wave relationships become ambiguous. Figure 5.22 is an example of a recent wave development in EURUSD.

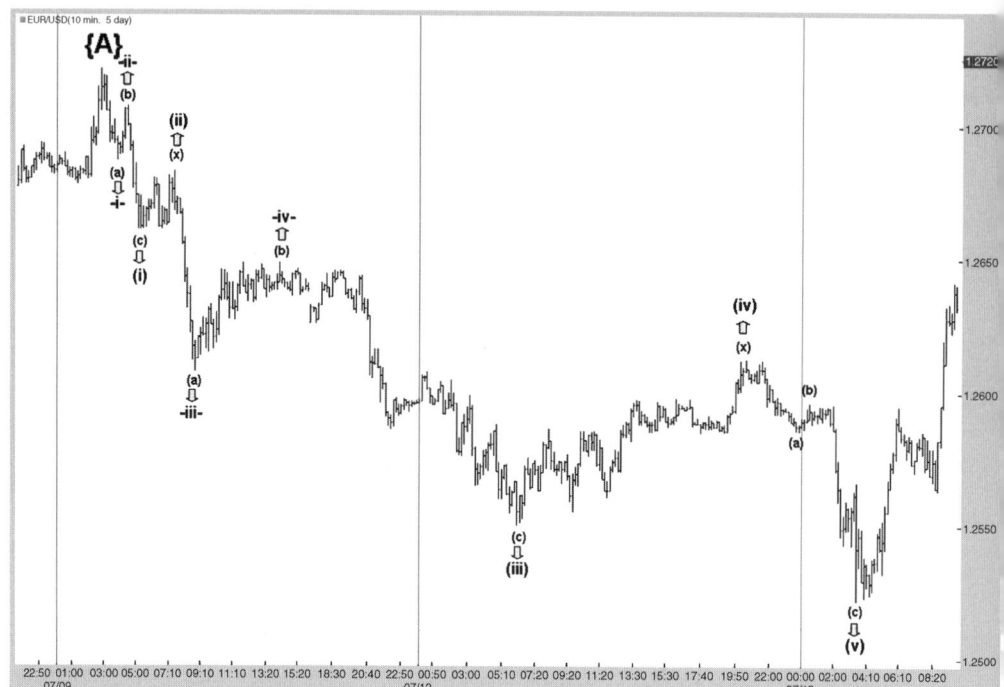

FIGURE 5.22 How Ratios can have Multiple Potential Relationships
Source: FXtrek IntelliChart™ in collaboration with FX-Strategy.com Pro Charts™

Working with the Modified Wave Structure in Forecasting

Figure 5.22 is the five-minute chart of EURUSD. This correction occurred within a rally from the June 2010 low at 1.1877, and is actually still in development at the time of writing. I judged this to be a correction, which is yet to be confirmed, but the rally has developed quite well within the general expectation of this being a large Wave (IV) correction.

The 1.2722 high labeled Wave {A} was anticipated as being the Wave {A} of Wave {III} of Wave (C) of the entire Wave (IV). The prior Wave {II} had been very brief and shallow, exceptionally so. This raised the risk that we may see a deep Wave {B}.

As this Wave {B} commenced there was no way of knowing whether this would be a simple ABC decline, a Double Zigzag, Triple Three, or possibly even a more complex correction. Thus the initial stages of the decline were more about judging what structure may develop. This was complicated by the fact that there were multiple retracement ratios with a minimum of 50%:

$$50.0\% = 1.2518$$
$$58.6\% = 1.2482$$
$$61.8\% = 1.2469$$
$$66.7\% = 1.2449$$

The first move lower from the 1.2722 peak certainly had more of a look of a five-wave move and was labeled Wave (a). This was followed by a pullback in Wave (b) and a decline logically in Wave (c) at 1.2661. This represented a 161.8% projection.

This was followed by a shallow correction in Wave (x) and sharp decline to 1.2608, which was then labeled as a second Wave (a). The appearance therefore was that the correction was developing in a multiple ABC move. However, an interesting development was that 1.2608 was just three points below the 261.8% projection of Wave (a). Consideration should be given to the possibility that Wave (a) should have been labeled Wave -i- and thus we had seen a 261.8% projection in Wave -iii-. To verify this, the wave relationships between the decline from the labeled Wave (x) high to the second Wave (a) should be a common extension ratio of the decline from the labeled Wave (b) to the first Wave (c). In fact, this turned out to be 161.8% also . . .

This opens an ambiguous interpretation. Either the multiple ABC decline will work through, or perhaps this was part of a five-wave decline in Wave (a) to be followed by a retracement in Wave (b) and final decline in Wave (c) as a large Zigzag. Given the potential for this to be a deep Wave {B}, it certainly had reasonable grounds for consideration.

The next measurement to take to try to clarify which structure was developing was to look for between a 41.4% and 50% retracement in what could be Wave (b) or Wave -iv-. The possible Wave -ii- had retraced around 61.8% and this tended to imply a greater chance of a 41.4% retracement. It met that perfectly at 1.2649.

Let's just recap what has occurred until this point.

Figure 5.23 displays the initial decline with ratios displayed. Clearly there are two possible interpretations but with differing expectations. If the 1.2649 high was a Wave (b) then a five-wave decline in Wave (c) will be expected; if this is a Wave -v- decline then

FIGURE 5.23 Reviewing the Wave Relationships
Source: FXtrek IntelliChart™ in collaboration with FX-Strategy.com ProCharts™

Working with the Modified Wave Structure in Forecasting **157**

we must expect a three-wave decline and with projection ratios calculated from the distance from the 1.2722 high to the 1.2608 low extended from 1.2649. These would be:

$$61.8\% = 1.2579$$
$$66.7\% = 1.2573$$
$$76.4\% = 1.2562$$
$$85.6\% = 1.2552$$

Therefore there is a need to observe how the beginning of the decline develops to judge from the structure whether it develops in three waves or five. At the end of the decline price stalled at 1.2550, just two points below the 85.6% projection.

Figure 5.24 displays the decline from 1.2649 appeared more to be like a five-wave move which swayed the wave count in favor of a Triple Three, with this being the second Wave (c) that had stalled 32 points above the 50% retracement in Wave {B} at 1.2518. This would

FIGURE 5.24 Reviewing the Wave Relationships
Source: FXtrek IntelliChart™ in collaboration with FX-Strategy.com ProCharts™

allow a further ABC decline that could stretch to 1.2518 or even perhaps one of the deeper Wave {B} retracement levels.

However, there was a further complication. Now that the decline has come in two sets of ABC moves this will mean the 1.2661 low may well be a Wave (i), which in turn could imply a larger ABC decline with this being Wave A. The first Wave (c) was 161.8% of Wave (a). The second Wave (c) was between 123.6% and 138.2% and also represented a 223.6% extension of the Wave (i).

Once again, verification of the possibility of a Wave (iv) is required. Wave (ii) had retraced close to 38.2% and therefore the Wave (iv) should be around 50%. In fact it stalled at 1.2613, which was just short of 50% but could still provide a projection in Wave (v), the common projections being:

$$61.8\% = 1.2507$$
$$66.7\% = 1.2498$$
$$76.4\% = 1.2482$$

Refer back to Figure 5.22. The final low was at 1.2522, which was four points above the 50% retracement level in Wave {B} and represented between a 50% and 58.6% projection in Wave (v). Wave (c) was a 276.4% extension of Wave (a).

At this point I forecast a recovery, and probably quite a deep one. However, there was still an ambiguity. This was after all a decline of three sets of ABC structures, and at the 50% retracement in Wave {B} could represent a completed correction. The alternative was that given the reasonably good wave relationships this could also be Wave A of a larger ABC decline that would see a deep Wave B and then Wave C decline to a level closer to one of the deep Wave {B} retracement levels.

In fact, price maintained the recovery to new highs to confirm the 1.2522 low as Wave {B}, and thus a rally in Wave {C} of Wave {III} was underway. There is a further validation to be made here. This was assumed to be a Wave {iii} and therefore there would be projections in Wave {III}, and these will need to match with a valid projection in Wave {C}.

CHAPTER 6

A Case Study in EURUSD

BEING CAUGHT WITH THE WRONG WAVE COUNT

For anyone attempting to forecast markets, there is absolutely no possibility of being right 100% of the time. In some cases the underlying larger degree forecast may be correct, but due to the sheer variety of developmental structures, especially in corrective patterns, there will always be errors of judgment, unseen alternatives, and just plain mistakes in the positioning of the lower wave degrees. It is inevitable and part of the process of being a forecaster.

Quite often, once a forecast is made for an extension or retracement to a level or perhaps a series of possible targets, the fact that the call was wrong is quite obvious. In many cases, since a forecast will always imply a particular wave development, in three waves or five, the error may be evident in the approach to the target and perhaps be anticipated with a particular retracement level providing a very obvious level where the structure completely breaks down.

For example, consider the situation where a Wave (ii) retracement has been seen in a larger rally. The call was for Wave (a) of

Wave (iii) to commence. This development is tracked in a lower degree Wave -i-, Wave -ii-, and followed by Wave -iii- perhaps to the area around the Wave (i) high. The forecast is for a (say) 50% retracement in Wave -iv-. This occurs, and a reversal higher is seen which prompts a forecast for Wave -v- to develop in three waves to complete Wave (a).

However, price fails to extend the gains and drops back below the 50% retracement in Wave -iv- and collapses back to the Wave (ii). What has occurred is a Flat correction. If this occurs in the weekly chart it looks like an awful piece of analysis . . . . As I mentioned, as much as we try it will always be a risk. What is important is the speed with which the analyst reacts to such an event.

However, it should be added that during the process it is quite possible to forecast correctly for much of the move but actually only break down when targets are achieved. The analysis may well be logical and drawn from alternative sources of analysis but still break down. In this section I shall detail a period in which I did get key calls incorrect but for much of the time still made successful forecasts during much of the move.

I will go through a series of long-term forecasts that I made which overall didn't turn out that well, but within the moves I had a lot of success. The market is daily EURUSD from the 1.6036 high.

Figure 6.1 displays that the decline from the 1.6036 high was aggressive and quite direct for the degree of movement normally seen in the markets. Wave (c) was just over a 114.6% projection of Wave (a). This was followed by a correction high to just below the Wave (b) high, as would normally be expected.

At this stage the market was in turmoil after the subprime shock. From the earlier charts showing the long-term cycles I was clearly still bullish overall but noted the three-wave correction to 1.4717 and felt that the time was not quite right for a direct rally. Having seen a three-wave correction, the risk was for one of two things: either a period of consolidation in a complex correction, or we would see a second decline to new lows in a new three-wave decline before the underlying bullish monthly cycles triggered a longer-term rally into the 2012–13 time frame.

A Case Study in EURUSD

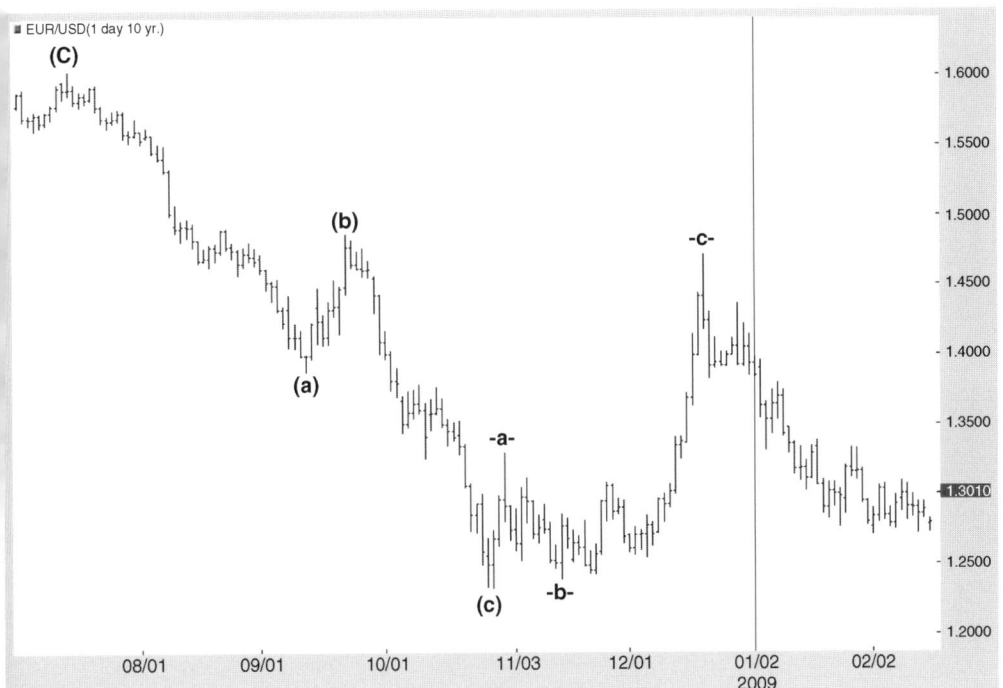

FIGURE 6.1 Decline from the 1.6036 high in EURUSD
Source: FXtrek IntelliChart™ in collaboration with FX-Strategy.com Pro Charts™

Therefore I was looking for the decline to end above the 1.2328 low in the second leg of a Triangle and then reverse higher in what would be Wave ^c.

Figure 6.2 displays the subsequent rally from the 1.2455 low. The 1.4717 high was labeled Wave ^A and the 1.2455 low as Wave ^B. The first rally stalled at 1.3737 and corrected to 1.2885. I labeled these points Wave (a) and Wave (b).

In a Triangle I would expect a projection in Wave ^C to be around 66.7%, but this being at 1.4048 I opted for the deeper 76.4% at 1.4280. It was comforting that a 109.2% projection in Wave (c) implied a target of 1.4280. However, as the rally progressed, the internal wave relationships did suggest a small extension beyond, which ended at 1.4338. There was a solid bearish divergence to add to the confidence of the call for a pullback in Wave ^D.

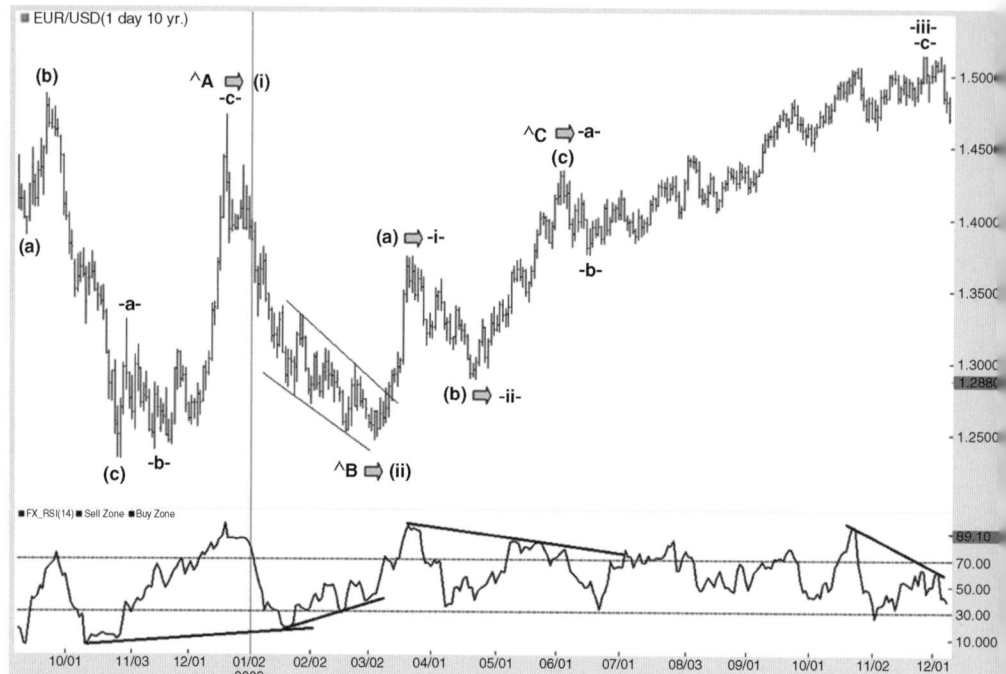

FIGURE 6.2 Rally to 1.5143 in EURUSD Daily Chart
Source: FXtrek IntelliChart™ in collaboration with FX-Strategy.com Pro Charts™

However, in spite of my confidence the wave count broke down, signaled by a break of the bearish divergence. At this point, having to adjust the wave count I began to wonder whether the larger bullish cycles were making their power felt much earlier than I had expected and I turned to a more bullish wave count which relabeled Wave ^A to Wave (i) and the 1.2455 low as Wave (ii). Given the confusion of the very erratic and choppy rally from the 1.2455 low, I relabeled the 1.3737 high as Wave -i- of Wave (a) and the 1.2885 low as Wave -ii-.

From these I generated a potential target at 1.5146, being a 176.4% projection in Wave -iii-. A 95.4% projection in Wave -c- implied a target of 1.5133. The rally from the 1.3747 Wave -b- low was exceptionally complicated. There were successful times and some more trying times during that rally, which fully tried my patience and confidence in the wave count. However, as price approached the 1.5146 target there was a strong bearish divergence and I called for a peak at 1.5146–60. Obviously I was delighted with the final peak at 1.5143.

A Case Study in EURUSD

FIGURE 6.3 Initial Decline from 1.5143 in EURUSD Daily Chart
Source: FXtrek IntelliChart™ in collaboration with FX-Strategy.com Pro Charts™

With the Wave -ii- being very close to a 66.6% correction I forecast for a correction in Wave -iv- to reach the 41.4% retracement at 1.4208.

Once again the forecast proved incorrect. The initial decline (shown in Figure 6.3) was actually quite good as it stalled at 1.4217, just nine points above the target I had quoted. However, at that point my RSI had dropped to below 10 and there was no sign of a bullish divergence. This caused me some concern. At that point I also had to consider the fact that the drop to 1.4217 was really quite brief, and in terms of the size and length of the rally from 1.2455 the correction was really much too short from a time perspective. There was a possibility that Wave -iv- would develop as a complex correction. However, I was quite certain at that time that this decline had come in five waves. The only way to count this was as a Wave A.

The implication of this could only be that it must be followed by a Wave B and then Wave C. However, after the rather brief correction to 1.4578 in Wave B, any target in Wave C must necessarily break any pullback in Wave -iv-.

Once again I had to readjust the wave count, and at that point, given the three-wave decline from 1.6036 and the fact that 1.5143 was very close to a 76.4% retracement of the entire decline, I decided that this may therefore be a Wave ^B after the Wave ^A at 1.2328. This implied a Wave ^C target at the 66.6% projection at 1.2671.

The next puzzle was identifying how this decline will develop. In a Wave ^C it is possible to see a simple Zigzag, Double Zigzag, or Triple Three, and within those structures there could be potential for some quite complex corrections.

This did indeed prove to be a challenge in attempting to identify the end of Wave C.

Without detailing every single segment of the decline I have shown how the 1.2671 target was eventually overshot in Figure 6.4.

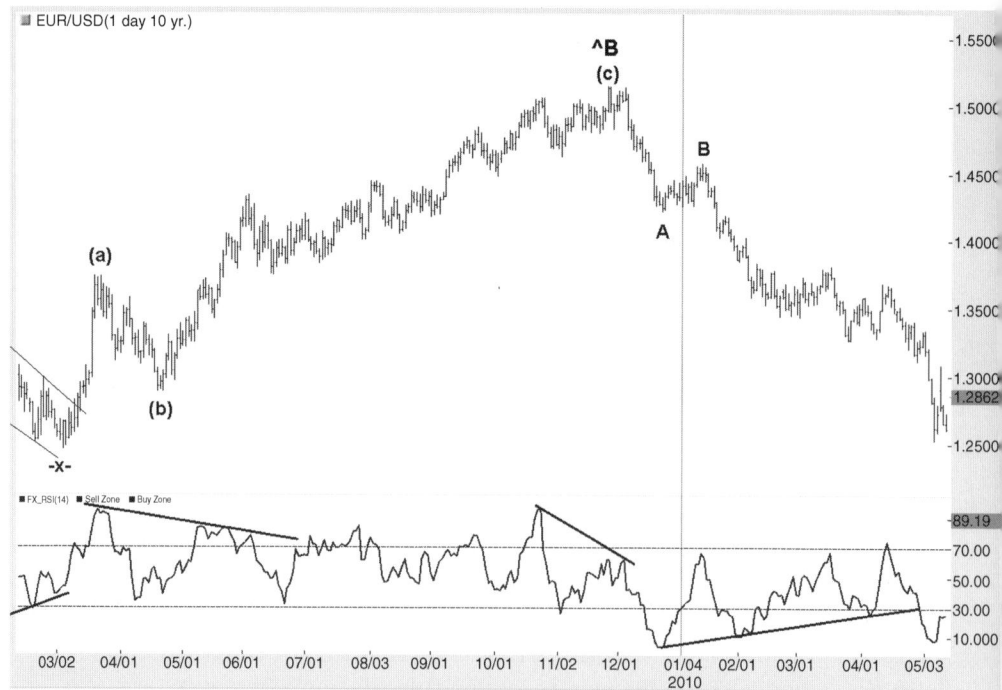

FIGURE 6.4 Decline from 1.5143 in EURUSD Daily Chart
Source: FXtrek IntelliChart™ in collaboration with FX-Strategy.com Pro Charts™

A Case Study in EURUSD

The break below the two lows around 1.3267 coincided with a break of the bullish divergence that had, for a while, begun to risk an earlier reversal. Breaks of divergences such as this one have a common result of seeing the trend accelerate, and this occurred.

A break of the 1.2671 Triangle target could only mean one thing: price would now have to break below the 1.2328 low.

It would be useful at this point just to refer back to Figure 6.1, which displays the initial three-wave decline from the 1.6036 high. The key point here is that it developed in three waves. The correction higher that ended at 1.5143 developing in a Double Zigzag, together with the break below 1.2671 which excluded a Triangle and the fact that the dollar has bearish cycles into the end of 2012, implies that the decline from 1.5143 must develop in a three-wave move.

As mentioned above I was confident that the decline from 1.5143 to 1.4217 developed in five waves. This implied that the end of Wave C must be below 1.2328. This is logical since it would be impossible for an ABC move to end above 1.2328 unless a descending Triangle was developing. However, that scenario would imply a strong dollar.

In Figure 6.5 I have provided what was my interpretation of the decline to the 1.1877 low. It can be seen that I opted to label the final 1.1879 low as Wave (iii) and not the end of Wave C. This type of extreme extended Wave C is not something I like to call but I couldn't really find any workable wave relationship to Wave A to suggest the decline had made a final low. When I come to these conclusions I can only work with the wave count and identify the levels that would prove me wrong. By doing this I generally find the initial wave development works in my favor and it is around the final critical area where the fine-tuning tends to be required.

I shall work through the logic used here with a view to providing a reasoned approach that can be applied to working through these ambiguous situations.

Firstly, the downward move under consideration is from the Wave B high at 1.4578 which is expected to decline in five waves to complete Wave C. If I simply take a 290.2% projection in Wave C it generates a target of 1.1891. That is close enough to the final 1.1879 low to satisfy a Wave C target. However, there is also a need to generate a harmonic five-wave decline which has internal relationships that also imply the

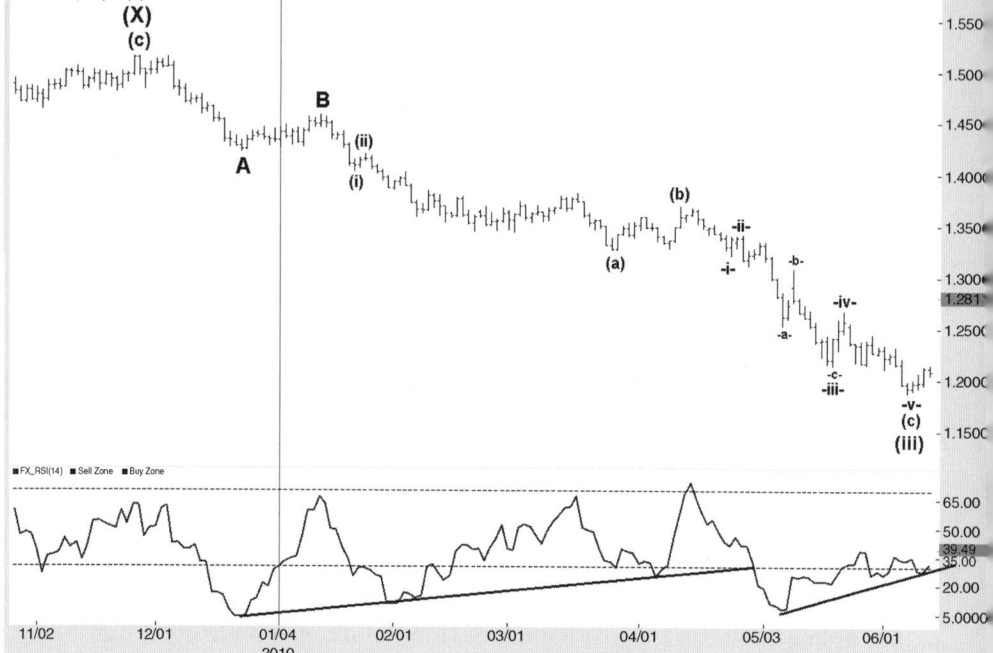

FIGURE 6.5 Decline from 1.5143 in EURUSD Daily Chart
Source: FXtrek IntelliChart™ in collaboration with FX-Strategy.com Pro Charts™

end of Wave C has been seen. This is where I had problems. Indeed, there were a few unusual issues that made the analysis quite problematic during its development and only really become clear in the final decline from 1.3691.

Referring to Figure 6.5, I was also quite confident of the Wave (i) and Wave (ii) count as internally the Wave (i) was quite clear. Obviously, at the time this occurred I was still looking for an eventual Wave ^C in a daily Triangle and therefore the expectations of a low at 1.1877 were not at the forefront of my mind. Thus the count in Figure 6.6 was generated after completion.

However, the wave relationships in the decline did not entirely conform to the usual ratios, as can be seen in Table 6.1.

In particular Waves -iii-, -iv-, Wave -b- of Wave -v-, and Wave -v- did not possess the accuracy I prefer to see in a wave development. This

A Case Study in EURUSD

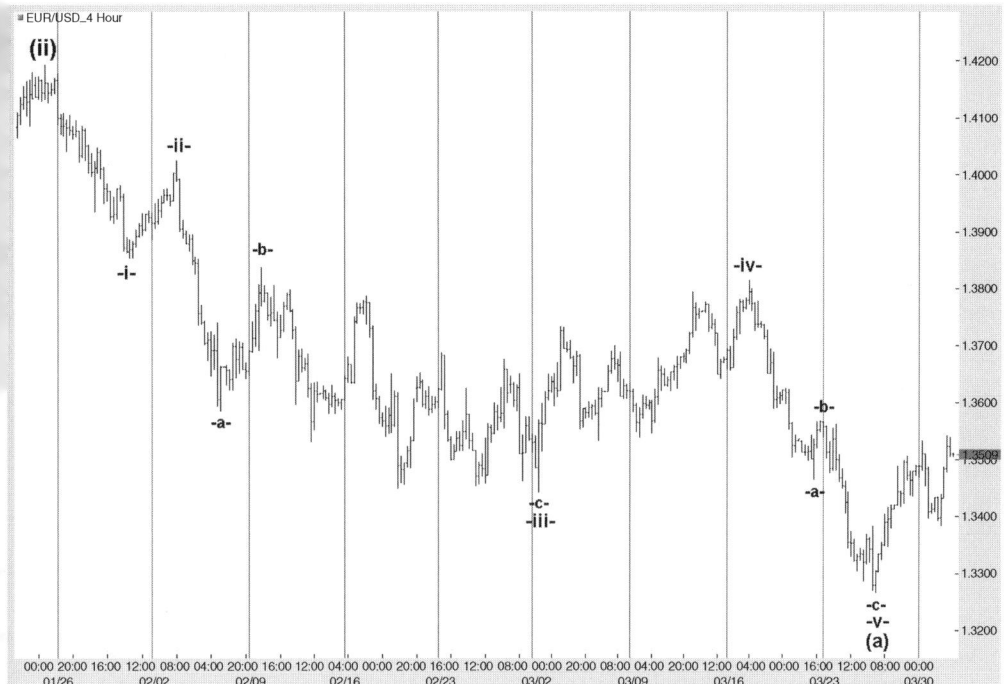

FIGURE 6.6 Decline from 1.4192 in a Daily Wave (a) of Wave (iii)
Source: FXtrek IntelliChart™ in collaboration with FX-Strategy.com Pro Charts™

TABLE 6.1 Wave Relationships from Figure 6.6

Wave (a)		Ratio	Projection	Actual
Wave -i-	1.3853			1.3853
Wave -ii-	1.3853 +	Wave -i- * 50.0% =	1.4023	1.4025
Wave -a-	1.3585			1.3585
Wave -b-	1.3585 +	Wave -a- * 58.6% =	1.3843	1.3838
Wave -c-	1.3838 −	Wave -a- * 90.2% =	1.3441	1.3442
Wave -iii-	1.4025 −	Wave -i- * 166.7% =	1.3458	1.3442
Wave -iv-	1.3442 +	Wave -iii- * 61.8% =	1.3802	1.3814
Wave -a-	1.3465			1.3465

(continued)

TABLE 6.1 (Continued)

Wave (a)		Ratio	Projection	Actual
Wave -b-	1.3465 +	Wave -a- * 61.8% =	**1.3681**	**1.3568**
Wave -c-	1.3568 −	Wave -a- * 85.4% =	**1.3270**	**1.3267**
Wave -v-	1.3814 −	Wave -i- > Wave -iii- * 76.4% =	**1.3240**	**1.3267**

lack of accuracy always leads to doubts, and again, looking back at the daily chart in Figure 6.5, there was a significant bullish divergence which suggested risk of a deeper correction. Keeping in mind that at this point, without particularly good wave relationships in the decline, the potential for this to be a Wave (a) of Wave (iii) was somewhat uncertain. The prior Wave -iv- of this decline was at 1.3814. A 50% retracement of the decline from Wave (ii) was at 1.3730. The recovery stalled at 1.3691.

Once price dropped below 1.3267 and the bullish divergence support line broke, the next stage was to see where the Wave (iii) could eventually stall. Through a simple spreadsheet I note the normal wave relationships, and Figure 6.7 displays this.

This may be difficult to see but basically the spreadsheet generates projections in Wave (iii) and for Wave (c) of Wave (iii) so that common stalling points can be identified. There were three areas which tended to match:

Wave (iii)
185.4%   @1.2622
298.6%   @1.2550
423.6%   @1.1862

Wave (c)
114.6%   @1.2631
123.6%   @1.2548
195.4%   @1.1884

The two that attract most are the 185.4% projection in Wave (iii) and the 298.6% projection at 1.2550. In practical terms the issue of the extension in Wave C would tend to cause a more conservative target.

Start	Wave (i)	Wave (ii)	Wave (iii)	Wave (iv)	Wave (v)		Wave (a)	Wave (b)	Wave (c)		Wave (a)	Wave (b)	Wave (c)
1.4578	1.4028	1.4192					1.3267	1.3691					
Wave (ii) Retracements	9.02% 1.4078	14.60% 1.4108	23.60% 1.4158	33.30% 1.4211	38.20% 1.4238	41.40% 1.4256	50.00% 1.4303	58.60% 1.4350	61.80% 1.4368	66.66% 1.4395	76.40% 1.4448	85.40% 1.4498	90.02% 1.4523	95.40% 1.4553	98.60% 1.4570
Wave (iii) Projections	161.80% 1.3302	166.70% 1.3275	176.40% 1.3222	185.40% 1.3172	190.20% 1.3146	198.40% 1.3101	238.20% 1.2882	261.80% 1.2752	276.40% 1.2672	285.40% 1.2622	290.00% 1.2597	295.40% 1.2567	298.60% 1.2550	323.60% 1.2412	361.80% 1.2202	423.60% 1.1862
Wave (c) Projections	76.40% 1.2984	85.40% 1.2901	94.40% 1.2818	100.00% 1.2766	105.60% 1.2714	109.20% 1.2681	114.60% 1.2631	123.60% 1.2548	138.20% 1.2413	161.80% 1.2194	166.70% 1.2149	176.40% 1.2059	185.40% 1.1976	194.40% 1.1893	223.60% 1.1623	261.80% 1.1269

FIGURE 6.7 Normal Wave Relationships

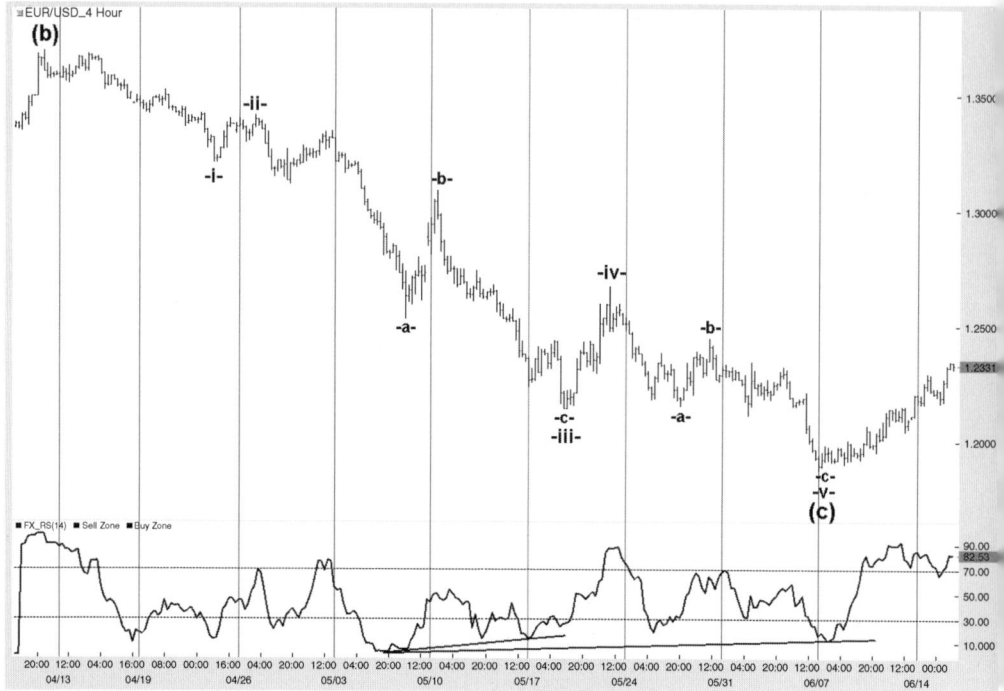

FIGURE 6.8 Decline from 1.3691 in a Daily Wave (c) of Wave (iii)
Source: FXtrek IntelliChart™ in collaboration with FX-Strategy.com Pro Charts™

A Wave (iii) in this area would obviously imply a correction in Wave (iv) and final extension in Wave (v) that should drop below 1.2328 . . .

The next chart shows the decline in Wave (c).

Figure 6.8 displays the decline from 1.3691. The closer target for Wave (iii) at 1.2622–31 was broken quite easily with momentum declining sharply. It was therefore quite clear that this would not hold at the time, while it was just about impossible to generate a five-wave count.

The low marked Wave -a- was at 1.2530, just 20 points below the second Wave (iii) projection, but momentum here had merely registered a very low level. While it is not impossible to see a reversal without a divergence, it is unusual. It was also difficult to see any five-wave pattern in the decline from 1.3691 to 1.2530. Therefore the chance this would provide the Wave (iii) low was quite low.

A Case Study in EURUSD

TABLE 6.2 Wave Relationships from Figure 6.8

Wave (c)		Ratio	Projection	Actual
Wave -i-	1.3206			1.3206
Wave -ii-	1.3206 +	Wave -i- * 41.4% =	**1.3407**	1.3412
Wave -a-	1.2530			1.2530
Wave -b-	1.2530 +	Wave -a- * 61.8% =	**1.3075**	1.3086
Wave -c-	1.3086 −	Wave -a- * 105.6% =	**1.2155**	1.2143
Wave -iii-	1.3412 −	Wave -i- * 261.8% =	**1.2142**	1.2143
Wave -iv-	1.2143 +	Wave -iii- * 41.4% =	**1.2668**	1.2670
Wave -a-	1.2153			1.2153
Wave -b-	1.2153 +	Wave -a- * 58.6% =	**1.2456**	1.2446
Wave -c-	1.2446 −	Wave -a- * 109.2% =	**1.1881**	1.1877
Wave -v-	1.2670 −	Wave -i- > -iii- * 50.0% =	**1.1896**	1.1877

Therefore, quite against initial expectations the next harmonic area at 1.1862–84 became the next target. By this time the wave count was becoming firmer, with the correction from 1.2530 being a deep Wave -b- of around 61.8% and followed by Wave -iii-, Wave -iv-, and Wave -v-. The full harmonic relationships are displayed in Table 6.2.

It can be seen that the harmonic wave relationships were quite standard ratios, with the final stalling point right in the lower Wave (iii) projection target at 1.1862–84. In addition, daily momentum was providing a solid bullish divergence so the call for a low here was quite strong. The only possible alternative would have been a more normal Wave -v- projection of 61.8%, which would have implied a target at 1.1713.

At this point we can refer back to Figure 6.5. Even I was rather astounded at the wave count. The required projection in Wave C was of a degree that must raise doubts as it has to be in excess of the 290% extension, which the 1.1879 low has already reached . . .

In these circumstances it is only possible to forecast a Wave (iv) retracement and observe momentum at that point to judge whether the count is correct. This situation was no different to the beginning of this move at 1.5143 from where I had (incorrectly) anticipated only a correction. The Wave (iv) should be a retracement of the decline from the Wave (ii) high at 1.4192. Given Wave (ii) was very brief and retraced only around 30% of Wave (i), I judged that we should at least see a 58.6% retracement, and an extreme at 61.8%. These generated targets at 1.3234 and 1.3308 respectively.

Once price had demonstrated a short-term confirmation of a reversal I announced the 1.3200–50 area as the target.

Figure 6.9 displays the correction in Wave (iv). Of course, the first challenge is to understand how this will develop. As a corrective wave it has the potential to become a simple Zigzag (and then with the risk of being a complex correction), a Double Zigzag, or even a Triple Three. If the first move is ambiguous this can generate confusion and uncertainty for the remainder of the move, or until

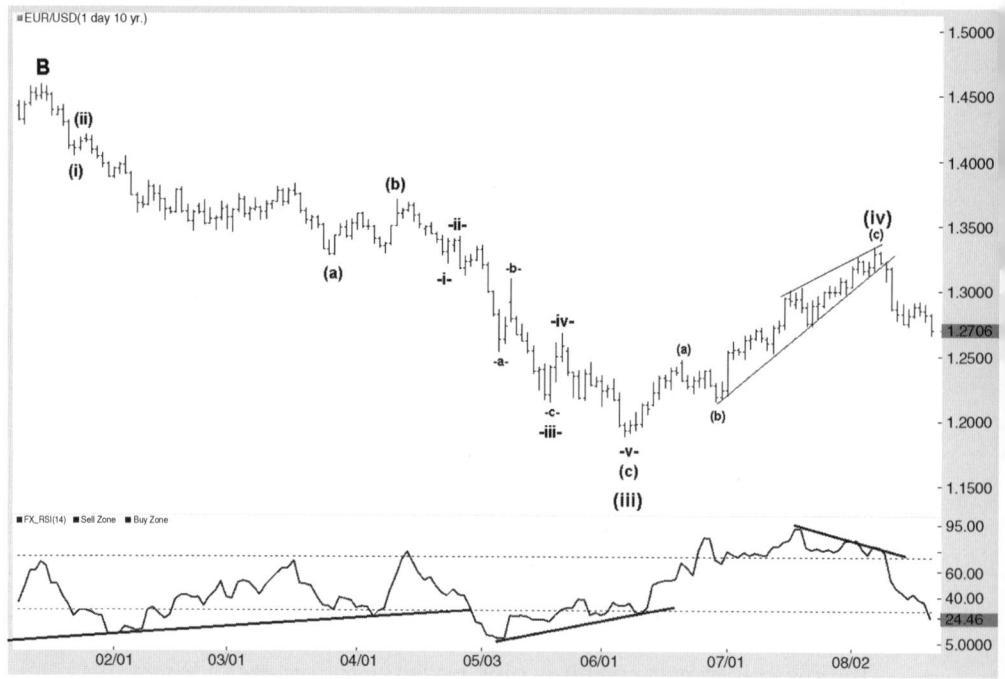

FIGURE 6.9 Correction in Wave (iv) in Daily EURUSD
Source: FXtrek IntelliChart™ in collaboration with FX-Strategy.com Pro Charts™

A Case Study in EURUSD

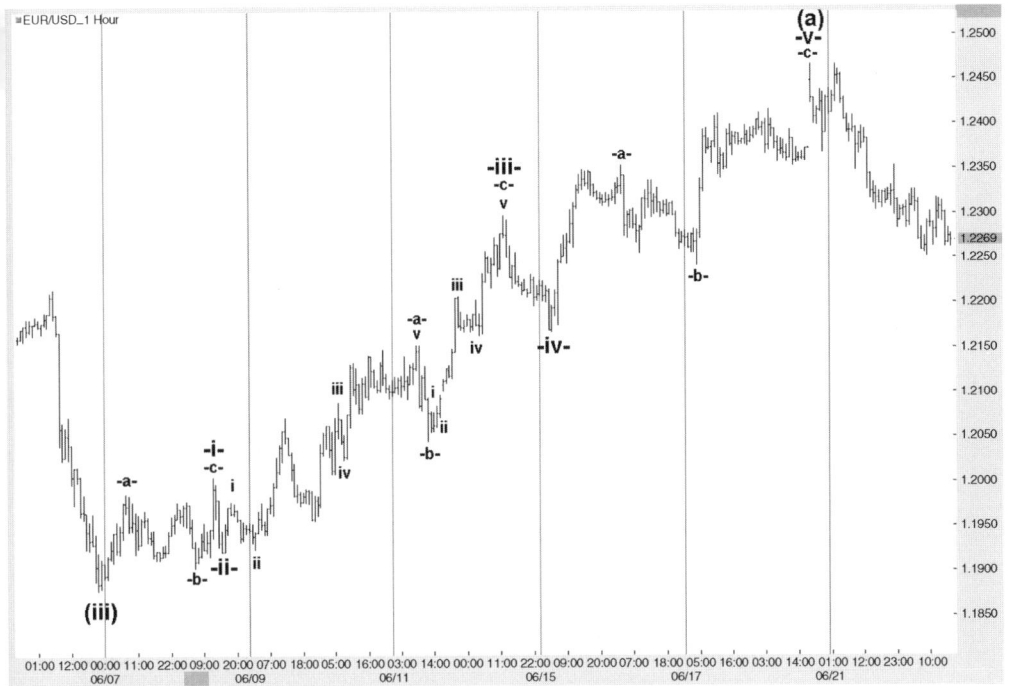

FIGURE 6.10 Rally in Wave (a) of Wave (iv) in Daily EURUSD
Source: FXtrek IntelliChart™ in collaboration with FX-Strategy.com Pro Charts™

the structure has become clear. I have labeled this as an (a)(b)(c) move with the Wave (a) quite clearly having developed in five waves.

Just to clarify this as it does represent the first hurdle in any correction, Figure 6.10 provides the Wave (a) rally that ended at 1.2466.

While the Wave -i- was easily recognized by the ABC structure, the subsequent Wave -iii- was a little more complex as Wave b of Wave iii was an exceptionally deep retracement. With the normal retracement for a Wave b being at most 58.6%, the depth of a deep Wave b can really provide a degree of confusion and tend to push the mind toward a Triple Three type structure. However, this was far too soon to begin to expect individual ABC structures given the expected target was still 1,000 points away.

While this type of development will always add doubt, the discipline of measurement to identify related waves remains vital. In this way the

TABLE 6.3 Wave Relationships from the Rest of the Move

Wave (a)		Ratio	Projection	Actual
Wave -a-	1.1986			1.1986
Wave -b-	1.1986 −	Wave -a- * 76.4% =	1.1904	1.1903
Wave -c-	1.1903 +	Wave -a- * 95.4% =	1.2005	1.2005
Wave -i-	1.2005			1.2005
Wave -ii-	1.2005 −	Wave -i- * 66.7% =	1.1921	1.1921
Wave -a-	1.2152			1.2152
Wave -b-	1.2152 −	Wave -a- * 50.0% =	1.2037	1.2045
Wave -c-	1.2045 +	Wave -a- * 109.2% =	1.2297	1.2297
Wave -iii-	1.1921 +	Wave -i- * 298.4% =	1.2297	1.2297
Wave -iv-	1.2297 −	Wave -iii- * 33.3% =	1.2172	1.2167
Wave -a-	1.2352			1.2352
Wave -b-	1.2352 −	Wave -a- * 61.8% =	1.2238	1.2241
Wave -c-	1.2241 +	Wave -c- * 123.6% =	1.2470	1.2466
Wave -v-	1.2167 +	Wave -i- > -iii- * 66.7% =	1.2446	1.2466

correct count is normally achieved. The rest of the move was fairly straightforward, with the wave relationships shown in Table 6.3.

It can be seen that the wave relationships began with a great deal of precision. While there is always an element of error in forecasting, the count can be established once the underlying move has begun to be established.

So now, having established the Wave (a) of Wave (iv), the next move is to identify the Wave (b), and this occurred at 1.2150 which was just over a 50% retracement. At this point it would be possible to judge whether the rest of the anticipated move to the 1.3234 target can be made by a single Wave (c) or whether there could be a series of ABC moves . . .

Again, Figure 6.11 may not be easy to view, but the answer was not particularly obvious. It is not impossible for a projection in

ABC WAVES	Trend end															
	1.1879	9.00%	14.60%	23.60%	33.30%	38.20%	41.40%	50.00%	58.60%	61.80%	66.66%	76.40%	85.40%	90.02%	95.40%	98.60%
Wave A	1.2466	1.2413	1.2380	1.2327	1.2271	1.2242	1.2223	1.2173	1.2122	1.2103	1.2075	1.2018	1.1965	1.1938	1.1906	1.1887
53.83% Wave B	1.2150		85.40% 1.2651	94.40% 1.2704	100.00% 1.2737	105.60% 1.2770	109.20% 1.2791	114.60% 1.2823	123.60% 1.2876	138.20% 1.2961	161.80% 1.3100	166.70% 1.3129	176.40% 1.3185	185.40% 1.3238	195.40% 1.3297	223.60% 1.3463
184.67% Wave C	1.3234	76.40% 1.2598														

FIGURE 6.11 Wave Projections

Wave (c) to be as short as 85.4% or as long at 261.8%. Of note was the 185.4% projection, which implied a target at 1.3238, so just four points above the 58.6% retracement in Wave (iv).

Therefore, from this 1.2150 Wave (b) low it would still require care to judge whether the move would end in a simple Zigzag or as much as a Triple Three. From this point, more uncertainties can cloud judgment of the wave structure until it becomes clearer. Eventually this ended not at 1.3234 but at 1.3333, which was just above a 61.8% retracement in Wave (iv). Referring back to Figure 6.9, the risk of a high developing was rising by the 1.3234 area as a bearish divergence was developing. There was also a rising wedge, and when this finally broke the reversal became clear.

Of course, on the assumption that the wave interpretation is correct, the next step is to identify potential targets in Wave (v) and then follow the wave structure to ensure that it develops in an (a)(b)(c) structure with the first Wave (a) stalling just above or below the 1.1879 low.

Taking the following confirmed levels:

> Wave B   1.4578
> Wave (i)   1.4028
> Wave (ii)   1.4192
> Wave (iii) 1.1879
> Wave (iv)   1.3333

The following projections in Wave (v) can be identified:

> 61.8%   1.1665
> 66.7%   1.1533
> 76.4%   1.1271

In addition, a suitable projection in Wave C must coincide with the Wave (v) of Wave C:

> Wave A   1.4217
> Wave B   1.4578

Given that the anticipated Wave C must be below 1.1879, one method of attempting to find common targets would be by calculating

A Case Study in EURUSD

the extension in Wave C required to reach those three Wave (v) targets. These generated the following projection ratios:

    1.1665   314.6%
    1.1533   328.8%
    1.1270   357.24% (which if adjusted to a 361.8% projection would imply 1.1228)

Therefore the two areas to be observed are the 1.1665 area—which being 25 points above a major weekly swing low should be treated with respect—and the 1.1228–70 area.

That's all well and good, but given the extreme nature of the Wave C projection it will be vital to ensure that the decline proceeds in a manner that would confirm a three-wave decline in Wave (v). While I like the idea of a new low, I do have reservations due to the monthly dollar bearish cycles which appear to suggest a new high above 1.6036. Any delay in a decline needs to be identified at an early stage to ensure that full advantage can be made of the anticipated resumption of dollar losses.

PROGRESSION SINCE THE ORIGINAL ANALYSIS

As mentioned above I was always concerned about the extreme projections in making this count work, and observed the decline from the 1.3333 high very closely. This began to develop quite constructively, and reached 1.2586 which was just above a 50% correction of the entire rally from the 1.1879 low.

The 50% area provided an early warning that if further losses were not seen promptly then the decline may well be corrective in nature. It was not really deep enough to be the Wave (a) of Wave (v) and therefore the break areas for the reversal were fairly obvious.

Figure 6.12 indicates the decline did provide a bullish divergence (not shown) from where a recovery was seen. It was not possible to consider the 1.2586 low to be Wave efb of an Expanded Flat as

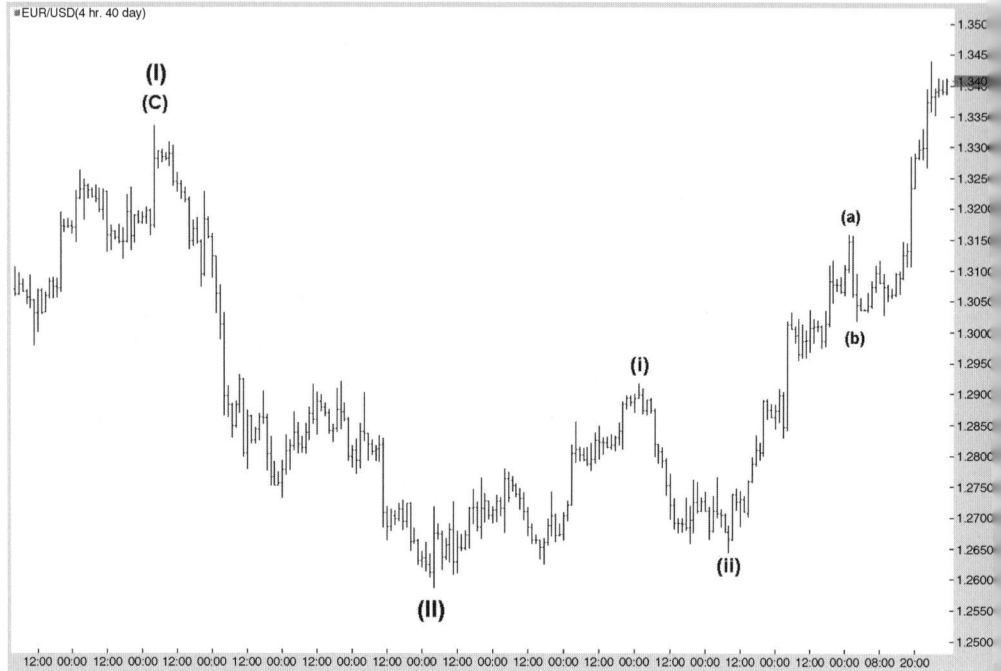

FIGURE 6.12 Pullback from 1.333 and Reversal Higher
Source: FXtrek IntelliChart™ in collaboration with FX-Strategy.com Pro Charts™

the expansion was just too large. Therefore, while it may have been possible to make an argument for the low to be Wave (a) and the peak (labeled Wave (ii)) Wave (b), this would have been stretching the imagination. It wasn't impossible, but the subsequent break higher would (and did) break down any chance of a Wave (v) developing.

At this point I had to concede that the 1.1879 low was the final low, and with monthly cycles now pointing higher for two years the overall risk must be higher. Therefore the 1.3333 high, having developed in three waves, is labeled Wave (I) and the 1.2586 low Wave (II), following which we appear to have seen Wave (i) and Wave (ii) of Wave (A) with Wave (iii) under development. This does imply a minimum 176.4% projection in Wave (III) above 1.50.

CONCLUSION

The reasoning for including this analysis, which in many ways I did not handle too well, was to highlight two important issues.

Firstly, this sort of thing still happens even with the harmonic structure. However, what I hope has been demonstrated is that with a greater understanding of structure and relationships, while the underlying recognition of the entire structure lacked on several occasions, for the majority of the move it was possible to adjust my outlook based on structure and this enabled correct analysis for much of the move. It was recognizing the key areas that would alter the overall structure and the implications that generated the next targets. This ability to shift perception and understand where a structure changed also allows the analyst to recognize quickly when a new structure needs to be employed.

Secondly, I was able to identify key turning points with accuracy throughout, even if the ultimate assumption would prove incorrect. This enables the analyst to provide a more consistent view and avoid chopping and changing an outlook between bullish and bearish too frequently. Using good momentum tools can also warn of when a structural count is breaking down, so a full gamut of technical tools can guide the analyst through many difficult situations.

At all times, even when allowing for the decline in the euro to much lower levels than I had originally expected, I remained with an overall bullish view from a cyclic perspective. Well, that is still to be proven and perhaps I shall be wrong again. However, this type of background expectation proves invaluable in maintaining perspective when movements go against the preferred analysis. Perhaps some will be able to combine this with fundamental analysis, but I still note the broad spread of fundamental opinions on the dollar in general.

CHAPTER 7

The Modified Structure in Other Markets

The vast majority of examples I have provided, naturally because I am primarily a forex analyst, are from the forex market. However, for the modifications I am proposing to be relevant they clearly need to be applicable to all markets and all time frames.

At first I was uncertain whether this would be the case. However, from the markets I have studied I have been pleasantly surprised by the soundness of the modified harmonic structure. In this chapter I shall present a range of examples with, in most cases, the outlook as I feel things are developing.

DOW JONES INDUSTRIAL AVERAGE

A first choice must naturally be a major stock index, and given the turmoil over the past two years I have taken a look at the Dow Jones Industrial Average (DJIA) to try to ascertain whether the decline from the 14,198.10 high was merely a correction or whether there are further losses to come.

FIGURE 7.1 DJIA Decline from the 14,198.10 High in a Triple Three
Source: Created with TradeStation. ©TradeStation Technologies, Inc. All rights reserved.

I have chosen the daily chart (Figure 7.1) to highlight what I feel is the likelihood that the entire decline from the peak was a complete correction and not just a complex correction that could keep it trading in a range for some years. I have counted this as a Triple Three which therefore implies the next larger move will be a rally that will reach new highs. I did find that some ratios were not quite as precise as I have found in the forex markets, but the vast majority of projections and retracements were within a reasonable variance of the calculated levels (Table 7.1).

The first ABC decline worked quite well, although the 141.4% projection in Wave (c) has never been a common ratio seen in Wave (c). However, the 58.6% retracement in Wave (x) is very common and came close to the actual final stalling point.

Table 7.2 lists the next two ABC declines.

The Modified Structure in Other Markets

TABLE 7.1 DJIA Projections

DJIA First (a)(b)(c)(x)		Ratio	Projection	Actual
Wave (a)	12724.09			12724.09
Wave (b)	12724.09 +	Wave (a) * 66.67% =	13706.67	13780.11
Wave (c)	13780.11 −	Wave (a) * 141.4% =	11695.86	11634.82
Wave a	12676.74			12676.74
Wave b	12676.74 −	Wave a * 90.02% =	11738.80	11731.60
Wave c	11731.60 +	Wave a * 138.2% =	13171.53	13136.69
Wave (x)	11634.82 +	(a) > (c) * 58.6% =	13136.90	13136.69

TABLE 7.2 ABC Declines

DJIA Second (a)(b)(c)		Ratio	Projection	Actual
Wave i	12442.59			12442.59
Wave ii	12442.59 +	Wave i * 41.4% =	12729.95	12726.66
Wave iii	12726.66 −	Wave i * 276.4% =	10808.17	10827.71
Wave iv	10827.71 +	Wave iii * 58.6% =	11940.49	11867.11
Wave v	11867.11 −	Wave i > iii * 61.8% =	10440.16	10459.44
Wave (a)	10459.44			10459.44
Wave (b)	10459.44 +	Wave (a) * 38.2% =	11482.15	11483.05
Wave i	10753.57			10753.57
Wave ii	10753.57 +	Wave i * 58.6% =	11181.05	11168.06
Wave iii	11168.06 −	Wave i * 223.6% =	9536.94	9525.32
Wave iv	9525.32 +	Wave iii * 38.2% =	10152.85	10124.03
Wave v	10124.03 −	Wave i > iii * 141.4% =	7945.97	7882.51
Wave (c)	11483.05 −	Wave (a) * 133.3% =	7914.28	7882.51

(continued)

TABLE 7.2 (Continued)

DJIA Second (a)(b)(c)		Ratio	Projection	Actual
Wave (x)				
Wave efa	7882.51 +	Wave (a)(b)(c) * 38.2% =	9889.61	9794.37
Wave efb	9794.37 −	Wave efa * 23.6% =	7431.31	7449.38
Wave efc	7449.38 +	Wave efa * 85.4% =	9082.11	9088.86
Wave (x)	9088.86			9088.86
DJIA Third (a)(b)(c)				
Wave (a)	7909.03			7909.03
Wave (b)	7909.03 +	Wave (a) * 41.4% =	8397.48	8405.87
Wave i	7845.31			7845.31
Wave ii	7845.31 +	Wave i * 85.4% =	8324.03	8315.07
Wave iii	8315.07 −	Wave i * 223.6% =	7061.66	7105.94
Wave iv	7105.94 +	Wave iii * 23.6% =	7391.29	7404.94
Wave v	7404.94 −	Wave i > iii * 76.4% =	6411.79	6469.95
Wave (c)	8405.48 −	Wave (a) * 161.8% =	6496.91	6469.95

The rest of the ratios were quite convincing to me that the index has seen a Triple Three, and thus overall we should be looking for a new high at some point.

Monthly Chart from Inception

Having seen that the decline to the 6,469.95 low was corrective I was rather surprised. All I had been hearing were extremely pessimistic forecasts, plenty of doom and gloom, and how the index would remain subdued for perhaps a decade or more. The prospect of new highs intrigued me, and I knew I should include the analysis for the super-cycle picture. I have to say that once again I was wondering

The Modified Structure in Other Markets 185

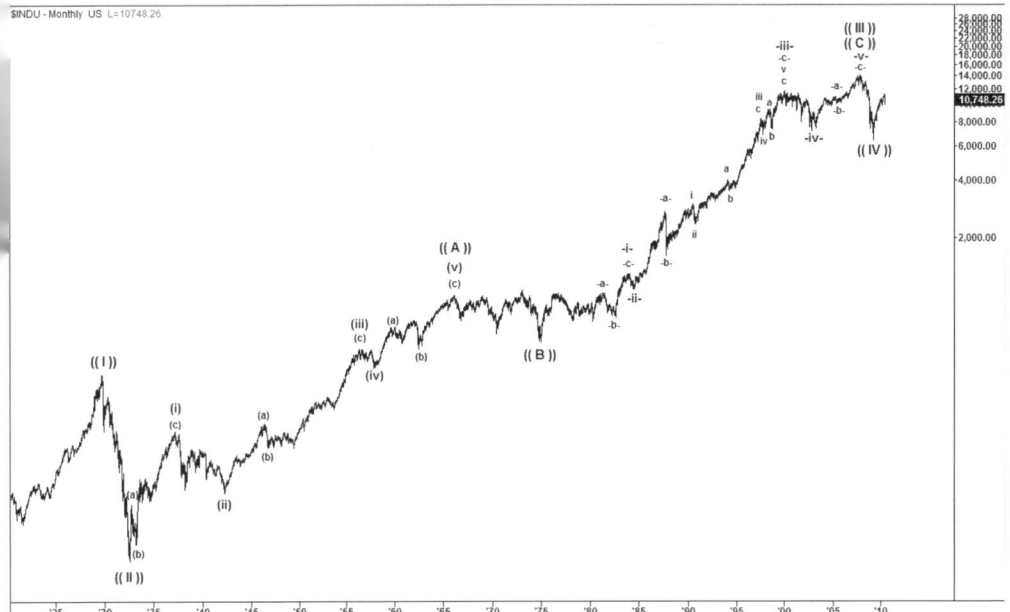

FIGURE 7.2 DJIA Rally from just before the 1930s Crash
Source: Created with TradeStation. ©TradeStation Technologies, Inc. All rights reserved.

what I would discover and had no real prior expectation of what I would find.

I found the result partly gratifying because the monthly chart confirmed the harmonic structure and also that a new price high is to be expected. However, I was rather shocked with the outcome.

Figure 7.2 displays the monthly DJIA chart from just before the 1930s crash. In looking at the chart for the first time with harmonic glasses the remarkable clarity of the harmonic structure hit me immediately. As much as I was convinced by merely eyeballing the chart, I wanted to confirm this to ensure the projection ratios were valid and the projection targets across the different wave degrees matched.

I had to decide on the starting value. I searched on the Internet and discovered that the first quotation for the DJIA wasn't until some time after Charles Dow compiled the original constituent members of the index. When this was quoted it was already above the 40.56 low that eventually occurred following the 1930s crash. Clearly it

TABLE 7.3 DJIA Wave Relationships from Figure 7.2

DJIA MONTHLY		Ratio	Projection	Actual
Wave ((I))	386.10			386.10
Wave ((II))	386.10 −	Wave ((I)) * 95.43% =	41.50	40.56
Wave ((A))	1001.11			1001.11
Wave ((B))	1001.11 −	Wave ((A)) * 50.0% =	520.84	570.01
Wave ((C))	570.01 +	Wave ((A)) * 1414% =	14152.19	14198.10
Wave ((III))	40.56 +	Wave ((I)) * 3902% =	14130.68	14198.10
Wave ((IV))	14,198.10 −	Wave ((III)) * 50.0% =	7119.33	6469.95
Wave ((V)) projections				
58.60%	6,469.95 +	Wave ((I)) > ((III)) * 58.6% =	14775.39	
61.80%	6,469.95 +	Wave ((I)) > ((III)) * 61.8% =	15288.93	
66.70%	6,469.95 +	Wave ((I)) > ((III)) * 66.6% =	15923.41	
76.40%	6,469.95 +	Wave ((I)) > ((III)) * 76.4% =	17298.20	

had to begin below 40.56, and I did discover a quote of 25.56. The accuracy is open to debate, but what I found is that in projecting a Wave ((III)) target the variance in projections with a starting value from as low as 10.00 made minimal difference to the final targets.

My findings imply that the 14,198.10 high is only Wave ((III)) while the correction in Wave ((IV)) was just over a 50% retracement of Wave ((III)). Table 7.3 shows the ratios.

In general, the retracement ratios were similar to any other wave development, with many close to either 50% or 66.6%. Note that using the assumed starting value of 25.56 the 1930s crash retraced a steep 95.43%, and Wave ((B)) and Wave ((IV)) were both close to 50%.

However, the biggest issue with such an extensive five-wave move was in justifying the projection ratios in the extensions. I found it interesting that while in forex a very deep extension in Wave (iii) could project by 290.02% or even 390.02%, in this case Wave ((III))

The Modified Structure in Other Markets **187**

had extended by a multiple of 10 times this larger figure—a 3,902% projection.

What was therefore important for me to feel comfortable with in this ratio is that the intrinsic wave relationships in Wave ((A)) and Wave ((C)) should also confirm this same area. The 1,414% projection in Wave ((C)), which appears to be a 10 times multiple of 141.4%, is also unusual. This is another area that I wanted to confirm more closely.

Table 7.4 shows Wave ((A)) and Wave ((B)).

The retracement and projection ratios throughout Wave ((A)) are all very common and generated targets very close to the actual

TABLE 7.4 Wave ((A)) and Wave ((B))

Wave ((A))		Ratio	Projection	Actual
Wave (a)	81.39			81.39
Wave (b)	81.39 −	Wave (a) * 76.4% =	50.20	49.68
Wave (c)	49.68 +	Wave (a) * 361.8% =	197.40	195.59
Wave (i)	195.59			195.59
Wave (ii)	195.59 −	Wave (i) * 66.6% =	92.25	92.69
Wave (a)	213.36			213.36
Wave (b)	213.36 −	Wave (a) * 41.4% =	163.40	160.49
Wave (c)	160.49 +	Wave (a) * 296.5% =	518.28	524.37
Wave (iii)	92.69 +	Wave (i) * 276.4% =	521.19	524.37
Wave (iv)	524.37 −	Wave (iii) * 23.6% =	422.49	416.15
Wave (a)	688.21			688.21
Wave (b)	688.21 −	Wave (a) * 58.6% =	528.78	524.55
Wave (c)	524.55 +	Wave (a) * 176.4% =	1004.46	1001.11
Wave (v)	416.15 +	Wave (i) > (iii) * 123.6% =	1014.14	1001.11
Wave ((B))				
Wave ((A))	1001.11			1001.11
Wave ((B))	1,001.11 −	Wave ((A)) * 50.0% =	520.84	570.01

respective wave terminations. If there are any that deviated very far from the norm then the 123.6% projection in the extended Wave (v) is more than I would normally expect in forex. The retracement in Wave ((B)) was also a deviation from an exact 50%. However, this is not uncommon and does not really detract from the overall structure.

Table 7.5 shows the relationships in Wave ((C)).

TABLE 7.5 Wave ((C))

Wave ((C))		Ratio	Projection	Actual
Wave -a-	1030.98			1030.98
Wave -b-	1,030.98 −	Wave -a- 23.6* % =	922.19	910.96
Wave -c-	910.96 +	Wave -a- * 85.4% =	1304.63	1296.95
Wave -i-				1296.95
Wave -ii-	1,296.95 −	Wave -i- * 33.3% =	1054.88	1078.95
Wave -a-				2746.65
Wave -b-	2,746.65 −	Wave -a- * 66.6% =	1634.96	1616.21
Wave -c-	1,616.21 +	Wave -a- * 609.02% =	11772.84	11749.97
Wave -iii-	1078.95	Wave -i- * 1460% =	11692.27	11.749.97
Wave -iv-	11749.97	Wave -iii- * 41.4% =	7332.17	7197.49
Wave -a-	10984.46			10984.46
Wave -b-	10,984.46 −	Wave -a- * 23.6% =	10086.49	10000.46
Wave -c-	10,000.46 +	Wave -a- * 109.02% =	14148.64	14198.10
Wave -v-	7,197.49 +	Wave -i- > -iii- * 61.8% =	14106.71	14198.10
Wave -c-				
Wave i	3024.26			3024.26
Wave ii	3,024.26 −	Wave i * 50.0% =	2320.24	2344.31
Wave iii	2,344.31 +	Wave i * 423.6% =	8308.81	8340.14
Wave iv	8340.14 −	Wave iii * 23.6% =	6925.12	6927.12
Wave v	6,927.12 +	Wave i > iii * 109.02% =	14257.55	14198.10

Once again the ratios are mostly very commonly seen, with just a few exceptions. Wave -iii- and the Wave -c- projection in Wave -iii- are really the two which stand out as being more questionable. The Wave -c- projection of 609.02% is one I can accept as being in line with commonly seen 109.02% ratios. The Wave -iii- of 1,460% can only be described as unusual. While it has a link to the 14.6%, the multiple of 100 in a Wave -iii- position is not one I would expect.

For this to be considered acceptable I need the resultant wave ratios connected with Wave -iii- to conform more closely to normal values. The 41.4% retracement in Wave -iv- is very common. The 61.8% projection in Wave -v- (from the Wave -iv- corrective low) is also very common. Equally the intrinsic ratios of the Wave -b- and Wave -c- of Wave -v- are also common.

Therefore I consider the entire wave count from the inception of the index to the Wave ((III)) high to have a strong chance of being correct. That being the case, the implication is for a five-wave rally in Wave ((a)) to around the 14,198.10 area followed by a pullback in Wave ((b)) and then Wave ((c)) to match with one of the Wave ((V)) projection targets.

This will effectively see the completion of what will then be labeled Wave {A} of higher degree, to be followed by what may well be an extensive Wave {B} that could indeed extend over at least two decades and potentially more.

Progression since the Original Analysis

Several months have passed since I began writing this book and therefore the initial stages of the anticipated Wave (A) of Wave ((V)) have already begun to develop, and in a constructive manner. I shall therefore present the subsequent waves since the Wave ((IV)) low at 6,496.95. As mentioned, the ultimate target for this first move in Wave ((V)) would normally complete just below or just above the Wave ((III)) high. This information should be kept in mind in order that appropriate stalling areas for each leg are in approximately the right levels that would imply this sort of target area.

At this stage I wasn't actively analyzing this market and can only offer comments on the characteristics. Indeed, it was only soon after the low that I even began to look at the chart. At that point I had not analyzed the decline and, influenced by the general pessimism, I had assumed that this was just a Wave (a) lower. Therefore when I began to look at the recovery I was looking more for corrective patterns. I finally made the analysis of the decline in the preparation for this book around January 2010, and was so taken aback by my findings that I decided to obtain monthly history dating back as far as I could. This is when I first saw the monthly chart in Figure 7.2. My first impression was that it looks exactly like a Harmonic move, with the sweep higher following the 1930s crash resembling a three-wave Wave ((III)). When I went through the wave relationships I was again astounded at the projections, but could find no other way to effectively rationalize the wave development.

Thus, it was only around the peak in Wave iii of Wave (a) of Wave (iii) that I began to reappraise the wave structure with bullish eyes. It was only after the peak at Wave (a) that finally I had access to intraday data and began to observe movements more closely and formulate targets. I shall provide that after the description of the rally to Wave (a) of Wave (iii).

Figure 7.3 displays the initial Wave (i), Wave (ii), and Wave (a). The initial recovery after the Wave ((IV)) low quickly moved higher and it was quite difficult to judge from the daily chart exactly where Wave -a- ended. At this point the focus should be on where the Wave (i) is mostly likely going to end. The area around the last swing highs within the decline would normally provide natural price resistance, and using momentum as a possible indication of an exhaustion of the rally, efforts should be made to tie up the possible Wave -a-, Wave -b-, and final Wave -c- in a manner that would identify a target in this area. As can be seen in Figure 7.3, there was a solid bearish divergence between the Wave iii and Wave (i) peaks.

The next problem would be identifying where Wave (ii) will complete. This is probably one of the most difficult points of the early wave structure as a Wave (ii) can retrace as little as 14.6% or as much as 100%. It is not uncommon for the internal wave count to be

The Modified Structure in Other Markets   **191**

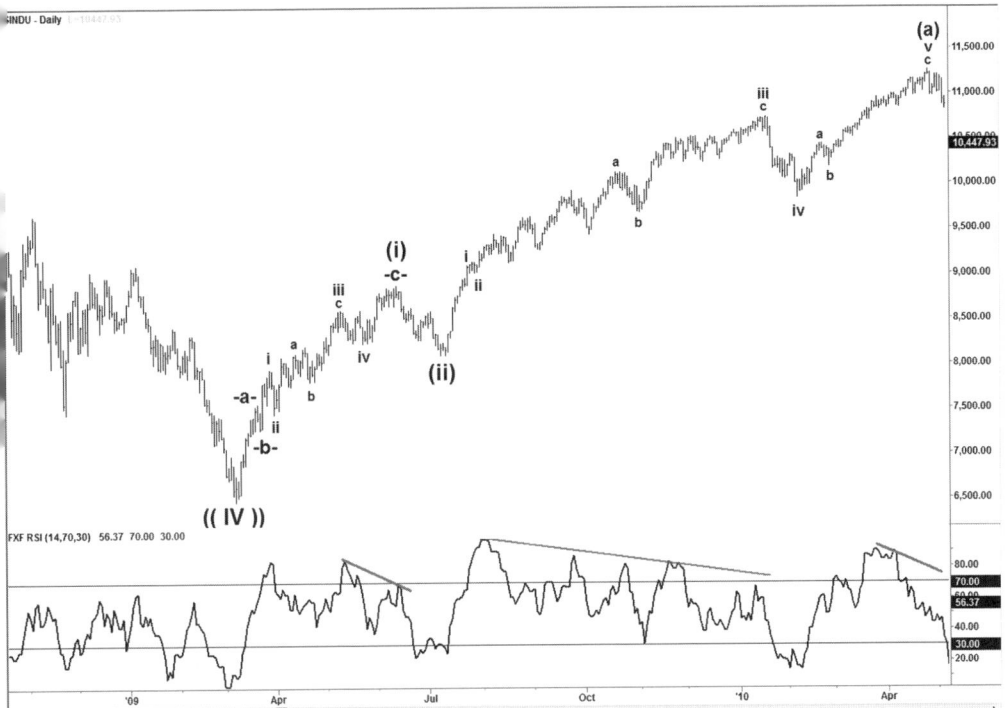

FIGURE 7.3 DJIA Rally in Waves (i), (ii), and Wave (a) of Wave ((a))
Source: Created with TradeStation. ©TradeStation Technologies, Inc. All rights reserved.

erratic, causing confusion as to whether it has completed a Double Zigzag or even a simple Zigzag that could be followed by a Triangle, Flat, or Expanded Flat. In the last case it can cause a defensive approach to allow for an Expanded Flat, which delays confirmation of the resumption of the rally, which occurred in this case where Wave (a) developed sharply. However, once the 38.2% expansion had been overcome there could be more confidence in the analysis.

Table 7.6 displays the wave relationships for Waves (i) and (ii) with the breakdown of the five-wave rally in Wave -c- provided at the bottom of the table.

While the correction in Wave -b- was close to a 33.3% retracement, the projection in Wave -c- was more approximate, with the final stalling point a little in excess of a 138.2% extension. These tend

TABLE 7.6 Waves (i) and (ii) with the Breakdown of the Five-Wave Rally in Wave -c-

DJIA Daily Wave (i) & (ii)		Ratio	Projection	Actual
Wave -a-	7571.64			7571.64
Wave -b-	7571.64 −	Wave -a- * 33.3% =	7204.78	7257.83
Wave -c-	7257.83 +	Wave -a- * 138.2% =	8780.37	8877.93
Wave (i)	8877.93			8877.93
Wave (ii)	8877.93 −	Wave (i) * 33.3% =	8076.07	8087.34
Wave i	7931.33			7931.33
Wave ii	7931.33 −	Wave i * 76.4% =	7416.78	7437.59
Wave a	8190.66			8190.66
Wave b	8190.66 −	Wave a * 50.0% =	7814.13	7791.95
Wave c	7791.95 +	Wave a * 105.6% =	8587.19	8587.55
Wave iii	7437.59 +	Wave i * 166.7% =	8560.31	8587.55
Wave iv	7437.59 −	Wave iii * 33.3% =	8204.61	8221.01
Wave v	8221.01 +	Wave i > iii * 50.0% =	8885.57	8877.93

to be a little disconcerting, but what made this situation provide more confidence was the common wave relationships through the entire five-wave rally. I have noted that compared to forex the DJIA has a tendency toward 50% projections in Wave (v), and sometimes less. In this case the Wave v was almost exactly 50%.

Wave (ii) stalled at the 33.3% retracement, and from there the rally resumed in a very aggressive manner. This again made the identification of Wave i very difficult indeed. While potential targets in Wave (iii) could be generated at this point that would slot into a subsequent Wave (iv) and Wave (v) that would imply a final high in Wave ((a)) around the 14,198.10 high, the problem is that the Waves (a), (b), and (c) could hold any number of ratios and thus there is no real way of working out how this would finally develop.

The Modified Structure in Other Markets   **193**

Thus, the uncertainty of where Wave i actually ended will have caused confusion for the rest of the rally. Momentum for much of the gains was displaying a bearish divergence but none of the pullbacks penetrated a prior swing low. This was also true of the Wave iv. Rather ironically, the final high in Wave v and Wave (a) produced only a minor bearish divergence. If there were any clues along the way, then the 50% retracement in Wave b of Wave iii was one that could have provided stronger evidence that there would be a Wave c to complete Wave iii. It would also be possible to link the correction in Wave b and also Wave iv to a possible Wave ii low since they both have direct relationships with Wave ii.

As I mentioned earlier, it was only from just after the Wave iii of Wave (a) when I made the analysis of the decline from the 14,198.10 high and then the entire rally from the 1880s that I personally started to become bullish. I can only look at the chart and feel the bullish analysis may have been hard to follow.

After the peak of Wave iii and having analyzed the monthly chart I became bullish. By the time the Wave (a) peak had been confirmed I found the wave structure much clearer, and observation of the hourly charts made the entire analysis come together. The clear conclusion was that Wave (b) would retrace the rally from the Wave (ii) low at 8,087.34. The rally until this point has been quite direct, so while Wave (b) can be shallow the potential for a 50% retracement, perhaps more to 58.6% or 61.8%, was quite possible.

As shown in Figure 7.4, the correction in Wave (b) developed very sharply in the initial stages, eventually seeing a choppy decline in a Triple Three to 9,614.32. The 50% retracement was at 9,672.68 and 58.6% at 9,400.00. At this point many fund managers were talking about the 200-day moving average, which was penetrated several times toward the lows, and discussing whether the index would extend losses or recover.

This decline had reached around 15%, which I understand is a general rule-of-thumb to indicate a bear market and based on the historic moves from the 1880s. Looking back at Figure 7.2, it is quite obvious that corrections have been shallow and this will increase the potential for deeper retracements as price moves higher. The drop to

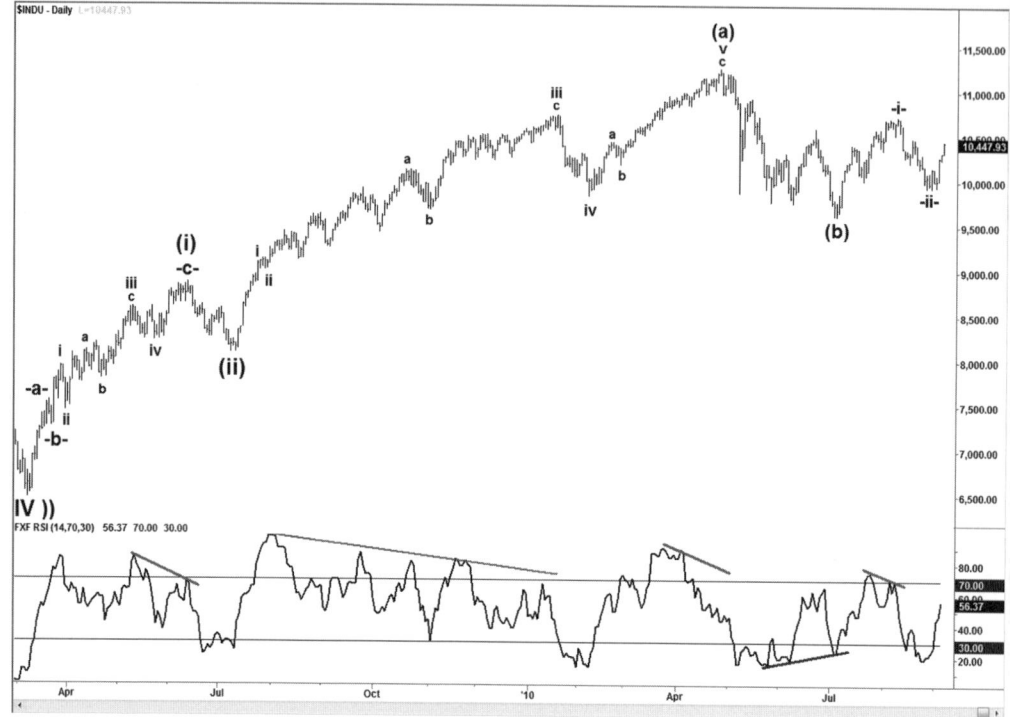

FIGURE 7.4 Correction in Wave (b) of Wave (iii)
Source: Created with TradeStation. ©TradeStation Technologies, Inc. All rights reserved.

the 2009 low at 6,496.95 is ample evidence of this. I suspect the risk is we shall see deeper retracements as we move to the final high that will repeatedly provoke corrections of over 15% that will cause not only the rule to cause some confusion but also see the 200-day moving average to be whipsawed on many more occasions. Thus, around the Wave (b) low, Harmonic Elliott Wave was indicating a recovery was due.

Figure 7.5 displays the hourly chart from the 9,614.32 Wave (b) low. According to the implied wave count there should be a five-wave rally to new highs to reach a projection drawn from the daily Wave (i) that should match a projection in Wave (c). Therefore the initial move should begin with a three-wave Wave -i-.

The Modified Structure in Other Markets

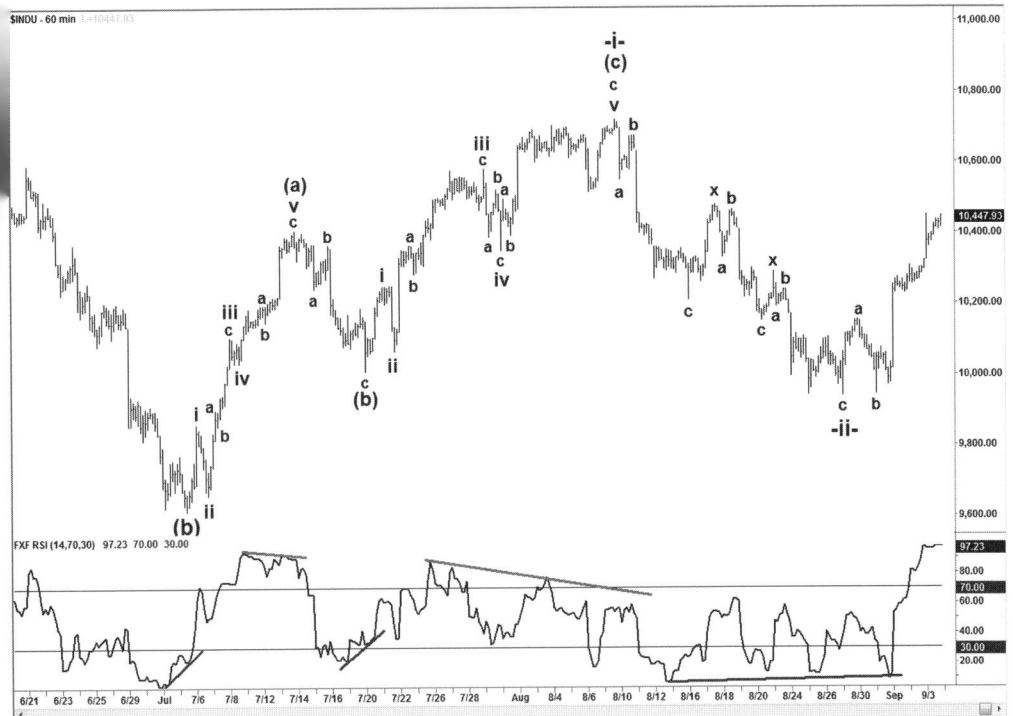

FIGURE 7.5 Development in Wave -i- and Wave -ii- of Wave (c)
Source: Created with TradeStation. ©TradeStation Technologies, Inc. All rights reserved.

The first rally would most probably stall just below the last Wave -b- in the decline from 11,258.01. Indeed, the Wave (a) of Wave -i- did just that, and provoked a correction in Wave (b) that slipped just below the previous Wave iv of Wave (a) to a 50% retracement. From there a further five-wave rally developed that extended 90.2% of Wave (a) to complete Wave -i- and generate a pullback in Wave -ii- that corrected between 66.7% and 76.4%.

The following tables provide the wave relationships for each section of the entire rally and correction.

Table 7.7 shows Wave (a) and (b) of Wave -i-. All the projections were reflective of the normal ratios for each respective move, with the exception of Wave c of Wave v which extended by an unusual

TABLE 7.7 Wave (a) and (b) of Wave -i-

Wave (a) & (b) of Wave		Ratio	Projection	Actual
Wave i	9857.60			9857.60
Wave ii	9857.60 −	Wave i * 85.4% =	9649.90	9659.16
Wave a	9898.24			9898.24
Wave b	9898.24 −	Wave a * 23.6% =	9841.82	9854.20
Wave c	9854.20 +	Wave a * 109.2% =	10115.28	10115.08
Wave iii	9659.16 +	Wave i * 185.4% =	10110.07	10115.08
Wave iv	10115.08 −	Wave iii * 14.6% =	10048.52	10032.73
Wave a	10216.64			10216.64
Wave b	10216.64 −	Wave a * 38.2% =	10146.39	10146.56
Wave c	10146.56 +	Wave a * 141.4% =	10406.51	10407.52
Wave v	10032.73 +	Wave i > iii * 76.4% =	10415.26	10407.52
Wave (a)	10407.52			10407.52
Wave a	10240.56			10240.56
Wave b	10240.56 +	Wave a * 85.4% =	10383.14	10378.98
Wave c	10378.98 −	Wave a * 223.6% =	10005.66	10008.21
Wave (b)	10407.52 −	Wave (a) * 50.0% =	10010.96	10008.21

141.4%, representing a harmonic extension. However, this was within 10.00 of the 76.4% projection in Wave v. The correction in Wave (b) was just about exactly 50%, with a 223.6% projection in Wave c, a ratio that doesn't occur frequently but one I have also noted in the forex market.

Table 7.8 shows Wave (c) of Wave -i-. The five-wave rally in Wave (c) developed with greater correlation of projected targets throughout, culminating in a 66.7% projection in Wave v, implying a target 12.6 above the final stalling point which matched with the 90.2% projection in Wave (c) after a solid bearish divergence.

The Modified Structure in Other Markets

TABLE 7.8 Wave (c) of Wave -i-

Wave (c) of Wave -i-		Ratio	Projection	Actual
Wave (a)	10008.21			10008.21
Wave i	10264.85			10264.85
Wave ii	10264.85 −	Wave i * 76.4% =	10068.78	10065.66
Wave a	10363.09			10363.09
Wave b	10363.09 −	Wave a * 23.6% =	10292.90	10282.45
Wave c	10282.45 +	Wave a * 100.0% =	10579.88	10584.69
Wave iii	10065.66 +	Wave i * 198.4% =	10574.83	10584.69
Wave a	10388.22			10388.22
Wave b	10388.22 +	Wave a * 66.7% =	10519.19	10522.25
Wave c	10522.25 −	Wave a * 90.2% =	10345.03	10347.50
Wave iv	10584.69 −	Wave iii * 41.4% =	10369.81	10347.50
Wave a	10495.99			10495.99
Wave b	10495.99 −	Wave a * 66.7% =	10397.01	10393.59
Wave c	10393.59 +	Wave a * 223.6% =	10725.61	10719.94
Wave v	10347.50 +	Wave i > iii * 66.7% =	10732.01	10719.94
Wave (c)	10008.21 +	Wave (a) * 90.2% =	10723.61	10719.94
Wave -i-	10719.94			10719.94

With Wave (a) and Wave (b) completed it was possible to generate projection targets in Wave (c) through my spreadsheet (shown in Figure 7.6).

At this point it would not be possible to know the final stalling area, but through the development of the Wave (c) the Wave v should provide a target close to one of these areas. This high was then Wave -i- of the Wave (c) of one higher degree, being part of the anticipated daily Wave (iii). Using the spreadsheet again the potential targets can be generated (Figure 7.7).

ABC WAVES	Trend end	9614.39									
	Wave A	10407.52	9.02%	14.60%	23.60%	33.30%	38.20%	41.40%	50.00%	58.60%	61.80%	66.66%
50.35%	Wave B	10008.21	10335.98	10291.72	10220.34	10143.41	10104.54	10079.16	10010.96	9942.75	9917.37	9878.82
90.20%			76.40%	85.40%	90.20%	100.00%	105.60%	109.20%	114.60%	123.60%	138.20%	161.80%
	Wave C	10723.61	10614.16	10685.54	10723.61	10801.34	10845.76	10874.31	10917.14	10988.52	11104.32	11291.49

FIGURE 7.6 Projection Targets in Wave (c)

Wave (A) of Wave (III)		32.83%	189.48%	277.25%	0.00%			51.84%		95.74%
Start	Wave (i)	Wave (ii)	Wave (iii)	Wave (iv)	Wave (v)			Wave (a)	Wave (b)	Wave (c)
6469.95	8877.93	8087.34	12650.00	0.00	0.00			11258.01	9614.32	12650.00
Wave (ii)	9.02%	14.60%	23.60%	33.30%	38.20%		41.40%	50.00%	58.60%	61.80%
Retracements	8660.73	8526.36	8309.65	8076.07	7958.08		7881.03	7673.94	7466.85	7389.80
Wave (iii)	161.80%	166.70%	176.40%	185.40%	190.20%		195.40%	223.60%	261.80%	276.40%
Projections	11983.45	12101.44	12335.02	12551.73	12667.32		12792.53	13471.58	14391.43	14743.00
Wave (c)	76.40%	85.40%	95.40%	100.00%	105.60%		10.20%	114.60%	123.60%	138.20%
Projections	12036.71	12322.07	12639.14	12784.99	12962.55		13076.69	13247.91	13533.27	13996.19

FIGURE 7.7 Three Prospective Target Areas

The Modified Structure in Other Markets **199**

Here it can be seen that there are three prospective target areas: at 12,322–35, being the 176.4% projection in Wave (iii) and 85.4% projection in Wave (c); at 12,639–67, being the 190.2% projection in Wave (iii) and 95.4% projection in Wave (c); and finally at 12,784–92, being the 195.4% projection in Wave (iii) and wave equality target in Wave (c). Therefore, as a general target area this wave structure implies a Wave (iii) stalling between 12,322 and 12,792.

Finally, the next move to cover is that of the Wave -ii- correction. A Wave -ii- is again one of the unknowns as it could stall after a very short retracement or a very deep one. In this case the decline came as a Triple Three and between the 66.7% and 76.4% retracement, as shown in Table 7.9.

TABLE 7.9 Triple Three Decline

Wave -ii-		Ratio	Projection	Actual
Wave -i-	10719.94			10719.94
Wave a	10552.30			10552.30
Wave b	10552.30 +	Wave a * 90.2% =	10703.21	10700.26
Wave c	10700.26 −	Wave a * 290.2% =	10213.77	10210.06
Wave x	10210.06 +	Wave abc * 50.0% =	10465.00	10480.44
Wave a	10330.09			10330.09
Wave b	10330.09 +	Wave a * 95.4% =	10473.52	10472.15
Wave c	10472.15 −	Wave a * 214.6% =	10149.50	10147.47
Wave x	10147.47 +	Wave abc * 50.0% =	10313.96	10304.70
Wave a	10191.37			10191.37
Wave b	10191.37 +	Wave a * 50.0% =	10248.04	10253.43
Wave c	10253.43 −	Wave a * 276.4% =	9940.19	9936.99
Wave -ii-	10719.94 −	Wave -i- * 66.7% =	9982.93	9936.09

The same process of estimating where Wave -iii- will stall may be made, bearing in mind the subsequent Wave -iv- and Wave -v- should imply a target close to the Wave (iii) targets. Once Wave -a- of Wave -iii- has been identified, a stronger idea of the potential projections in Wave -iii- can be generated, followed by Wave -iv-, and through this method it will be possible to home in on the most likely stalling point.

As a final point on this analysis it is imperative to understand where the wave count breaks down, and compared to Elliott's original structure it is normally much easier to identify this with greater accuracy. For me the early break level will be the 9,614.32 low that I have marked as Wave (b) of Wave (iii), as this will imply the rally from there to the 10,719.94 high then becomes a three-wave correction.

GOLD

I was asked by a subscriber about my view of gold in August 2009. This was the first time I had looked at a gold chart in many years, and therefore obviously the first time I offered any opinion on gold. I have to say that I was not prepared for what I found, or at least what I thought I found, in the wave structure. It is still a wave count that I look at and think, "Is this *really* correct?"

At that time my first target was between $1,215.64 and $1,221.00. The high for this move came in at $1,218.40, so I am cautiously encouraged by the development but I still remain somewhat cautious since, as you will see from the structure, it does look quite unusual.

Firstly, to get a larger perspective I provide the monthly chart (Figure 7.8).

Since I only have data back to around 1970 I cannot be 100% certain of the wave count. However, there does seem to be logic in the current rally being a Wave (C). I have also placed on this chart what I consider to be a sound cyclic representation that seems to match with the major price lows. I suspect the next larger cycle low occurred around the Wave (B) low. This would then imply a strong

The Modified Structure in Other Markets

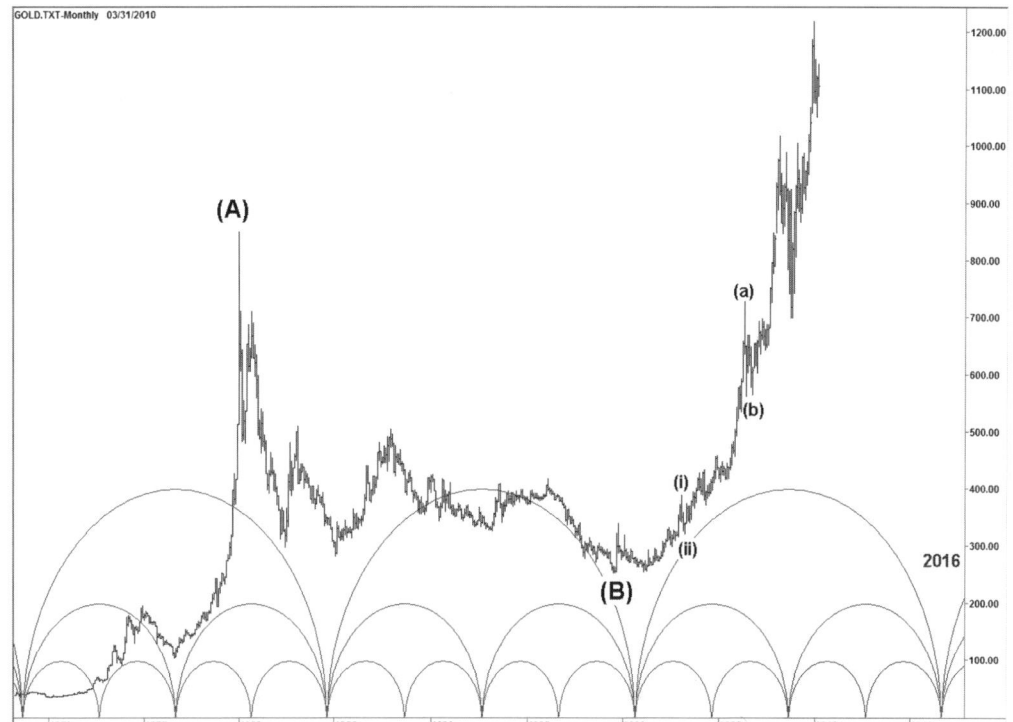

FIGURE 7.8 Monthly Gold with Underlying Cycles
Source: Created with TradeStation. ©TradeStation Technologies, Inc. All rights reserved.

major up-cycle and why we are still seeing gains at the top of the largest displayed cycle which next finds a low in 2016. That should mean that there is probably another two to three years (to 2012–2013) in the current up-cycle before a substantial correction.

In viewing this I am making a mental note that the anticipated 2012–2013 cycle high may only be the end of a major third wave with the 2016 low being the fourth. This would imply that the marked Wave (A) and Wave (B) may only be those within a larger Wave (III).

In adhering to the modified harmonic wave structure I found myself forced to look for an excessive projection in Wave (iii), otherwise the wave count just didn't make sense. As you can see in Figure 7.9, in August 2009 price had just poked above the Triangle

FIGURE 7.9 Weekly Gold Displaying an Unfinished Wave (iii) of Wave (C)
Source: Created with TradeStation. ©TradeStation Technologies, Inc. All rights reserved.

and my target was between $1,215.64 and $1,221.00. Although I was uncertain about the structure that would make up the target in Wave [c] of Wave [iii], I have been pleasantly surprised some seven months later when I updated the data that everything has held together.

Table 7.10 provides the ratios supporting the wave count.

In all instances the wave relationships are very similar to those I have found in the forex market, and the variance between projections and actual rates are within an acceptable amount.

It is perhaps the Wave (c) of Wave (iii) under development that requires a little more scrutiny with the deep Wave [b] of Wave [iii]. For this I shall also provide the daily chart (Figure 7.10).

Table 7.11 shows the wave relationships.

The Modified Structure in Other Markets

TABLE 7.10 Wave Relationships for Figure 7.9

GOLD Wave (i) & (ii)		Ratio	Projection	Actual
Wave a	338.00			338.00
Wave b	338.00 −	Wave a * 100% =	253.20	255.80
Wave c	255.80 +	Wave a * 161.80% =	393.00	384.50
Wave (i)	**384.50**			**384.50**
Wave (ii)	**384.50 −**	Wave (i) * 50.0% =	**318.85**	**320.10**
Wave (a) of Wave (iii)				
Wave -a-	374.70			374.70
Wave -b-	374.70 −	Wave -a- * 61.80% =	340.96	340.80
Wave -c-	340.80 +	Wave -a- * 166.70% =	431.80	433.00
Wave -i-	**433.00**			**433.00**
Wave -ii-	**433.00 −**	Wave -i- * 50.0% =	**376.55**	**372.00**
Wave -a-	458.20			458.20
Wave -b-	458.20 −	Wave -a- * 50.0% =	415.10	411.50
Wave -c-	**411.50 +**	Wave -a- * 194.43% =	**579.10**	**579.50**
Wave -iii-	**372.00 +**	Wave -i- * 185.40% =	**581.32**	**579.50**
Wave -iv-	**579.50 −**	Wave -iii- * 23.60% =	**530.53**	**534.50**
Wave -v-	**534.50 +**	Wave -i- > -iii- * 76.4% =	**732.68**	**728.00**
Wave (a)	728.00			728.00
Wave (b) of Wave (iii)				
Wave (a)	728.00			728.00
Wave (b)	728.00 −	Wave (a) * 41.40% =	**559.13**	**561.50**

FIGURE 7.10 Daily Gold Displaying an Unfinished Wave [c] of Wave [iii] of Larger Wave (iii)
Source: Created with TradeStation. ©TradeStation Technologies, Inc. All rights reserved.

TABLE 7.11 Wave Relationships for Figure 7.10

GOLD Wave (c) of (iii)		Ratio	Projection	Actual
Wave (b)	561.50			561.50
Wave [a]	669.00			669.00
Wave [b]	669.00 −	Wave [a] * 100% =	561.50	563.50
Wave [c]	63.50 +	Wave [a] * 123.60% =	696.37	698.00
Wave [i]	698.00			698.00
Wave [ii]	698.00 −	Wave [i] * 41.40% =	641.49	642.80

The Modified Structure in Other Markets **205**

Wave [a]	1017.50			1017.50
Wave [b]	1017.50 −	Wave [a] * 85.40% =	697.51	698.50
Wave [c] of [iii]				
Wave i	830.50			830.50
Wave ii	830.50 −	Wave i * 66.67% =	742.51	742.00
Wave a	1005.00			1005.00
Wave b	1005.00 −	Wave a * 50.0% =	873.50	866.60
Wave c	866.60 +	Wave a * 133.34% =	1217.18	1218.40
Wave iii	742.00 +	Wave i * 361.80% =	1219.58	1218.40
Wave iv Retracements				
	1218.40 −	Wave iii * 33.30% =	1059.76	
	1218.40 −	Wave iii * 38.20% =	904.53	
	1218.40 −	Wave iii * 41.4% =	896.12	
Wave [c] Projections				
	698.50 +	Wave [a] * 176.40% =	1359.47	
	698.50 +	Wave [a] * 185.40% =	1393.19	
	698.50 +	Wave [a] * 194.43% =	1427.03	
Wave [iii] Projections	642.80 +	Wave [i] * 576.4% =	1429.59	
If Wave iv = 1050.00				
Wave v	1050.00 +	Wave i > Wave iii * 61.8% =	1371.30	
Wave v	1050.00 +	Wave i > Wave iii * 66.7% =	1396.77	
	1050.00 +	Wave i > Wave iii * 76.4% =	1447.20	

The wave relationships work well, although there are two ratios that make me slightly nervous. The 85.4% retracement in Wave [b] of Wave [iii] is very, very deep, and the 361.8% projection in Wave iii of Wave [c] is likewise unusual but does work quite well.

It is not yet clear whether the Wave iv retracement is complete, although at 1,050.00 it was quite close to the 33.3% retracement at 1,059.76. I have also offered tentative potential projections for Wave [iii] and Wave v of Wave [c] which appear to point to the next target being around 1,393–1,396. However, this does include a 576.4% projection in Wave [iii], which again I am rather cautious about.

I have looked for an alternative count, but at this point the ratios are more extreme than those shown above. In terms of the wave count shown I am quite content with the implication of the target in Wave [iii], which should then be followed by a rally in Wave [v] to complete Wave (c) of Wave (iii).

Given the brief Wave (ii) and the fairly direct rally in Wave (iii), it does imply a deeper and longer lasting Wave (iv) that should finally allow a Wave (v) to develop in time for the anticipated cycle high in 2012–2013.

Progression Since the Original Analysis

As with the analysis I originally provided for the Dow Jones Industrial Average, over the time I have been writing this book the structural development of this rally has been developing in line with the analysis. Again, at the time of the original analysis I was working only with daily data, but since then I have sourced the intraday data and I shall present this later in this update. For now Figure 7.11 shows the progression since the Wave iv low.

I recall the Wave iv low shown in Figure 7.11 as a time when many analysts were exceptionally bearish, with a common target being around 860. I had one trader to whom I revealed my counting method angrily berate me, declaring that I could not change Elliott's impulsive wave structure. It seems I lost a potential subscriber as I never heard from him again!

However, price rallied well from that Wave iv low, initially in five waves to complete Wave a of Wave v and then a correction in Wave b. I also noted that my RSI was quite consistent in identifying market turns through bullish and bearish divergences.

The Modified Structure in Other Markets

FIGURE 7.11 Daily Gold Displaying the Development of Wave a and Wave b of Wave v
Source: Created with TradeStation. ©TradeStation Technologies, Inc. All rights reserved.

In Figure 7.12 I expanded the daily chart to show the rally in Wave a and correction in Wave b more clearly.

In Figure 7.12 the rally in Wave a of Wave v can be seen with more clarity. Wave (ii) developed as an Expanded Flat, following which the normal development of Wave (iii), Wave (iv), and Wave (v) was seen. The correction in Wave b developed in three waves, and from there price has pushed back to the 1,265 high but with a bearish divergence having developed in my RSI. From this perspective, due to the tendency for divergences to provoke a reversal I must allow for a (possible) Flat Wave b or even an Expanded Flat that would imply a recycling from either the old 1,265 high or from a limited overshoot in a Wave efb to generate a decline back to the same area around marked Wave b or Wave Fa.

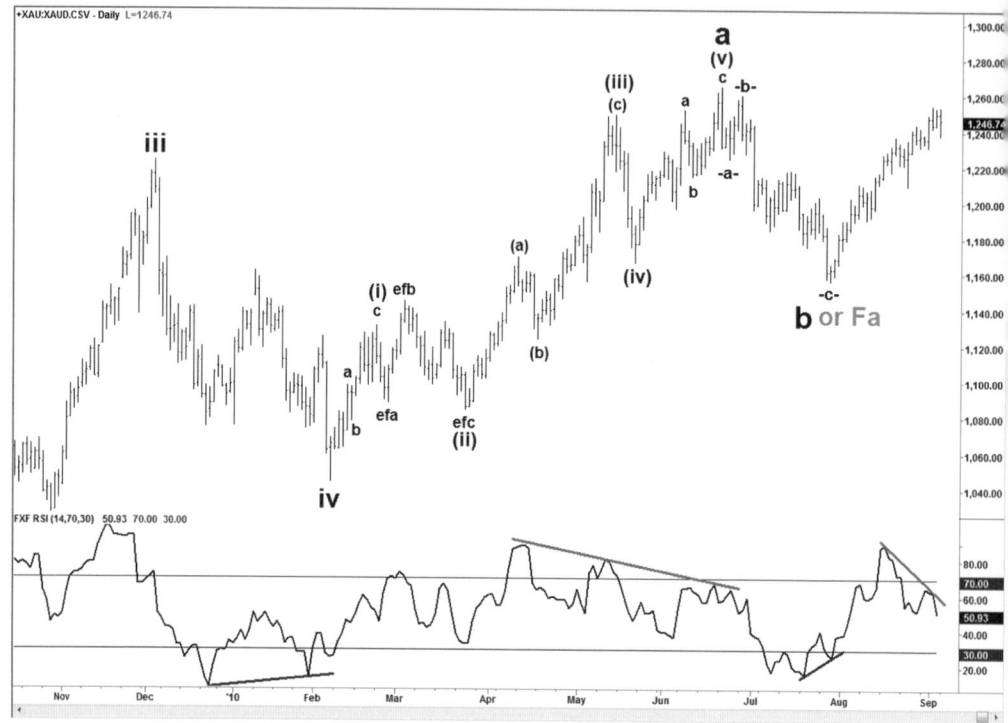

FIGURE 7.12 Daily Rally in Wave a and Wave b of Wave v
Source: Created with TradeStation. ©TradeStation Technologies, Inc. All rights reserved.

Table 7.12 provides the wave relationships in Wave a and Wave b.

There were some very accurate retracements and projections throughout this move, with the maximum deviation from normal projections being around $8.00. However, the projections that certainly caught me by surprise were the 58.6% projection in Wave c of Wave (v) and the 50% projection in Wave (v) itself. The correction in the larger Wave b was very close to the exact 50% retracement, and if this turns into a Flat correction, it may well move down to test the full 50% level and perhaps a small overshoot.

In terms of the 1,390–1,395 Wave [iii] target I highlighted in the original analysis, and using the levels of the current Wave a and Wave b of Wave v, it is possible to see the potential projection in

The Modified Structure in Other Markets

TABLE 7.12 Wave Relationships for Figure 7.12

GOLD Wave a of Wave v		Ratio	Projection	Actual
Wave a	1097.67			1097.67
Wave b	1097.67 −	Wave a * 38.2% =	1077.26	1077.79
Wave c	1077.79 +	Wave a * 100% =	1131.22	1130.91
Wave (i)	1130.91			1130.91
Wave efa	1088.14			1088.14
Wave efb	1088.14 +	Wave efa * 133.3% =	1145.15	1144.81
Wave efc	1084.51			1084.51
Wave (ii)	1130.91 −	Wave (i) * 50.0% =	1087.58	1084.51
Wave (a)	1169.50			1169.50
Wave (b)	1169.50 *	Wave (a) * 50.0% =	1127.01	1123.67
Wave (c)	1123.67 +	Wave (a) * 138.2% =	1241.13	1249.29
Wave (iii)	1084.51 +	Wave (i) * 190.2% =	1249.36	1249.29
Wave (iv)	1249.29 −	Wave (iii) * 50.0% =	1166.90	1166.19
Wave a	1251.69			1251.69
Wave b	1251.69 −	Wave a * 41.4% =	1216.29	1214.58
Wave c	1214.58 +	Wave a * 58.6% =	1264.68	1265.00
Wave (v)	1166.19 +	Wave (i) > (iii) * 50.0% =	1268.72	1265.00
Wave a	1265.00			1265.00
Wave -a-	1224.55			1224.55
Wave -b-	1224.55 +	Wave -a- * 95.4% =	1263.14	1262.48
Wave -c-	1262.48 −	Wave -a- * 261.8% =	1156.58	1156.69
Wave b or Fa	1265.00 −	Wave a * 50.0% =	1154.62	1156.69

Wave c:

$$105.6\% = 1,389.81$$
$$109.2\% = 1,397.76$$

Therefore, even if Wave b develops as a Flat (or Expanded Flat) correction that could test the 50% retracement at 1,154.62, the 109.2% projection will imply a target at around the 1,395 area and therefore I feel we are on the right course to see this target achieved.

FRENCH CAC 40 INDEX

I'd like to add two more examples of equity markets, starting with the French CAC 40 Index, just to provide more than a single equity market. However, there is still the final forecast for this which may or may not occur, but by the time this book is published the result will be known. I will highlight the key break areas that would render my forecast as incorrect.

In Figure 7.13 the French CAC 40 Index is displaying what appears to be a weekly Zigzag lower from the September 2000 high at 6,944.77.

At this point I find it hard to conceive any other wave count, with the decline to Wave -iii- in Wave (c) having stalled just 64.00 above Wave (a) and the pullback in Wave -iv- being just a little less than 50% of Wave -iii-. Still, this outlook needs to be confirmed and only time will tell. The following tables provide the wave relationships in the three legs.

As shown in Table 7.13, there are some quite accurate relationships in the Wave (a) decline and some not quite so accurate, but overall the general correlation of target levels, in particular the final 2,401.15 low, is quite convincing. Where perhaps there are more mild deviations from normal ratios is in the corrective waves, but that is not an uncommon observation. The correction in Wave -ii- of Wave (a) generated a difference of 50.0 between the 33.3% retracement and final stalling point, but still only represented less than a 1% deviation. In Wave -c- of Wave -v- there were also two other instances of a 50.0

The Modified Structure in Other Markets

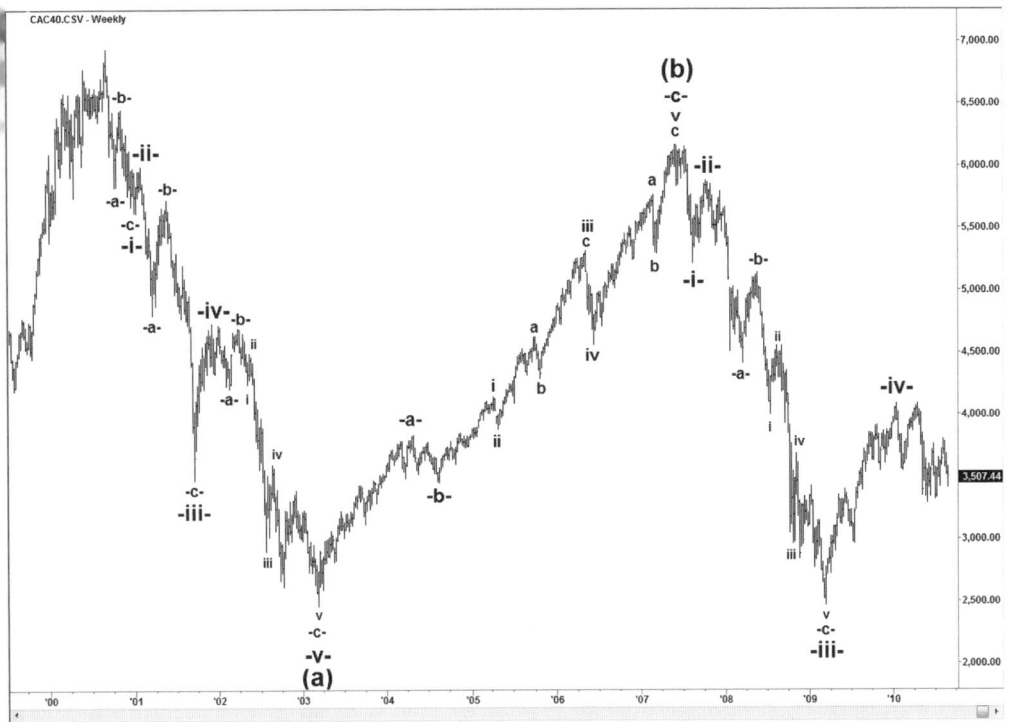

FIGURE 7.13 An Incomplete (a)(b)(c) Decline in CAC 40 Index
Source: Created with TradeStation.©TradeStation Technologies, Inc. All rights reserved.

TABLE 7.13 Decline in Wave (a) in the CAC 40 Index

CAC 40 Wave (a)		Ratio	Projection	Actual
Wave -a-	5828.24			5828.24
Wave -b-	5828.24 +	Wave -a- * 58.6% =	6482.13	6459.50
Wave -c-	6459.50 −	Wave -a- * 76.4% =	5606.85	5603.92
Wave -i-	5603.92			5603.92
Wave -ii-	5603.92 +	Wave -i- * 33.3% =	6050.42	5999.18
Wave -a-	4804.40			4804.40

(continued)

TABLE 7.13 *(Continued)*

CAC 40 Wave (a)		Ratio	Projection	Actual
Wave -b-	4804.40 +	Wave -a- * 76.4% =	5717.21	5728.52
Wave -c-	5728.52 −	Wave -a- * 190.2% =	3456.05	3463.07
Wave -iii-	5999.18 −	Wave -i- * 190.2% =	3448.88	3463.07
Wave -iv-	3463.07 +	Wave -iii- * 50.0% =	4731.13	4735.21
Wave -a-	4210.30			4210.30
Wave -b-	4210.30 +	Wave -a- * 90.2% =	4682.81	4696.18
Wave -c-	4696.18 −	Wave -a- * 438.2% =	2395.50	2401.15
Wave -v-	4735.21 −	Wave -i- > -iii- * 66.7% =	2412.92	2401.15
Wave -c- of Wave -v-				
Wave i	4239.72			4239.72
Wave ii	4239.72 +	Wave i * 58.6% =	4507.21	4497.46
Wave iii	4497.46 −	Wave i * 361.8% =	2845.99	2898.60
Wave iv	2898.60 +	Wave iii * 41.4% =	3650.53	3601.41
Wave v	3601.41 −	Wave i > iii * 66.7% =	2402.15	2401.15

difference between the final result and closest normal retracement/projection. However, overall I feel this does represent a solid reflection of the harmonic structure.

As shown in Table 7.14, the Wave (b) correction was very deep, just short of an 85.6% retracement. Again, I can't say the relationships developed with the level of consistency I prefer to see, but without any doubt this was a correction and should therefore be labeled as a Wave (b).

The decline in Wave (c) has been constructive, and I feel the weight of evidence does still point to a new low that should be in place by the time this book is published.

The Modified Structure in Other Markets

TABLE 7.14 Correction in Wave (b) in the CAC 40 Index

CAC 40 Wave (b)		Ratio	Projection	Actual
Wave -a-	3831.54			3831.54
Wave -b-	3831.54 −	Wave -a- * 23.6% =	3496.26	3452.41
Wave i	4143.93			4143.93
Wave ii	4143.93 −	Wave i * 38.2% =	3879.77	3882.42
Wave a	4651.11			4651.11
Wave b	4651.11 −	Wave a * 50.0% =	4266.77	4288.15
Wave c	4288.15 +	Wave a * 138.2% =	5350.48	5329.16
Wave iii	3882.42 +	Wave i * 198.4% =	5254.40	5329.16
Wave iv	5329.16 −	Wave iii * 50.0% =	4605.79	4564.69
Wave a	**5771.69**			5771.69
Wave b	5771.69 −	Wave a * 38.2% =	5310.62	5295.58
Wave c	5295.58 +	Wave a * 76.4% =	6217.73	6168.15
Wave v	4564.69 +	Wave i > iii * 85.4% =	6167.43	6168.15
Wave -c-	3452.41 +	Wave -a- * 190.2% =	6173.01	6168.15

As shown in Table 7.15, again while the wave relationships aren't particularly spot-on, the projection in what I feel is Wave -iii- and pullback in Wave -iv- appear quite convincing. I feel there is still a small risk of a slightly deeper retracement in Wave -iv- since the full 50% retracement was not met, but the balance of the rough 66.7% retracement in Wave -ii- and the mild shortfall in the 50% retracement in Wave -iv- do tend to complement each other in terms of alternation.

Should the current Wave -iv- high at 4,088.18 remain intact, as I feel it may, then a 66.7% projection in Wave -v- will target the 1,618.49 area. Equally, a wave equality target implies a target at 1,624.53, which is obviously very close.

TABLE 7.15 Decline in Wave (c) in the CAC 40 Index

CAC 40 to Wave -iii- of (c)		Ratio	Projection	Actual
Wave -a-	5837.14			5837.14
Wave -b-	5837.14 +	Wave -a- * 95.4% =	**6152.92**	**6156.16**
Wave -c-	6156.16 −	Wave -a- * 285.4% =	**5211.46**	**5217.70**
Wave -i-	5217.70			5217.70
Wave -ii-	5217.70 +	Wave -i- * 66.7% =	**5851.27**	**5882.07**
Wave -a-	4416.71			4416.71
Wave -b-	4416.71 +	Wave -a- * 50.0% =	**5149.39**	**5142.10**
Wave -c-	5142.10 −	Wave -a- * 185.4% =	**2425.32**	**2465.46**
Wave -iii-	5882.70 −	Wave -i- * 361.8% =	**2443.34**	**2465.46**
Wave -iv-	2465.46 +	Wave -iii- * 50.0% =	**4173.77**	**4088.18**

If this outlook is incorrect then a break above the 50% retracement in Wave -iv- at 4,173.77 and the 58.6% retracement at 4,467.59 would imply a deeper recovery that would require an adjustment to the entire structure.

JAPANESE NIKKEI 225 INDEX

Another equity index which I thought would make for an interesting analysis is the Japanese Nikkei 225, which made its high in December 1989 and has seen a general decline from there which thus far has lasted over 20 years. I think we can say without too much argument that this was a strategic high and probably also the end of a five-wave rally. Therefore I'd like to present what looks to me to be the structure of the decline from then.

The Modified Structure in Other Markets

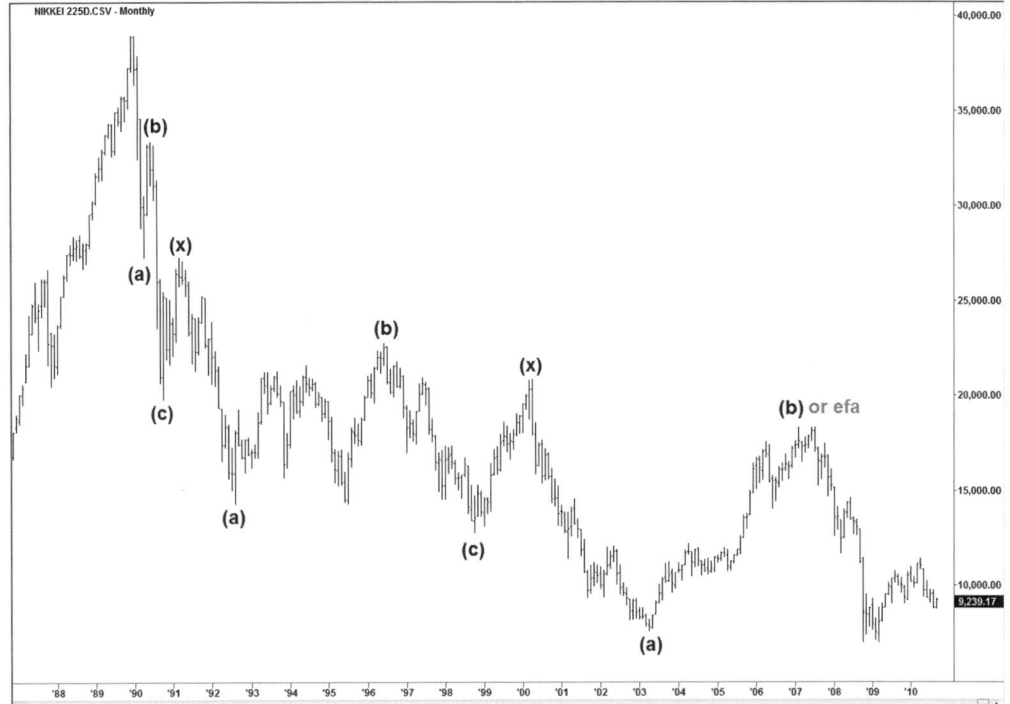

FIGURE 7.14 Decline in the Japanese Nikkei Index since the 1989 High
Source: Created with TradeStation. ©TradeStation Technologies, Inc. All rights reserved.

I shall cover the initial basic moves first and then break down the movement seen during the past 10 years in more detail to highlight the harmonic structure.

Figure 7.14 displays the monthly chart of the Nikkei 225 Index, from which it can be seen that the structure appears to be a Triple Three. The first two (a)(b)(c) declines are complete, while the third is either on its final Wave (c) or alternatively the Wave (b) may be developing as a complex correction. The first two (a)(b)(c) declines are recorded in the following tables.

Table 7.16 displays an accuracy that sees a variance from standard retracement and projection ratios of around 1% or less. I therefore feel there is a strong argument for this wave count to probably represent the correct structure.

TABLE 7.16 Decline in Nikkei 225

Monthly decline in Nikkei 225		Ratio	Projection	Actual
Wave (a)	27251			27251
Wave (b)	27251 +	Wave (a) * 50.0% =	33104	33345
Wave (c)	33345 −	Wave (a) * 114.6% =	19930	19782
Wave (x)	19782 +	Wave (a) > (c) * 38.2% =	27107	27270
Wave (a)	14194			14194
Wave (b)	14194 +	Wave (a) * 66.7% =	22910	22757
Wave (c)	22757 −	Wave (a) * 76.4% =	12767	12788
Wave (x)	12788 +	Wave (a) > (c) * 50.0% =	20732	20833
Wave (a)	7604			7604
Wave (b)	7604 +	Wave (a) * 76.4% =	17711	18300

Since the third Wave (a) has already developed, followed by a correction higher, the question of whether we are in a final decline in Wave (c) that would generate a reversal higher, or whether this will develop as a complex Wave (b), is very critical. I have therefore provided these waves in more detail.

Figure 7.15 shows the five-wave harmonic decline in Wave (A) followed by the three-wave correction. This may have completed Wave (B) or possibly be the first wave of a complex correction. Given that the low from the Wave (B) peak has moved below Wave (A) it may be possible to alternatively label the Wave (B) high as Wave efa. This would imply that the current decline is Wave efb.

As can be seen from Table 7.17, the Wave (A) decline developed with all retracement and projection ratios being common harmonic relationships and the variance from those being extremely limited. From that point of view, I am confident this was a valid Wave (A).

The Modified Structure in Other Markets   217

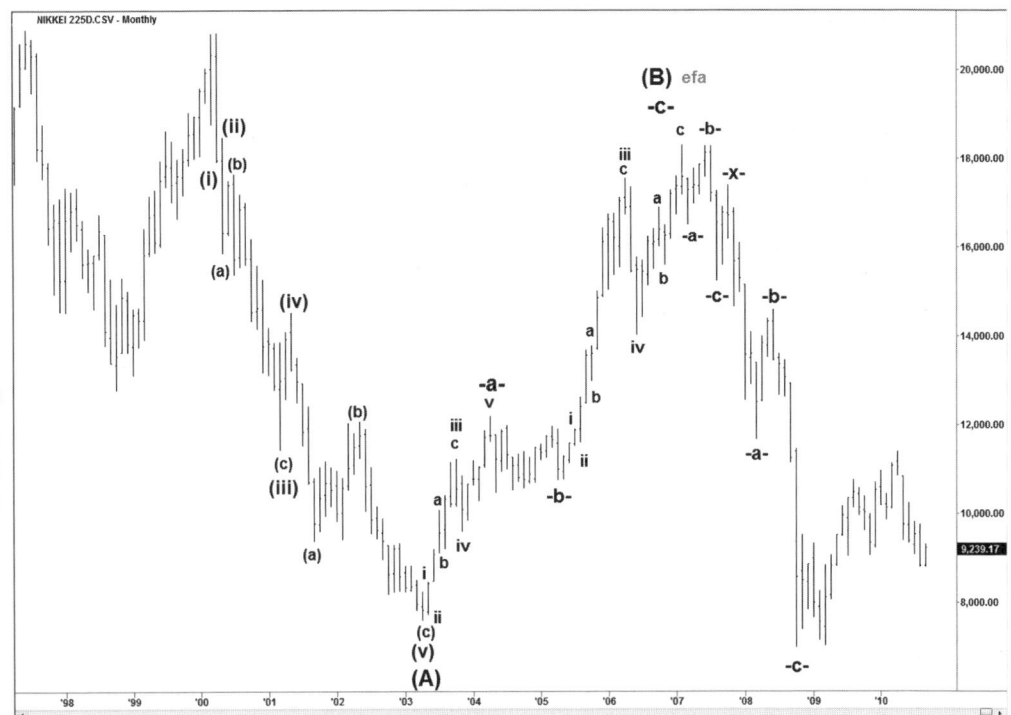

FIGURE 7.15 Wave (A) Decline and Correction in Wave (B) or Wave efa
Source: Created with TradeStation. ©TradeStation Technologies, Inc. All rights reserved.

TABLE 7.17   Wave (A) Decline

Wave (A) decline in Nikkei 225		Ratio	Projection	Actual
Wave (i)	18091			18091
Wave (ii)	18091 +	Wave (i) * 33.3% =	19003	18987
Wave (a)	15870			15870
Wave (b)	15870 +	Wave (a) * 58.6% =	17697	17661
Wave (c)	17661 −	Wave (a) * 198.4% =	11477	11434
Wave (iii)	18987 +	Wave (i) * 276.4% =	11405	11434

(*continued*)

TABLE 7.17 (Continued)

Wave (A) decline in Nikkei 225		Ratio	Projection	Actual
Wave (iv)	11434 −	Wave (iii) * 41.4% =	14561	14556
Wave (a)	9383			9383
Wave (b)	9383 +	Wave (a) * 50.0% =	11969	12081
Wave (c)	12081 −	Wave (a) * 85.4% =	7663	7604
Wave (v)	14556 −	Wave (i) > (iii) * 76.4% =	7375	7603

The correction in Wave (B) developed in three waves; Table 7.18 provides the wave relationships.

Again the majority of wave relationships are common harmonic ratios. There are one or two more unusual ratios—for example, the Wave iii in Wave -a- at 441.4% is not one I would normally expect to see—but the 95.4% projection in Wave c of Wave iii is very common. In general the levels of variance between the ideal harmonic ratios and actual stalling points were limited.

TABLE 7.18 Wave (B) Relationships

Nikkei 225 Wave (B) of efa		Ratio	Projection	Actual
Wave i	8339			8339
Wave ii	8339 −	Wave i * 50.0% =	7971	7962
Wave a	10070			10070
Wave b	10070 −	Wave a * 41.4% =	9197	9224
Wave c	9224 +	Wave a * 95.4% =	11235	11239
Wave iii	7962 +	Wave i * 441.4% =	11208	11239
Wave iv	11239 −	Wave iii * 50.0% =	9601	9615

The Modified Structure in Other Markets **219**

Wave v	9615 +	Wave i > iii * 66.7% =	12039	12195
Wave -a-	12195			12195
Wave -b-	12195 −	Wave -a- * 33.3% =	10785	10770
Wave i	11913			11193
Wave ii	11913 −	Wave i * 23.6% =	11643	11615
Wave a	13784			11784
Wave b	11784 −	Wave a * 38.2% =	12955	12996
Wave c	12996 +	Wave a * 209.2% =	17529	17563
Wave iii	11615 +	Wave i * 523.6% =	17529	17563
Wave iv	17563 −	Wave iii * 58.6% =	14077	14045
Wave a	16901			16091
Wave b	16901 −	Wave a * 41.4% =	15719	15616
Wave c	15616 +	Wave a * 95.4% =	18341	18300
Wave v	14045 +	Wave i > iii * 61.8% =	18243	18300
Wave -c-	10770 +	Wave -a- * 161.8% =	18200	18300

Therefore, we have had a Wave (A) lower followed by a deep correction in three waves that consequently raises the potential for the Wave (B) to develop in a complex manner. To try to decide whether the decline from there will be the final Wave (C) or whether it will be an Expanded Flat, I have detailed the wave relationships in the decline so far (Table 7.19).

It can be seen this time that to judge whether this decline is corrective or impulsive I have added the alternative count next to the preferred count shown in Figure 7.15. If the Wave -c- low at 7,021.00 was actually Wave (iii), it would have implied a projection of 344.4% and the correction from there which reached 11,408 would suggest a Wave (iv) retracement of 41.4%. I can't say 344.4% is a projection ratio I would expect, but there were one or two unusual projections so possibly retaining an open mind may well be preferable.

TABLE 7.19 Wave Relationships in the Decline So Far

Decline in Nikkei 225		Ratio	Projection	Actual
Wave -a-	16533			16533
Wave -b-	**16533 +**	Wave -a- * 100.0% =	**18300**	**18297**
Wave -c- or (Wave (i)	**18297 −**	Wave -a- * 166.7% =	**15351**	**15262**
Wave -x- or Wave (ii)	17489			17489
Wave -a-	11691			11691
Wave -b-	**11691 +**	Wave -a- * 50.0% =	**14591**	**14601**
Wave -c- or Wave (iii)	**14601 −**	Wave -a- * 33.3% =	**6872**	**7021**
Retracement	**11408**			**11408**

If this turns into an Expanded Flat then ratios we may look for would be:

$$14.6\% \quad 6,041$$
$$23.6\% \quad 5,078$$
$$38.2\% \quad 3,517$$

If an assumption is made that the correction at 11,408 was a Wave (iv) then projections in Wave (v) could be estimated at:

$$61.8\% \quad 4,437$$
$$66.7\% \quad 3,884$$
$$76.4\% \quad 2,790$$

Furthermore, the common projections in Wave (C) can also be generated:

$$105.6\% \quad 4,330$$
$$109.2\% \quad 3,854$$
$$123.6\% \quad 1,949$$

I would suggest that if this turns out to be an Expanded Flat then the 14.6% or 23.6% expansions at 5,078–6,041 are the most likely. However, what is striking are the 61.8% projection in alternate Wave (v) at 4,437 that matches closely with the 105.6% projection in Wave (C) and the 66.7% projection in Wave (v) at 3,884 that matches closely with the 109.2% projection in Wave (C). I am open to either alternative.

WHEAT FUTURES

To include an example of a commodity future I was able to obtain the history for wheat futures. This is still what I feel is probably an incomplete decline as it has mapped out a three-wave decline in the weekly chart thus far which I feel completes only Wave (iii).

Figure 7.16 displays a decline in the wheat futures contract that looks very much like having generated Wave (iii) of Wave (C) lower. Table 7.20 shows the wave relationships.

From this table it can be seen that the wave relationships are generally represented by harmonic relationships, and the variances between the exact ratios and the actual stalling points are also quite close.

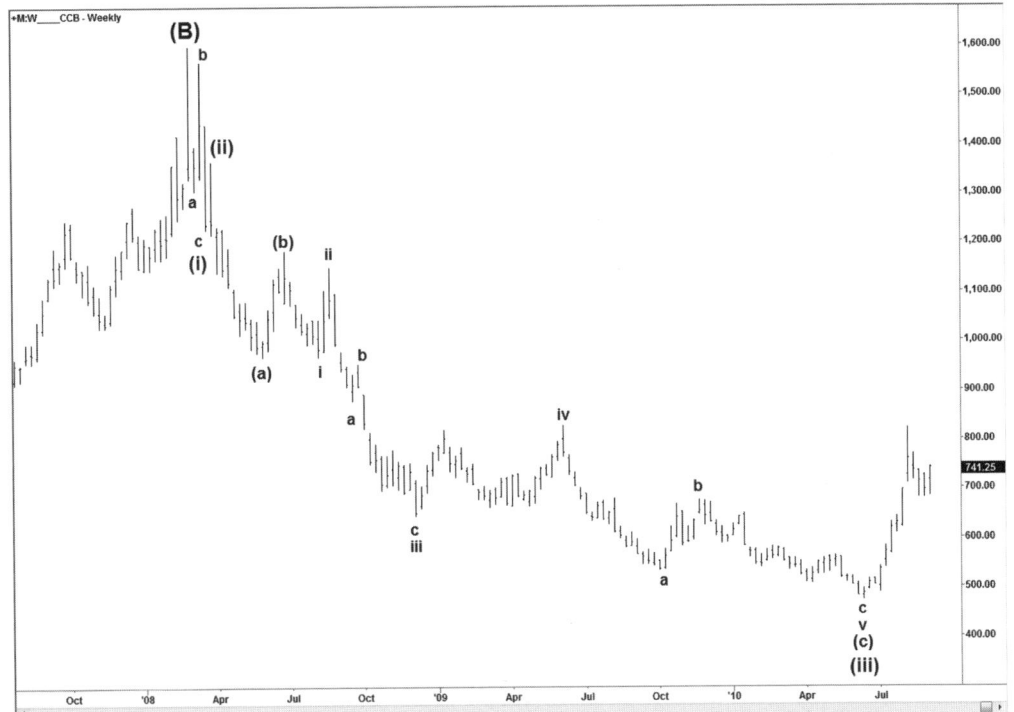

FIGURE 7.16 Decline to Wave (iii) in the Weekly Wheat Future Contract
Source: Created with TradeStation. ©TradeStation Technologies, Inc. All rights reserved.

TABLE 7.20 Wave Relationships for Figure 7.16

Wave (C) decline in Wheat		Ratio	Projection	Actual
Wave a	1304.50			1304.50
Wave b	1304.50 +	Wave a * 90.2% =	1568.75	1566.50
Wave c	1566.50 −	Wave a * 114.6% =	1230.25	1225.50
Wave (i)	1225.50			1225.50
Wave (ii)	1225.50 +	Wave (i) * 38.2% =	1367.75	1363.50
Wave (a)	965.75			965.75
Wave (b)	965.75 +	Wave (a) * 85.4% =	1187.50	1187.75
Wave i	965.75			965.75
Wave ii	965.75 +	Wave i * 76.4% =	1135.50	1147.75
Wave a	877.75			877.75
Wave b	877.75 +	Wave a * 23.6% =	941.27	951.75
Wave c	951.75 −	Wave a * 114.6% =	642.25	643.75
Wave iii	1147.75 −	Wave i * 223.6% =	651.25	643.75
Wave iv	643.25 +	Wave iii * 38.2% =	836.25	826.25
Wave a	533.75			533.75
Wave b	533.75 +	Wave a * 50.0% =	680.00	675.25
Wave c	675.25 −	Wave a * 66.7% =	480.15	472.75
Wave v	826.25 −	Wave i > iii * 66.7% =	463.50	472.75
Wave (c)	1187.75 −	Wave (a) * 176.4% =	469.75	472.75
Wave (iii)	1363.50 −	Wave (i) * 238.2% =	476.25	472.75

Following this decline, price has recovered to 822.25, and I note the ideal 50% retracement in Wave (iv) would imply a corrective peak close to the 918.00–25 area. In turn, this type of Wave (iv) peak would imply a minimum target of a 50% projection at 355.75 with the 61.8% projection at 222.75. At this point I do not have the peak of the original high and cannot match this with a projection of the original Wave (A), which would help to identify a most likely area where the decline will stall.

COTTON FUTURES

As a second example of a commodity future I have included the (A)(B)(C) rally in cotton from the 1985 low to the 1995 high. The results display a slightly larger variance from normal harmonic ratios in some instances, but overall the combination of the ratios across the wave degrees do tend to confirm the harmonic structure.

To support the chart shown in Figure 7.17, Table 7.21 provides the ratios during the rally.

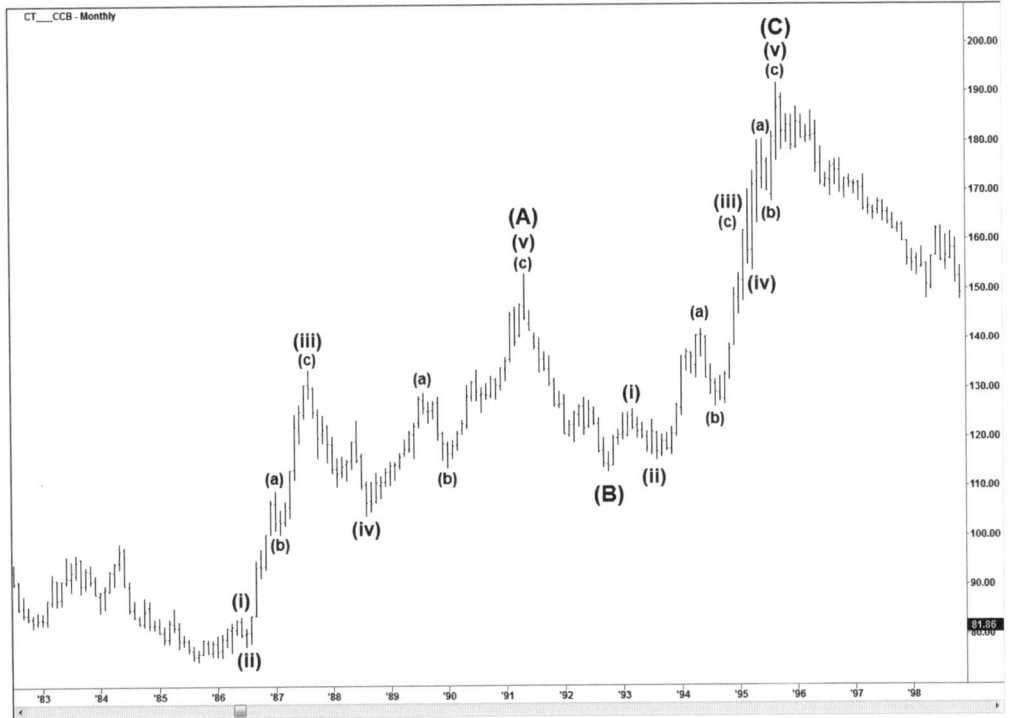

FIGURE 7.17 (A)(B)(C) Rally in Cotton Futures
Source: Created with TradeStation. ©TradeStation Technologies, Inc. All rights reserved.

TABLE 7.21 Ratios for (A)(B)(C) Rally in Cotton Futures

(A)(B)(C) rally in Cotton		Ratio	Projection	Actual
Wave (i)	83.81			83.81
Wave (ii)	83.81 −	Wave (i) * 66.67% =	**77.77**	77.80
Wave (a)	109.30			109.30
Wave (b)	109.30 −	Wave (a) * 33.3% =	**98.81**	100.42
Wave (c)	100.42 +	Wave (a) * 105.6% =	**133.68**	133.70
Wave (iii)	77.80 +	Wave (i) * 614.6% =	**133.48**	133.70
Wave (iv)	133.70 −	Wave (iii) * 50.0% =	**105.69**	103.99
Wave (a)	133.70			133.70
Wave (b)	133.70 −	Wave (a) * 33.3% =	**123.81**	125.10
Wave (c)	125.10 +	Wave (a) * 95.4% =	**153.44**	153.08
Wave (v)	103.99 +	Wave (i) > (iii) * 85.4% =	**154.22**	153.08
Wave (A)	153.08			153.08
Wave (B)	153.08 −	Wave (A) * 50.0% =	**113.92**	113.09
Wave (i)	147.98			147.98
Wave (ii)	147.98 −	Wave (i) * 76.4% =	**116.08**	115.48
Wave (a)	141.88			141.88
Wave (b)	141.88 −	Wave (a) * 61.8% =	**125.56**	125.74
Wave (c)	125.74 +	Wave (a) * 138.2% =	**162.73**	161.70
Wave (iii)	115.48 +	Wave (i) * 366.7% =	**161.87**	161.70
Wave (iv)	161.70 −	Wave (iii) * 14.6% =	**154.95**	153.75
Wave (a)	180.27			180.27
Wave (b)	180.27 −	Wave (a) * 66.7% =	**167.89**	167.76
Wave (c)	167.76 +	Wave (a) * 133.3% =	**192.51**	191.65
Wave (v)	153.75 +	Wave (i) > (iii) * 76.4% =	**190.89**	191.65
Wave (C)	113.09 +	Wave (A) * 100% =	**191.42**	191.65

Index

A

Alternation
  Elliott, 13, 58
  harmonic, 12, 28
Alternative wave relationships, 77
Ambiguous projections in Wave (c) of Wave (i), 128–130
Ambiguous wave counts, 153–158

B

Being caught with the wrong wave count, 159–177

C

Common wave relationships, 40, 77–82, 104, 192
Complex corrections, 13, 16–18, 20, 25, 28, 31, 33, 34, 35, 53, 78, 79, 80, 134, 139, 146, 153, 155, 160, 163, 164, 172, 182, 215, 216
Complex wave structure, 3, 4
Complications in corrective structures, 16–26
Corrective ratios, 163, 167–168, 198, 220
Corrective waves, 2, 3, 8, 13, 16–35, 53, 58, 80, 172, 210
Cotton Futures, 223–224

D

Diagonal Triangles, 7, 8, 9, 13, 32, 33, 38, 39, 40
Difference between a modified impulse wave and a Triple Three, 120, 131
Divergences, 51, 127, 143, 145–148, 161–163, 165, 168, 170, 171, 176, 177, 190, 193, 196, 206, 207
Double Zigzag, 17–18, 25–27, 30–32, 34, 132, 150, 155, 164, 165, 172, 191
Dow Jones Industrial Average, 181–200, 206

E

Elliott, Ralph Nelson, 1–2, 43
Elliott's guidelines, 12–14
Elliott's unbreakable rules, 56
Expanded Flat corrections, 22, 23, 24, 32, 33, 54, 55, 81, 129, 148, 151, 210

Extended fifth wave
  Elliott, 141
  harmonic, 171
Extended waves
  Elliott, 194
  harmonic, 216
  Wave 1, 43
  Wave 3, 49, 50, 86, 106, 142
  Wave 5, 7, 10, 38, 79, 89, 139, 141

F
Failed fifth waves, 10
Fibonacci, Leonardo, 72
Fibonacci ratios, 37, 71, 74–77, 85, 154
Flat corrections, 22, 23, 81, 148
French CAC 40 Index, 210

G
General Observations on Using Ratios, 81
Gold, 200

H
Harmonic impulsive structure versus Triple Three, 18–21, 26–28, 52–56
Harmonic ratios, 15, 26, 43, 47, 68, 71, 76, 114, 218, 223
Harmonic structure background, 37–41
Harmonic wave extensions, 46, 49, 51

I
Identifying Wave (ii), 127
Identifying Wave (iv), 79
Impulsive waves
  comparison of Elliott versus harmonic, 41, 51
  Elliott, 5, 8, 9, 11, 84
  harmonic, 84, 94, 201

J
Japanese Nikkei 225 Index, 214, 215
Judging when a complex correction is more likely to occur, 25

M
Matching projections in Wave v, Wave (c) and impulsive wave targets, 126

O
Overlap of Wave (i) and Wave (iv), 56

P
Prechter's Special Wave A, 38
Projection ratios
  corrections, 79
  impulsive, 71, 119

S
Simple wave structure, 2
Square root of two, 71, 76, 77

INDEX

Strength and accuracy of the harmonic structure, 96
Structural relationships–Elliott versus harmonic, 97, 102
Superior results of the harmonic wave structure, 82

T

The wave structure of one higher degree, 117, 131
Three waves–Wave A, 3, 16, 25, 28, 55, 216, 219
Triangles, 24, 64, 81
Triple Three, 13, 18–21, 23–28, 30, 32, 34, 40, 52, 53, 55, 56, 64, 78, 80, 106, 108, 131, 155, 157, 164, 172, 173, 176, 182, 184, 193, 199, 215

U

Using cycles, 148
Using momentum to confirm projection targets, 146

W

Wave (a) – potential stalling points, 176
Wave (b), 18, 20, 21, 22, 25, 27, 28, 30–34, 40, 45, 47, 51, 53–57, 59, 60, 63–68, 78–81, 87, 88, 99, 101, 104, 106, 108, 109, 111, 114, 121, 122, 125, 127–129, 131–138, 140–143, 147, 151, 152, 155, 156, 160, 161, 174, 176, 178, 193–197, 201, 212, 216, 218, 219
Wave (b) – deep, 20, 45, 55, 59, 60, 62, 63, 68, 87, 88, 99, 108, 110, 114, 115, 125, 131, 133, 155, 158, 173, 202
Wave (b) in the harmonic wave structure, 14, 176, 201
Wave (b) retest, 64, 135
Wave (c), 7, 10, 16, 27, 33, 47, 55, 57, 65, 80, 87, 89, 96, 106, 111, 114, 121, 125, 126, 131, 137, 139, 142, 147, 155, 161, 176, 199, 220
Wave (i) – targets, 48, 62, 88, 121, 125, 140, 141
Wave (ii) – targets, 62
Wave (iii) – targets, 63, 80, 88, 120, 125, 126, 131, 135, 137, 186, 192, 200, 206
Wave (iv) – targets, 143
Wave (iv) retracements - reference to Wave (b) of Wave (iii), 64
Wave (v) – targets, 63, 66, 80, 88, 91, 99, 120, 126, 131, 137, 139, 141, 151, 176, 189, 213
Wave (x), 17, 18, 20, 21, 32, 53, 68, 80, 81, 106, 108, 111, 132, 134, 142, 150, 155
Wave degrees, 116, 119, 120, 159, 185, 223
Wave relationships, 27, 40, 41, 51, 61, 77, 93, 97, 104, 115, 157, 171, 191, 218, 221

Wave relationships in Expanded Flats, 13, 22, 26–30, 54, 58
Wave relationships in Triangles, 24, 64, 81
Wheat Futures, 221

Z

Zigzag, 13, 16, 17, 21, 22, 25–28, 30–34, 57, 58, 79–81, 96, 97, 99, 131, 132, 150, 155, 156, 164, 165, 172, 176, 191, 210